ALL KINGDOM ALL THE TIME

How to Stay Tuned-In To the Frequency of Heaven

DR. JAMES BREWTON

WestBow Press books may be ordered through booksellers or by contacting:

WestBow Press
A Division of Thomas Nelson & Zondervan
1663 Liberty Drive
Bloomington, IN 47403
www.westbowpress.com
844-714-3454

ISBN: 978-1-6642-6454-0 (sc)
ISBN: 978-1-6642-6456-4 (hc)
ISBN: 978-1-6642-6455-7 (e)

Library of Congress Control Number: 2022907522

Print information available on the last page.

WestBow Press rev. date: 05/17/2022

Other definitions are taken from Wikipedia and Wiktionary.
Emphasis or italics have been placed on certain words and Scriptures at the author's discretion to amplify the meaning of the text.

To contact the Author: brewton4@breezeline.net; pastorbrewton@gmail.com; www.community-empowerment-ministries.com

But the saints of the Most High shall receive the kingdom, and possess the kingdom forever, even forever and ever.

—Daniel 7:18 NKJV

CONTENTS

FOREWORD

"All Kingdom... All the Time." Here is a statement of faith, a statement of power and a statement of purpose that should be the signature DNA of every kingdom citizen! This book captures both the fundamental and developmental aspects of kingdom life and what it takes to live a consistent life of victory.

> **Acts 9:19 KJV**
> "...And when he had received meat, he was strengthened."

If I may take the liberty to use creative license, I'd like to quote the passage above. This book is truly a document of divine design and is full of "meat" to strengthen every believer!

The missing link in many believer's lives is the consistency of kingdom dynamics. This "ebb and flow" is often due to the lack of understanding in how to find, function, flow and follow through in the kingdom DNA that makes consistent victory possible. One of the best solutions in this hour is to go "All Kingdom, All the Time!" There is a popular saying that suggests that "Whatever you are, you do it all of the time," and another that suggests "Everywhere you go, you are there." When believers develop the motivation to be Kingdom Level Citizens "all of the time," that is when true victory is experienced.

Dr. James Brewton, as a scholar, Apostolic Ministry Leader and teacher/trainer has done a thorough and masterful job in mapping out each step of kingdom life development with this great blueprint for victory! This is by far one of the most concise and precise works about Kingdom development and lifestyles that I have seen in my nearly fifty years of ministry. Frequently found in this book is the important phrase,

"...Holy Spirit wavelength that transmits the frequency of Heaven to Earth." Realizing that there is such a thing as "frequency" within the framework of Kingdom language and communications should awaken a level of interest and excitement in believers that suggests there is more to the kingdom life than they've first believed!

After learning from this book, believers won't simply stockpile "memory verses" and quotes that don't generate progress and power that is so badly needed in traditional ministry.

This prevents the "loss in translation" that often plagues the "church" lifestyle. This lifestyle cannot be steeped in guesswork or groping about in the darkness of misunderstanding or misinformation. Make no mistake about it, we must be clear! We must "be" the Kingdom! Luke 17:21 KJV is clear! "The kingdom of God is within you."

> **James 1:5-8 KJV**
> **5** "If any of you lack wisdom, let him ask of God, that giveth to all men liberally, and upbraideth not; and it shall be given him.
> **6** But let him ask in faith, nothing wavering. For he that wavereth is like a wave of the sea driven with the wind and tossed.
> **7** For let not that man think that he shall receive any thing of the Lord.
> **8** A double minded man is unstable in all his ways."

Asking in faith is predicated on the fact that the information upon which we base our beliefs must be Biblically accurate. *"There is no premise without a promise."* GEB

Wavering is guaranteed without a solid Biblical framework on which to develop a healthy expectation or outcome. Many believers, unfortunately, base their expectations on traditional quotes and quips that often have no accurate Biblical construct or connection. Even if they are steadfast and repetitive in their expectations there are limited results because there is no direct relationship with the Logos Word of God, and therefore not necessarily an endorsement from Heaven. The Biblical text noted above lets us know that we have an opportunity to gain wisdom on this journey, and it's freely given to us, but only if we obtain it by faith. Nearly every good student of the Bible has heard how we obtain faith. "Faith cometh by hearing and hearing by the word of God" -Rom. 10:17 KJV. Therefore, the Word of God and an accurate expression and exegesis of it is not optional.

A clear perspective and understanding of what kingdom life is actually about greatly reduces the tendency for believers to "phase" in and out of the opportunity for victorious life. This book helps to develop "staying power" in the believer's life. I believe this book should be in the library of every ministry leader and believer who is looking to abandon repetitive traditional thinking and lethargic mindsets and ignite the energy of end-time advancement that is essential today. The world and the church need to see what the kingdom of God actually looks like! This is the blueprint for that! As for the kingdom… Let's get in and stay in! All Kingdom... All the Time!

Dr. Gordon E. Bradshaw
Founder/President - Global Effect Movers & Shakers Network and The Demonstration Nation
Founder/ President - The Misrah Academy Governmental Empowerment Center
Author: The Technology of Apostolic Succession - Transferring the Purposes of God to the Next Generation of Kingdom Citizens,
Authority for Assignment: Releasing the Mantle of God's Government in the Marketplace,
I SEE THRONES! - Igniting and Increasing Your Influence in the Seven Mountains of Culture
Co-Creator of Community Civility Counts and World Civility Day,
Ambassador - IChange Nations

INTRODUCTION

As I look back over the thirty years I've been an ordained minister, there have been many people who Abba (Father) used to help develop me, spiritually, into a commissioned kingdom-compliant servant-leader—one who strictly adheres to the Word of God as opposed to the evil systems of the world. I've become a "current progressive" kingdom leader by dwelling in the secret place of the Most High.

It is in his presence that the Father transforms believers into the image of Jesus Christ; it's where he consistently moves us from one level of glory to the next level of glory. Dwelling in the secret place of God should be and must be prioritized in the life of every believer for reasons that are imperative to a sustained intimate relationship with God, in which he assigns to our lives "pleasures forevermore."

If we carefully examine the life of Jesus, we will find he spent quality time in the presence of God—Jesus stayed tuned-in to the frequency of heaven. Jesus received instructions from his Father and was led by the Holy Spirit; he had to rely on the Holy Spirit just as saints do today.

Like Jesus, we, too, should spend quality time in God's presence, where we become "presence dwellers." In that place, Abba communes in fellowship with us and gives us revelations and instructions via the Holy Spirit. This becomes the frequency through which he gives us comprehensive insight into our Father's plans and purpose with clarity—in supernatural high definition. He opens our mind's eye and illuminates it with the Gospel of the kingdom—its laws, principles, and systems pertaining to heaven's government.

Frequency relates to the number of occurrences of a repeating event per unit of time. For example, if a newborn baby's heart beats at a frequency of 120 beats per minute, its period—the interval between beats—is half a second—sixty seconds divided by 120 beats.

Frequency is defined as the state or fact of being frequent—frequent occurrence or rate of occurrence. For example, the doctor has increased the frequency of his visits.

Frequency, as it is defined in accordance with the theme of this book, means being God conscious, Christ centered, and Holy Spirit focused—that is, the ability to access a sustainable, regular, or consistent mind filled with God's Word, God thoughts, and meditation on the Word and the goodness of God—a mind at peace, knowing we have "access on demand" to the wisdom and power of God in "supernatural high definition."

> *You will keep him in perfect peace, whose mind is stayed on You, because he trusts in You.*
>
> **—Isaiah 26:3 NKJV**

I could easily frame the above verse to read: Abba keeps me in perfect peace because my mind stays tuned-in to his frequency.

God's process toward spiritual maturity is usually slow and steady. The Holy Spirit is always moving "upon the face" of every single believer to bring forth God's original plan that he intended in his eternal mind before he created the world. God is a God of order; therefore he is very methodical. He moves us from one place to another place, which is always a place of higher standards and levels of surrender, struggle, and godly suffering. God never moves backward; he is always in forward motion. His steps toward spiritual maturity are deliberate. They are intricate, they are sure, and they are pure.

In each phase of spiritual growth, God tests our commitment, loyalty, and character "to humble you and test you, to know what was in your heart, whether you would keep His commandments or not" (Deuteronomy 8:2 NKJV). His desire is for his children to fulfill the kingdom assignment and destiny he ordained for us, where life is enjoyable, and the rewards are great and abundant.

As an apostle, a bishop, and a pastor (shepherd) of Jesus Christ, I am blessed to share with readers throughout the pages of this book what probably is the most significant scheme Satan has used to stunt the saints' spiritual growth and render them as spiritual babies. Satan knows that baby Christians cannot become wise master builders. His deception involves keeping the saints busy with religious duties but never embracing God's process toward spiritual maturity, where saints become commissioned commanders and kingdom-compliant servant-leaders.

Kingdom-compliant servant-leaders have discovered their kingdom assignment and have submitted themselves to the teaching, training, equipping, and obedience that will meet the standard of the kingdom—the lofty position of subduing earthly kingdoms that become the kingdoms of our Lord and of his Christ, according to Revelation 11:15.

Like many contemporary saints, the prophet Jeremiah was deluged by a flood of complaints questioning God's sovereignty. "Why does the way of the wicked prosper? Why are those happy who deal so treacherously?" (Jeremiah 12:1 NKJV). How does a saint of God today come to this same place of complaint experienced by Jeremiah over twenty-five hundred years ago? In part, it is because many saints have conformed to the celebrity mentality of the world's system of greatness. They have been duped by the devil, living as if they are of this world.

Jesus prayed to his Father, "I do not pray that You should take them out of the world, but that you should keep them from the evil one. They are not of the world, just as I am not of the world. Sanctify them by Your truth. Your word is truth" (John 17:15–17 NKJV).

Yes, we live in the world, but we are not of the world. Jesus taught us how to distinguish between the two—the word of truth. Many members of the body of Christ have succumbed to the devil's strategy—his quick fix, overnight sensation, and personality-driven claim to fame. For many, when the name-it-and-claim-it doctrine and formula for success did not work—mostly because people weren't properly taught and never received revelation of God's process and timing for their manifestation—they lost hope and began to "make things happen" by their might and power rather than by patiently awaiting God's perfect timing, "who gives us richly all things to enjoy" (1 Timothy 6:17 NKJV).

Not abiding the process of spiritual maturity and God's timing for our kingdom commission will always result in spiritual immaturity. Saints of God want very much to be spiritual giants possessing the kingly anointing of Jesus with authority and power, but not many are willing to surrender to the process by which this level of anointing is attained, or willing to pay the costly price for God's promotion, whose "blessing … makes rich, and He adds no sorrow with it" (Proverbs 10:22 ESV). So, like Jeremiah, they end up complaining and questioning God.

This is the place in which I found myself for so many years, in a regressive state filled with complaints and questioning God's love for me. One day, as I was trying to make sense of it all, desiring to be restored to my heavenly Father, the Holy Spirit led me to this scripture verse. It was as if God was speaking directly to me face-to-face. "If you have run with the footmen, and they have wearied you, then how can you contend with horses?" (Jeremiah 12:5 NKJV).

The difference between believers who are footmen and believers who are horsemen is significant, distinguished by a mark of honor, rank, eminence, or excellence.

My purpose in writing this book is to communicate through personal experiences the process toward spiritual maturity and how to endure it. It is a process that begins with total surrender to the development of saints from footmen and spiritual babes to horsemen—commanders, generals, officers, leaders, and spiritual parents.

Spiritual growth takes place when a believer learns to trust God completely, willingly obey his commands, heed his instructions, and serve God in the kingdom assignment he specifically ordained for that individual's life on earth. The process is relative to the purpose, and the experience is unique to the believer.

I am very transparent in sharing some of the experiences I've encountered and endured en route to spiritual maturity and becoming a commissioned kingdom-compliant servant-leader. Together we will traverse the spiritual growth process by learning how to stay tuned-in to the frequency of heaven, God's frequency, through his omnipotence, omnipresence, and omniscience. His very nature, power, and glory work in and through the believer. It is the same power Jesus exercised during his earthly ministry.

The church is now experiencing the kingdom age awakening, the era of kingdom compliance, and the era of God's glory being revealed in the earth through his saints—those who he knows are his. She is being reformed from the inside out as she embraces the twenty-first-century apostolic and prophetic reformation and transformation models—the many diverse global networks, applications and expressions, and the unity of the faith working together, allowing the church to mature to the measure of the full stature of Christ, speaking the truth in love and growing up in all things to Jesus Christ, her head (Ephesians 4:13–16 NKJV).

God is reaffirming the church's credibility and viability, and the saints will indeed be known as a powerful and reliable apostolic and prophetic people who speak to the seven mountains of culture with the authority of a king-priest. The church is standing at the crossroads of the conclusion of the age of grace. She must now fulfill her obligation, her mandate, to subdue the kingdoms of the world as a fully prepared bride adorned to wed the bridegroom. "Let us be glad and rejoice and give Him glory, for the marriage of the Lamb has come, and His wife has made herself ready" (Revelation 19:7 NKJV). She has learned to stay tuned-in to the frequency of heaven.

CHAPTER 1

God's Solid Foundation

> *Nevertheless, God's solid foundation stands firm, sealed with this inscription: "The Lord knows those who are his," and, "Everyone who confesses the name of the Lord must turn away from wickedness."*
>
> **—2 Timothy 2:19 NIV**

In this end-time harvest season, it is imperative that the body of Christ understand the foundation of God's kingdom. It is a substructure laid with the spirit of humankind, not the soul or body, as a basis for raising something greater: saints who are kingdom compliant, adhering strictly to the Word of God. The Lord knows those who are his—those who have turned away from wickedness; those who are true bond servants; those who express purity of heart, attitude, and action; and those who confess in order to know the Lord and continue in his word. They are his disciples indeed (John 8:31 NKJV).

The word *foundation*, as it relates to the law of first mention in the Bible, is derived from the Hebrew word *yacad*, a primary root word meaning to set, to found, or to sit down together—that is, to settle; to consult; to establish; to lay the foundation; or to instruct, set, or ensure.

In the New Testament, the Greek translation for *foundation* is the verb *themelioo*, which means to lay a foundation. Metaphorically, it means to be grounded in love and settled in faith.

God's very nature is incorporated in his foundation, which forms an indistinguishable whole—a legal corporation that stands firm, grounded in love and settled in faith. God's foundation is solid because it takes on the personality and character of the One who laid it: "For no other foundation can anyone lay than that which is laid, which is Jesus Christ" (1 Corinthians 3:11 NKJV).

In light of this revelation, we must understand that the kingdom of God is both a concept and a reality. A *concept* is defined as something conceived in the mind, while a *reality* is something in actual fact—a real event, entity, or state of affairs.[1] Jesus said, "My kingdom is not of this world. If it were, my servants would fight to prevent my arrest by the Jews. But now my kingdom is from another place" (John 18:35 NIV). Notice he never said it was not *in* this world. In essence, Jesus identifies his kingdom as a reality although it is from another place, heaven. Jesus further stated, "The kingdom of God does not come with observation … For indeed, the kingdom of God is within you" (Luke 17:20–21 NKJV). The implication is that the kingdom of God is a concept of the heart (mind) since it cannot be seen as a geographical location on the earth.

Before we go any further, let's define *kingdom*. A kingdom is the realm of the authority of a king, or the territory or people over whom a king bears rule. In short, it is the government of a king, a sovereign who exerts his influence over his territory, influencing it with his will and his purpose in order to develop a culture and society of subjects or citizens who reflect his nature and values. *Basileia* is the Greek word for kingdom, and it means sovereignty, royal power, and dominion.[2] Therefore, a kingdom is a government led by a king. The king is the government, and wherever the king is, his government is also present.

Let's also make a distinction between the kingdom of God and the kingdom of heaven in how each entity functions. The former is the

---

[1] *Merriam-Webster's Collegiate Dictionary: Eleventh Edition*, sv "concept."

[2] *Vine's Expository Dictionary of New Testament Words*, sv "*basileia*."

extension of God's rule and dominion—the government of God on the earth. The latter is the government of God in heaven. The kingdom of heaven is a clear depiction of where it is from, while the kingdom of God lets us know who runs it. Nevertheless, in the realm of the spirit, there is no difference between the two.

> *Then Jesus said to His disciples, "Assuredly, I say to you that it is hard for a rich man to enter the kingdom of heaven. And again I say to you, it is easier for a camel to go through the eye of a needle than for a rich man to enter the kingdom of God."*
>
> **—Matthew 19:23–24 NKJV**

The kingdom of God is the governing influence of our heavenly Father's will over the territory called earth—his affect and influence over his citizens whom he has chosen.

> *Just as He chose us in Him before the foundation of the world, to be holy and blameless before Him in love.*
>
> **—Ephesians 1:4 MEV**

> *Now, therefore, you are no longer strangers and foreigners, but are fellow citizens with the saints and members of the household of God.*
>
> **—Ephesians 2:19 NKJV**

> *Because God has from the beginning chosen you for salvation through sanctification by the Spirit and belief in the truth.*
>
> **—2 Thessalonians 2:13 NKJV**

The kingdom of God is a government based upon a constitution that governs the kingdom. The solid foundation of the kingdom stands sure, for it is built upon the eternal Word of God, which is established forever in heaven (Psalm 119:89 NKJV). In the beginning, God spoke. He used his words to bring everything into existence, including humankind. He created Adam in his own image and likeness and crowned him with words of dominion. He created Adam to rule and crowned him with his glory. This was the delegated authority conferred on humankind to be God's agent-representatives in the territory called earth (Genesis 1:26–31 NKJV).

As citizens of the kingdom of heaven, we were created to act like God on the earth because we were created in his image—his nature and creativity—and his likeness—his similarity, behavior, and capability. So God, our king, governs earth—his expanded territory or domain—from heaven through his people. It is the will of the King for his rule to be asserted throughout his territory by his citizens. Therefore, our kingdom assignment is the priority of God and the object of our pursuit. Through his nature, we are programmed to do his will on earth as it is in heaven. Jesus's top priority was to teach and preach the Gospel of the kingdom. His focus was solely on a kingdom, not a religion.

> *From that time on Jesus began to preach, "Repent, for the kingdom of heaven is near."*
>
> **—Matthew 4:17 NIV**

> *Jesus went throughout Galilee, teaching in their synagogues, preaching the good news of the kingdom, and healing every disease and sickness among the people.*
>
> **—Matthew 4:23 NKJV**

> *And He sent them out to preach the kingdom of God and to heal the sick.*
>
> **—Luke 9:2 KJV**

The kingdom message is fully disclosed in the Bible. The Bible is about a king, his kingdom, its citizens, and his will to be done on earth as it is in heaven. Our purpose, or kingdom assignment, is tied to the earth, not only in this life but also in eternity. Earth will always be our permanent home. God has created us in his image and likeness and has given us his authority to manage it according to the heavenly constitution. The Word of God is the constitution of the kingdom. The Word of God is the eternal foundation of the kingdom. Jesus is the brightness of the Father's glory, the express image of God, and upholds all things by the word of his power (Hebrews 1:3 NKJV).

THE ORIGIN OF GOD'S KINGDOM IS SPIRITUAL

That which is spiritual supersedes that which is physical. Everything visible and physical was made from that which is invisible and spiritual. "By faith we understand that the universe was formed at God's command [His Word], so that what is seen was not made out of what was visible" (Hebrews 11:3 NIV). Living in the kingdom of God requires a heavenly eternal perspective, not an earthly ephemeral one.

In the Gospel of Matthew, Jesus tells us to prioritize the kingdom of God, and all visible and physical things will be added (Matthew 6:33 NKJV). What we must understand is that God's kingdom and his sovereignty are one. From the moment we made Jesus Savior and Lord of our lives, we became citizens of the kingdom of heaven under our heavenly Father's sovereign rule. Our Father doesn't ask our permission concerning his sovereignty. He boldly affirms that he is sovereign. "God has set his throne in heaven; he rules over us all. He's the King" (Psalm 103:19 MSG).

"Our God is in heaven doing whatever he wants to do" (Psalm 115:3 MSG). It's high time the saints of God realize when we accepted Jesus we accepted the kingdom of God, his sovereignty, and his rule from heaven. We may look at earth as a colony of heaven, a colony created by God for humankind—the extension of his royal family. David wrote, "The earth is the Lord's, and the fullness thereof; the world, and they that dwell therein" (Psalm 24:1 KJV). God upholds the world by the word of his power. John affirms this in his Gospel and in the book of Revelation.

> *In the beginning was the Word, and the Word was with God, and the Word was God. He was with God in the beginning. All things were created through Him, and apart from Him not one thing was created that has been created.*
>
> **—John 1:1–3 TPT**

> *You are worthy, O Lord, To receive glory and honor and power; For You created all things, And by Your will they exist and were created.*
>
> **—Revelation 4:11 NKJV**

Everything God created he created for his glory. There is no one greater than God; therefore there is no one greater than God to receive glory. "For by Him all things were created that are in heaven and that are on earth, visible and invisible, whether thrones or dominions or principalities or powers. All things were created through Him and for Him. And He is before all things, and in Him all things consist" (Colossians 1:16–17 NKJV).

Jesus's Kingdom Prayer says, "Your kingdom come. Your will be done On earth as it is in heaven" (Matthew 6:10 NKJV), which suggests that the will of the King, whose throne is in heaven, be done or duplicated on earth by his citizens. Daniel assures us that God's dominion is everlasting, and his kingdom will never be destroyed (Daniel 7:14 NKJV). As citizens, our duty is to serve God and to do his will. He has delegated to us, through his Son, Jesus, his authority to rule his domain called earth. We are stewards of his earthly kingdom. And as such, our duty is to occupy until he comes: "Do business till I come" (Luke 19:13 NKJV).

Whenever we allow the evil systems of this world, through our flesh, to jeopardize our stewardship, we fail to adhere to the rules of the kingdom, living independently of God.

Sadly, there are still many saints who try to live independent of God, as if God doesn't exist. But a close look at their lifestyles would reveal that they are reaping the fruit of rebellion against God. They are saints, but broken saints. They are saints, but sick saints. They are saints, but undelivered saints. Although regenerated, born again by the Holy Spirit, many have never been baptized in the Holy Spirit. They have never made Jesus Lord of their life. There is a difference between regeneration and being filled with the Holy Spirit.

> "Have you received the Holy Spirit since you believed?"
> They said to him, "No, we have not even heard that there is a Holy Spirit."
> He said to them, "Into what then were you baptized?"
> They said, "Into John's baptism."
> Paul said, "John indeed baptized with the baptism of repentance, telling the people that they should believe in the One coming after him, that is, in Christ Jesus."

> When they heard this, they were baptized in the name of the Lord Jesus. When Paul had laid his hands on them, the Holy Spirit came on them, and they spoke in other tongues and prophesied. (Acts 19:2–6 MEV)

Regeneration is an *inward expression* of Jesus as Savior: "For you have been born again, not from perishable seed, but imperishable, through the word of God which lives and abides forever" (1 Peter 1:23 MEV). The renewing of the Holy Ghost, or being filled with the Holy Spirit, is an *outward manifestation* of Jesus as Lord lived through us on the earth. It is difficult to advance into new standards of kingdom living without a revelation of this truth. One cannot be completely faithful to God by regeneration alone; he or she must be filled with the Holy Spirit, the power of God, to live the kingdom life on the earth. The evidence of God in a person's life is not simply the fulfilled desire of that which is hoped for but the evidence of faith as proof by one who believes in a God who cannot lie and trusts him even when he or she still cannot see it happening in the natural world.

> *Not by works of righteousness which we have done, but according to His mercy He saved us, through the washing of regeneration, and renewing of the Holy Ghost; Which he shed on us abundantly through Jesus Christ our Saviour.*
>
> **—Titus 3:5–6 KJV**

As saints, citizens of the kingdom of heaven, we must commit to being faithful so that we also enjoy the benefits of the kingdom. The kingdom of heaven is full of benefits for its citizens. Some of these benefits include fullness of life, divine health, divine prosperity, and divine security and protection.

In God's kingdom, we are privileged. There is safety, security, and we are valued sons and daughters. He is our provider. This is not the case in earthly kingdoms. In earthly kingdoms, provision comes through either work or welfare. And when people get sick, they have special care through physicians who practice medicine. But in God's kingdom, he is our healer. In earthly kingdoms, we have a place to live. But in God's kingdom, God lives in us. As a result, there is no worry for citizens of the kingdom who trust God absolutely. It is our Father's, our King's, good pleasure to give us the kingdom (Luke 12:32 NKJV).

As we are faithful to obey the rules, principles, constitution of the kingdom—the Word of God—we may have to give up certain things along the way. In my book *From Footmen to Horsemen*, I share my personal story of things I was impressed by the Holy Spirit to give up along my journey of becoming obedient to the Word of God. I remained faithful, allowing the Father to develop me and equip me to become the commissioned kingdom-level servant apostle I am today. What I've learned since those days is that the Father will give back to us at the appointed time in another season of our spiritual growth. The things we gave up in our early walk with him will be exponentially multiplied. As we sometimes say, "A delay is not a denial."

Peter details the sacrifices he and the other eleven disciples had made in order to follow Jesus.

> Then Peter began to say to Him, "See, we have left all and followed You."
> So Jesus answered and said, "Assuredly, I say to you, there is no one who has left house or brothers or sisters or father or mother or wife or children or lands, for My sake and the gospel's, who shall not receive a hundredfold now in this time - houses and brothers and sisters and mothers and children and lands, with persecutions - and in the age to come eternal life. But many *who are* first will be last, and the last first. (Mark 10:28–31 NKJV)

Notice that Jesus draws upon a promise of God to calm Peter's anxiety: "And indeed there are last who will be first, and there are first who will be last" (Luke 13:30 NKJV). God's promises are always *yes* because they are a part of his covenant—his contractual agreement with humankind by which he administers his kingdom. And God's covenant is legally binding, "since there was no one greater for him to swear by, he swore by himself … And so after waiting patiently, Abraham received what was promised" (Hebrews 6:13–15 NIV).

Every Old Testament law was fulfilled in and through Jesus by a new covenant established upon better promises (Hebrews 8:6). God's character is unchanging. His word was, is, and always will be absolute and trustworthy. But in order to secure our fallen human condition, where man's word is not necessarily trustworthy, God condescended himself to our broken state, making his word—already totally trustworthy—twice dependable. And through our faith in Jesus Christ, we are indeed true spiritual descendants of Abraham. "If you belong to Christ, then you are Abraham's seed, and heirs according to the promise" (Galatians 3:29 NIV).

The "better covenant which was established upon better promises" (Hebrews 8:6b KJV) is preeminent over the old covenant in many ways: "For Christ is the end of the law for righteousness to every one that believeth" (Romans 10:4 KJV). The old covenant is full of rituals and demands, and the new covenant is full of gifts and supplies. One of the differences between the old covenant and the new covenant is seen in the context of servitude versus sonship. "And because you are sons, God has sent forth the Spirit of His Son into your hearts, crying out, 'Abba Father'" (Galatians 4:6 NKJV).

There is a cleansing and a refining taking place in the body of Christ—the church—involving the shift from religion (rules) to kingdom (relationship). The Father has preserved a remnant of kingdom-compliant saints who have not sold out to the evil systems of the world, who have not compromised the Gospel of the kingdom out of a self-righteous, covetous, and corrupt heart of flesh. This remnant is being called to "come up higher" into a realm of kingdom compliance—identification with our Lord in his suffering on earth as his bond servants and exercising our faith in him through our willing obedience and servitude, even as we are seated in heavenly places with him. Prioritizing the kingdom of God is the goal.

Saints must realize that the Lord greatly desires to introduce his body to his true kingdom, the kingdom of their hearts, through a Spirit-led life and walk—kingdom compliance. We will not have a part in this higher governmental realm of the kingdom of heaven until we have individually, collectively, and unconditionally submitted our lives to be governed by him, having learned in some measure and continuing to learn how to walk in the Spirit and live within God's kingdom economy.

The kingdom of God is a realm in which everything moves by divine order and purpose. There are kingdom benefits available to us that we never experience, because we fail to appropriate the Word of God to our desires, our situations, our problems. Too many saints tend to settle for less than the Lord's best provision. Their ignorance, relative to the promises of God, or their unwillingness to appropriate those promises, has deprived them of the Lord's best.

During this time of the saints' transition and transformation from the church age (religious bondage) into the kingdom age (freedom built upon grace and truth), there is a price the saints must pay if we are to perpetually experience the Lord's best. We cannot *overcome* unless there is something to overcome. The reward we receive for putting the Lord first is the prize that is beyond comparison, as we forget what's past and reach toward what lies ahead. We must "press toward the mark for the prize of the high calling of God in Christ Jesus" (Philippians 3:13–14 KJV).

CHAPTER 2

God's Nature Is Incorporated in the Foundation of His Kingdom

Father, I desire that they also whom You gave Me may be with Me where I am, that they may behold My glory which You have given Me; for You loved Me before the foundation of the world.
—John 17:24 NKJV

THE KINGDOM OF HEAVEN IS ESTABLISHED UPON LOVE

Love is a kingdom covenant law. The nature of someone or something expresses the essential features that lie within it. As believers, our heavenly Father has made us partakers of his divine nature through his exceedingly great and precious promises (2 Peter 1:4 NKJV), which begins with love, as God is love. Clearly, the solid foundation of the kingdom of God begins with love. Like the Word of God, love is eternal, and "love never fails" (1 Corinthians 13:8 NKJV).

The word *love*, in this context, is the Greek word *agape*, taken from *agapao*, which means love in a social or moral sense; affection or benevolence; a love feast: charity, dear, love.[3] Agape is unconditional love.

This description references the divine, self-sacrificial, unconditional love of God shown toward us and given from his heart of benevolence with pure motives. This same love has been shed abroad in our hearts by the Holy Spirit, who is given to us. Through New Testament commandment, we, too, are obligated to give to others the same love God has given to each of us "because the love of God has been poured out in our hearts by the Holy Spirit who was given to us" (Romans 5:5 NKJV).

Wow! How awesome is that? When we received Jesus Christ as Savior and Lord, the Holy Spirit (our comforter) was given to us as a gift, and with that gift came love—God himself. The very nature of God is love, which also is the primary fruit of the Holy Spirit in the life of the believer (Galatians 5:22 NIV).

I really don't believe people hate one another as much as they are afraid of one another. As humans, we tend to be intimidated by those who look, think, and behave differently than we do. The result, in many cases, can generally be seen in the form of some kind of defense bent on superiority and carried out in an evil way that tends to inflict some measure of harm—separation, discrimination, racism, prejudice, and bigotry. If only people could love one another. As stated in 1 John 4:18 NKJV, "There is no fear in love; but perfect love casts out fear, because fear involves torment. But he who fears has not been made perfect in love."

> Beloved, let us love one another, for love is of God; and everyone who loves is born of God and knows God. He who does not love does not know God, for God is love. In this the love of God was manifested toward us, that God has sent His only begotten Son into the world, that we might live through Him. In this is love, not that we loved God, but that He loves us and sent His Son to be the propitiation for our sins. Beloved, if God so loves us, we also ought to love one another. No one has seen God at any time. If we love one another, God abides in us, and His love has been perfected in us. By this we know

[3] *Strong's Exhaustive Concordance of the Bible, NT,* 4102.

> that we abide in Him, and He in us, because He has given us of His Spirit. (1 John 4:7–13 NKJV)

According to the above scripture, there is no getting around the fact that God is revealed through our love for one another. When love controls our thoughts and actions and is shown to others, it becomes the same benevolent gift God gave believers through his Son, Jesus. This means it is perfected in and through us by the indwelling Holy Spirit when genuinely shown toward others. To this end, it becomes the believer's primary obligation and his or her highest birthright, making love a foundation of the kingdom of heaven.

> *A new commandment I give to you, that you love one another; as I have loved you, that you also love one another. By this all will know that you are My disciples, if you have love for one another.*
>
> **—John 13:34–35 NKJV**

> *If you really fulfill the royal law according to the Scripture, "You shall love your neighbor as yourself," you do well.*
>
> **—James 2:8 NKJV**

Therefore, love is the primary wavelength, via the Holy Spirit, that transmits the frequency of heaven to earth.

THE KINGDOM OF HEAVEN IS ESTABLISHED UPON FAITH

Everything God does, he does by faith. First and foremost, faith is a spiritual force, which means its power is not predicated upon physical things. Faith is of God—what God knows to be truth. The Greek word for *faith* is *pistis*, which means persuasion, credence, conviction—truth or the truthfulness of God—reliance upon Christ for salvation; constancy in truth itself: assurance, belief, believe, faith, fidelity.[4]

The Word of God says that believers have been justified by faith (Romans 5:1 NKJV). In other words, we've been made righteous by our

[4] *Strong's Exhaustive Concordance of the Bible, NT*, 4102.

faith in Jesus Christ and his finished work. Justified is our status in life as born-again people who trust completely in Jesus's victory over Satan, death, and hell, which signifies our redemption through his precious blood, reconciling us back to God.

The Greek word for *justification* is *dikaiosis*, taken from *dikaioo*, which means to show or regard as just or innocent; an equitable deed; justification, acquittal for Christ's sake.[5] *Justification* is a legal term declaring the believer free from the penalty of death prescribed by the law. Justification is inclusive of repentance from dead works and faith toward God (Hebrews 6:1 NKJV), which undergirds the commandment that the just shall live by faith. Therefore, God is a faith God who can only be pleased by our lifestyle of faith.

> *Therefore, having been justified by faith, we have peace with God through our Lord Jesus Christ, through whom also we have access by faith into this grace in which we stand, and rejoice in hope of the glory of God.*
>
> **—Romans 5:1–2 NKJV**

> *Knowing that a man is not justified by the works of the law but by faith in Jesus Christ, even we have believed in Christ Jesus, that we might be justified by faith in Christ and not by the works of the law; for by the works of the law no flesh shall be justified.*
>
> **—Galatians 2:16 NKJV**

> *But that no one is justified by the law in the sight of God is evident, for "the just shall live by faith."*
>
> **—Galatians 3:11 NKJV**

Everything God does, He does by faith; from the creation of the world to the creation of a new heaven and a new earth. He calls those things which do not exist as though they did (Romans 4:17 NKJV).

Faith is a manifestation of supernatural power. It is not based on what we see or any of our other physical senses. Faith in God—his word, his name, the Holy Spirit, Jesus Christ, and his finished work on the cross—must be embraced by the believer as a title deed to all the promises of God that belong to the believer by covenant. It is our

[5] *Strong's Exhaustive Concordance of the Bible, NT*, 1344, 1345, 1347.

position of liberty as being citizens of the kingdom of heaven as long as we maintain our faith in Jesus Christ. "For we walk by faith, not by sight" (2 Corinthians 5:7 NKJV). "But without faith, it is impossible to please Him" (Hebrews 11:6 NKJV).

The most powerful element of faith is love. "For we through the Spirit eagerly wait for the hope of righteousness by faith. For in Christ Jesus neither circumcision nor uncircumcision avails anything, but faith working through love" (Galatians 5:5–6 NKJV). Here's where many believers miss it. Their faith life is weak because their love walk is insincere.

Love is God's first nature. All other character traits that flow from his love-nature is an offshoot of love and works through love, via the Holy Spirit, in helping the believer to keep the commandments of God as his new creation. This is a case to be made once we look at all the components of faith that can only work through the person, nature, character, and glory of God, which describes who God is—love!

Faith is present tense: "Now faith is …" (Hebrews 11:1 NKJV) the absence of doubt; grace through faith is a gift that leads to salvation. Faith is an impartation from God; faith comes by hearing the Word of God (Romans 10:17 NKJV). Faith is a fruit of the Holy Spirit that grows as godly character within the believer's heart. Faith speaks (Romans 10:6 NKJV), and the righteous must live by his faith (Habakkuk 2:4 NKJV; Romans 1:17 NKJV; Galatians 3:11 NKJV).

Faith is the fundamental law of the kingdom of heaven—belief in God as the sovereign king of all kingdoms. Fear is the opposite of faith. And as such, fear or unbelief or lack of faith is the supreme evil and enemy of the kingdom of heaven, but faith is a foundation for all things good.

Faith is a Holy Spirit wavelength that transmits the frequency of heaven to earth.

THE KINGDOM OF HEAVEN IS ESTABLISHED UPON GRACE

The kingdom of heaven is governed by the New Testament covenant of grace. Grace is one of the benefits believers enjoy as citizens. "The

Word became flesh and made his dwelling among us. We have seen his glory, the glory of the One and Only, who came from the Father, full of grace and truth ... From the fullness of his grace we have all received one blessing after another. For the law was given through Moses; grace and truth came through Jesus Christ" (John 1:14–17 NIV).

I believe grace is God's way of giving believers better than we deserve. Grace abounds to us from God's benevolence. Faith in Jesus Christ initiates his grace. It is a gift from him to us, not based on anything we've done to earn or deserve it. Since religion teaches that we have to work for God, perform some ritual, dress a certain way, never have fun or enjoy recreation or entertainment outside the church, and earn our way into heaven, many believers cannot simply receive grace. Grace makes them feel guilty or condemned, when it should make them feel a sense of freedom. For many believers who are entrenched in religion, freedom condemns them because it exposes them to the truth—their inability to "live right" through their own self-righteousness.

Grace is what believers receive when their level of spiritual maturity does not surpass the level of the lust of their flesh, even when it should.

The New Testament is a covenant of grace established upon better promises (Hebrews 8:6 NKJV). What exactly is grace, and why is it so important to living the Christian lifestyle successfully? Let's explore the word *grace* as it is rendered in the Greek text.

Charis is the Greek word for *grace*. It is taken from the verb *chairo* and can be defined as a gracious act or manner; a divine influence upon the heart that is reflected in the life of an individual. It is a benefit, favor, or gift of joy, liberality, and pleasure. It means to be cheerful, calmly happy, and Godspeed.[6] Grace is so much more than just unmerited favor.

Everything that grace stands for affords the believer a full and varied life substantiated by divine influence, which includes gracious acts of favor, joy, godly pleasure, and cheerfulness with Godspeed. Who wouldn't want this level of divine benefits? Only those whose mindset is closed to the knowledge of what God has already done through his Son, our apostle and high priest, Jesus Christ.

We receive God's grace by our faith in Jesus. He is full of grace. He is

---

[6] *Strong's Exhaustive Concordance of the Bible, NT*, 5485.

the God of all grace (1 Peter 5:10 NKJV). As we obtain more knowledge of God and of Jesus our Lord, the more grace we receive with peace. He pours upon us grace and peace multiplied so that we may grow in Christ, enjoying "all things that pertain to life and godliness, through the knowledge of Him who called us by glory and virtue" (2 Peter 1:3 NKJV).

False humility robs believers of God's grace. Religion is a grace killer. It robs us of God's best through its legalistic doctrine.

Grace is much deeper than unmerited favor from God. Not only is grace a gift that cannot be earned but it is also a bestowal of practical manifestations of goodwill. It is a divine favor of blessings for successful earthly living. It is the power of God to equip believers for ministry. And those who are determined to live by the Old Testament law cannot receive this grace. Why?

> *Christ is become of no effect unto you, whosoever of you are justified by the law; ye are fallen from grace.*
>
> **—Galatians 5:4 KJV**

There are still many pastors who refuse to teach their congregation the grace of God through the finished work of his Son, Jesus Christ. They think grace gives believers "a license to sin." I heard one well-known pastor say, "Believers don't need a license to sin. They're doing just fine without one."

I tend to agree with his assessment. Pastors have a charge to teach the entire Gospel. We cannot omit certain parts of the Gospel simply because we think our congregants will misunderstand or take advantage of it. We must hold baby Christians accountable to spiritual growth, knowing mistakes come with growth. We must hold one another accountable to the Word of God, and rather than trying our best not to sin, leave the renewing of our minds to the Holy Spirit. That is his job, when we allow him to do it. As we allow the Holy Spirit to renew our minds by revealing to us knowledge of who Jesus is, that God and his word are one, we will grow in grace and in the knowledge of Jesus Christ (2 Peter 3:18 NKJV).

God's Word is clear concerning the power of grace: "Where sin abounded, grace did much more abound" (Romans 5:20 KJV). The implication is that grace is more powerful than sin; therefore he warns us not to take grace for granted nor to use it as a cloak for sin. The standard for grace is righteousness. "Even so might grace reign through righteousness" (Romans 5:21 KJV).

"For you, brethren, have been called to liberty; only do not use liberty as an opportunity for the flesh, but through love serve one another. For all the law is fulfilled in one word, even in this: 'You shall love your neighbor as yourself.' But if you bite and devour one another, beware lest you be consumed by one another" (Galatians 5:13–15 NKJV). Believers must learn to live the Christian lifestyle from the inside out, through the power of the Holy Spirit, as living epistles known and read by all men (2 Corinthians 3:2 NKJV). To try any other way will expose a lack of spiritual maturity and reveal a life based on self-righteousness, which is religion. In Christ, we have liberty in accordance with the Word of God, in service (loyalty) to him. Only as we yield to the leadership and guidance of the Holy Spirit can we walk in his power and purge our flesh. "For if you live according to the flesh you will die; but if by the Spirit you put to death the deeds of the body, you will live. For as many as are led by the Spirit of God, these are sons of God" (Romans 8:13–14 NKJV).

If believers want to walk in God's unconditional favor, we must get into God's Word. We must seek, pursue, research, study, learn, meditate, and appropriate God's grace. His grace is without measure or limit. Once we receive a revelation of grace, we'll possess the boldness to walk confidently before God, our heavenly Father, knowing that as we trust him in all things his grace will abound in our lives.

> *But by the grace of God I am what I am, and His grace toward me was not in vain; but I labored more abundantly than they all, yet not I, but the grace of God which was with me.*
>
> **—1 Corinthians 15:10 NKJV**

As believers grow in grace, we cannot be afraid to make mistakes. God is not stunned or appalled when we make mistakes. He knows how he made us: "For He knows our frame; He remembers that we are dust" (Psalm 103:14 NKJV). Thank God we are saved by grace through faith and surrounded by his favor. We stand in the fullness of God's grace and live our lives in abundance being delivered, healed, prosperous, and equipped for the ministry of the Gospel of the kingdom to the world.

> *You therefore, my son, be strong in the grace that is in Christ Jesus.*
>
> **—2 Timothy 2:1 NKJV**

> *Therefore they stayed there a long time, speaking boldly in the Lord, who was bearing witness to the word of His grace, granting signs and wonders to be done by their hands.*
>
> **—Acts 14:3 NKJV**

> *So now, brethren, I commend you to God and to the word of His grace, which is able to build you up and give you an inheritance among all those who are sanctified.*
>
> **—Acts 20:32 NKJV**

Through grace we can learn to live in this world with liberty, unswayed by "the corruption that is in the world through lust" (2 Peter 1:4 NKJV). Understanding God's grace means we have access to receive his best through our faith in Jesus Christ, who receives us as if we never sinned and bestows upon us his grace to receive all the promises of God. As the ministry of grace is engrafted into our hearts, we become living epistles known and read by all people (2 Corinthians 3:2 NKJV).

Our ability to walk in the grace of God is joined together with understanding our right standing before him. Because of Jesus's sacrifice, we are the redeemed of the Lord, and we must say so (Psalm 107:2 NKJV). "We then, as workers together with Him also plead with you not to receive the grace of God in vain" (2 Corinthians 6:1 NKJV). In other words, let's not reject God's goodness by refusing to receive his bestowal of grace. It is his gift to us through the shed blood of Jesus. Also, let's not be guilty of grieving God's heart nor of insulting the blood of Jesus by not understanding, receiving, walking in, and growing in grace.

Grace works by faith; therefore believers must walk in full assurance of faith, knowing that God is faithful to his word. Like Paul, "I do not frustrate the grace of God" (Galatians 2:21 KJV), because grace is a foundation of the kingdom of heaven.

Grace is a Holy Spirit wavelength that transmits the frequency of heaven to earth.

THE KINGDOM OF HEAVEN IS ESTABLISHED UPON HUMILITY—TOTAL DEPENDENCE ON GOD

But he gives us more grace. That is why scripture notes, "God opposes the proud but gives grace to the humble" (James 4:6 NIV).

The apostle Peter admonishes believers to clothe themselves with humility. "Be clothed with humility, for 'God resists the proud, but gives grace to the humble'" (1 Peter 5:5 NKJV). Why is humility so important to kingdom compliance, and why do so many "saved people" tend to not be clothed with humility, which God condemns as pride? To the contrary, many believers wear self-righteousness as a badge of honor, esteeming themselves higher than others. "Be of the same mind toward one another. One should not set their mind on high things but associate with the humble. One should not be wise in their own opinion" (Romans 12:16 NKJV).

The Greek word for *humility* is *tapeinophrosune*, which means humiliation of mind, modesty, humble, to abase self.[7] But the world tends to view humility as being weak, reliant on something or someone. Many people associate humility with religion, dependence on an invisible God who keeps letting his people down because they are so weak, which also implies that God is a weak god.

> *The fear of the Lord is the instruction of wisdom, and before honor is humility.*
>
> **—Proverbs 15:33 NKJV**

> *Pride goes before destruction, and a haughty spirit before a fall. Better to be of a humble spirit with the lowly, than to divide the spoil with the proud.*
>
> **—Proverbs 16:18–19 NKJV**

> *By humility and the fear of the Lord are riches and honor and life.*
>
> **—Proverbs 22:4 NKJV**

As believers live in humility before the Lord, he opens the way that leads them to honor. Jesus himself is our best example of living a life of

[7] *Strong's Exhaustive Concordance of the Bible, NT,* 5012.

humility—total trust in God. And we can see the result of his humility. Jesus displayed no anxiety, no worry, and no concern for his own life. It was simply a life lived in total reliance upon God's grace. Dependence on God is our place of rest. In this place in him, he supplies all our needs according to his riches in glory by Christ Jesus (Philippians 4:19).

The apostle Paul gives this exhortation to humility. "Let nothing be done through selfish ambition or conceit, but in lowliness of mind let each esteem others better than himself" (Philippians 2:3 NKJV).

John the Baptist understood humility. He clothed himself, his physical person, with camel's hair, but his heart was clothed in humility. John was dependent on God for the fulfilling of his earthly assignment. Jesus never told John the Baptist that he should decrease so that he could increase (John 3:30 NKJV). No, John received a revelation from God that Jesus was indeed "the Lamb of God who takes away the sin of the world" (John 1:29 NKJV).

By relinquishing himself as the "prophet of the hour," John allowed Jesus to have full reign for the fulfillment of his purpose on earth. John showed spiritual maturity when he told his disciples to follow Jesus.

We, too, must receive the Holy Spirit revelation that Jesus can only increase in our lives as we decrease (relinquish) all of who we are through our flesh and sense knowledge and embrace his life lived in and through us. We must submit ourselves in total dependence on God. He will not force himself on us.

Shortly after he had fulfilled his earthly purpose and confirmed Jesus as the messiah, John was thrown into prison by Herod Antipas because John had reproved him concerning his immoral relationship with his sister-in-law. "Because John had said to him, 'It is not lawful for you to have her'" (Matthew 14:4 NKJV). And I believe that prior to his heinous death God led John into the place of his rest. Remember, God gives grace to the humble.

The rest of God is a place of peace that surpasses human understanding. Take for instance Stephen the evangelist. He was "a man full of faith and the Holy Spirit" (Acts 6:5 NKJV). He preached from Abraham to Jesus to the Sanhedrin. And the Sanhedrin was offended by his words. As a result, Stephen was stoned to death. But he never denied or renounced his dependence on God. He exhibited humility in the likeness of Jesus, leaving us yet another example of true humility. "But he, being full of the Holy Spirit, gazed into heaven and saw the glory of God, and Jesus standing at the right hand of God … And they stoned Stephen as he was calling on God and saying, 'Lord Jesus, receive my spirit.' Then he knelt down and cried out with a loud voice, 'Lord, do not charge them with this sin.' And when he had said this, he fell asleep" (Acts 7:55, 59–60 NKJV).

Jesus is not in heaven pacing the floor because he is worried. His humility before God also brought him to the place of his Father's rest. Jesus understands God's rest and has made it available to us. He promises that as we come to him, he gives us rest (Matthew 11:28 NKJV).

Jesus is seated at the right hand of God—the position of authority. And his position is our position. God has "raised us up together, and made us sit together in the heavenly places in Christ Jesus" (Ephesians 2:6 NKJV).

"Far above all principality and power and might and dominion, and every name that is named, not only in this age but also in that which is to come" (Ephesians 1:21 NKJV).

As saints of God, we must have the same attitude as John the Baptist, Stephen the evangelist, and Jesus.

> Let this mind be in you which was also in Christ Jesus, who, being in the form of God, did not consider it robbery to be equal with God, but made Himself of no reputation, taking the form of a bondservant, and coming in the likeness of men. And being found in appearance as a man, He humbled Himself and became obedient to the point of death, even the death of the cross. Therefore God also has highly exalted Him and given Him the name which is above every name. (Philippians 2:5–9 NKJV)

Humility is the bedrock of character in alignment with kingdom compliance. It is fundamentally foundational. As citizens of the kingdom of heaven, we are commanded to be humble, to walk in dependence of God, which ensures freedom from pride. Those who walk in pride or self-righteousness display false humility (Colossians 2:18 NKJV). But God humbles us to bring us—those who are his—to obedience. Let's live each day in total dependence on our king, who is all, has all, and is in all, serving him with all humility (Acts 20:19 NKJV).

> *Or do you think that the Scripture says in vain, "The Spirit who dwells in us yearns jealously"? But He gives more grace. Therefore He says: "God resists the proud, but gives grace to the humble."*
>
> **—James 4:5–6 NKJV**

As we humble ourselves, we step into a place of divine favor knowing that God, our Father, dwells with the humble. God's desire is for our complete loyalty, and humility opens the door to our completeness in him. Humility is the foundation of the kingdom of heaven.

Humility is a Holy Spirit wavelength that transmits the frequency of heaven to earth.

THE KINGDOM OF HEAVEN IS ESTABLISHED UPON FORGIVENESS

> *Giving thanks to the Father who has qualified us to be partakers of the inheritance of the saints in the light. He has delivered us from the power of darkness and conveyed us into the kingdom of the Son of His love, in whom we have redemption through His blood, the forgiveness of sins*
>
> **—Colossians 1:12–14 NKJV**

Nothing can be clearer than forgiveness when it comes to living in the kingdom of heaven as a kingdom-compliant saint. No one can argue, in good faith, that forgiveness is not the foundation of the kingdom of heaven. The Lord's Prayer is actually a "kingdom" prayer, which is inclusive of the need for kingdom citizens to ask God for forgiveness of our debts or trespasses, as we forgive others (Matthew 6:12). Jesus concludes his discourse on prayer with these words: "For if you forgive men their trespasses, your heavenly Father will also forgive you. But if you do not forgive men their trespasses, neither will your Father forgive your trespasses" (Matthew 6:14–15 NKJV).

The Greek word for *forgiveness* is *aphiemi,* which is taken from *aphesis.* It means freedom; pardon; deliverance, liberty, remission. To send away; separation, cessation, completion, and reversal.[8]

Forgiveness is a significant force for living the kingdom lifestyle. It displays God's righteousness, it makes salvation real, it establishes our freedom in Christ, and it must be taught and preached on this measure—seventy times seven (Matthew 18:21–22 NKJV), as forgiving one another is unlimited. We forgive as God, through Christ Jesus, forgave us.

> *For You, Lord, are good, and ready to forgive, And abundant in mercy to all those who call upon You.*
>
> **—Psalm 86:5 NKJV**

> *And be kind to one another, tenderhearted, forgiving one another, even as God in Christ forgave you.*
>
> **—Ephesians 4:32 NKJV**

> *Take heed to yourselves. If your brother sins against you, rebuke him; and if he repents, forgive him. And if he sins against you seven times in a day, and seven times in a day returns to you, saying, "I repent," you shall forgive him. And the apostles said to the Lord, "Increase our faith.*
>
> **—Luke 17:3–5 NKJV**

It is evident the apostles thought the measure of forgiving someone seven times in a day was over the edge—beyond their faith level. As they embraced Jesus's command to forgive, however, they began to reap the benefits that come with forgiveness.

As a mature believer and servant-leader with a kingdom mindset (strict adherence to the principles of the Gospel of the kingdom as taught by Jesus), it can be very difficult to walk in the realm of "seventy times seven forgiveness." But like so many other apostles, prophets, evangelists, pastors, and teachers who have had to learn how to forgive as often as is required, I, too, have learned to do the same, riding on the wave of the benefits that accompany forgiveness.

Forgiving others frees the believer from dwelling on a past wrong;

---

[8] *Strong's Exhaustive Concordance of the Bible, NT,* 863, 859, 575.

it takes away the fleshly desire of revenge, minimizes the offense, and allows the love of God, which is shed abroad in our hearts by the Holy Spirit, to be released as a reflection of our genuine forgiveness by an act of our own will. The Word of God says, "Love will cover a multitude of sins" (1 Peter 4:8 NKJV).

Too many saints live tattered lives as opposed to the best life the King has ordained for kingdom citizens. They are sickly because unforgiveness releases toxins into the physical body and is the most influential cause of disease, hardening arteries, destroying the liver, and affecting eyesight, among other ills. They don't understand that benefits of a kingdom are commensurate with the wealth of the king. Why live on earth in squalor, when the Word of God says we can have days of heaven on earth (Deuteronomy 11:21)?

Instead of days of heaven on earth, many saints experience days of doom and gloom. Saints must learn to walk in love and forgiveness. The benefits are spiritual cleansing and restored Christian fellowship, which are the means or necessity of forgiveness. "And whenever you stand praying, if you have anything against anyone, forgive him, that your Father in heaven may also forgive you your trespasses. But if you do not forgive, neither will your Father in heaven forgive your trespasses" (Mark 11:25–26 NKJV).

> But if anyone has caused grief, he has not grieved me, but all of you to some extent – not to be too severe. This punishment which was inflicted by the majority is sufficient for such a man, so that, on the contrary, you ought rather to forgive and comfort him, lest perhaps such a one be swallowed up with too much sorrow. Therefore I urge you to reaffirm your love to him. For this end I also wrote, that I might put you to the test, whether you are obedient in all things. Now whom you forgive anything, I also forgive. For if indeed I have forgiven anything, I have forgiven that one for your sakes in the presence of Christ. (2 Corinthians 2:5–10 NKJV)

> Is anyone among you sick? Let him call for the elders of the church, and let them pray over him, anointing him with oil in the name of the Lord. And the prayer of faith will save the sick, and the Lord will raise him up. And if he has committed sins, he will be forgiven. (James 5:14–15 NKJV)

That the prayer of faith will save the sick is truth, yet we see so many of our brothers and sisters in Christ who are sick and not healed. I believe we see too much of this reality in the life of many believers because sin is the root cause of sickness. But when the sin is addressed, forgiven, and repented of, saints of God will certainly receive not only healing but also forgiveness, along with the greater benefit, which is life more abundantly and days of heaven on earth.

Believers, kingdom citizens, must learn to live out the principles of the kingdom of heaven here on the earth. Along with love, faith, grace, and humility, forgiveness is also a foundation of the kingdom of heaven.

All these characteristics are a part of God's nature, and his glory saturates the believer who embraces and aligns their lives with them. God wants his sons and daughters to walk in forgiveness. In other words, your Christian lifestyle is one of pardoning or excusing a wrong, canceling a debt and giving up claim for revenge or resentment. Forgiving others opens us to receive forgiveness from God. Jesus forgave sins and encourages believers to forgive others the same way. "Therefore, as the elect of God, holy and beloved, put on tender mercies, kindness, humility, meekness, longsuffering; bearing with one another, and forgiving one another, if anyone has a complaint against another; even as Christ forgave you, so you also must do" (Colossians 3:12-13 NKJV).

When a believer harnesses a hurt and holds on to it without having forgiven the person who caused the hurt, he or she becomes entangled in that hurt and can no longer move forward in the liberty in which God has set him or her free. Not forgiving people only binds the believer to the injustice committed by the person they haven't forgiven or refuse to forgive.

One cannot let go of the past until he or she forgives those who wronged them. Genuine forgiveness through love is in the heart of the believer to be released to anyone who does him or her wrong. Forgiveness is too much weight. Why not cast that burden on the Lord, and he will sustain you. He will never permit the righteous to be moved (Psalm 55:22 NKJV). Forgiveness is a foundation of the kingdom.

Forgiveness is a Holy Spirit wavelength that transmits the frequency of heaven to earth.

THE KINGDOM OF HEAVEN IS ESTABLISHED UPON OBEDIENCE—SUBMISSION TO THE KING

The Greek word for *obey* is *hupakouo*, which literally means to listen to, to hear as a subordinate—that is, to listen attentively; to heed or conform to a command or authority: hearken, be obedient to, obey.[9]

To listen to one in authority and then submit to that authority is what it means to obey. Here's where many saints are not kingdom compliant. Saints must realize we are still human, and we have an independent will. When we feed our spirit consistently with the Word of God—spiritual nutrition—we become spiritually strong, and our soul tends to align itself with our spirit, forcing compliance from our physical body, our flesh. When our spirit is nutritionally sound, we are easily led by Holy Spirit. On the contrary, whenever we neglect to consistently feed our spirit with the Word of God, we tend to allow ourselves to be driven by our flesh rather than our spirit. In this state, driven by our flesh, we don't want to be told what to do. We want to maintain control over what we do and not submit to the will of our heavenly Father, our King. Somehow it seems easier to obey the king or a law we can see and are governed by in the natural sense, which carries immediate consequences, than to obey a king and the principles of his kingdom, neither of which we can see or fathom through our physical senses.

I believe obedience to the King—reverence, loyalty, trust—opens the treasures of heaven and pours out all the benefits of the kingdom—the promises of God—onto those who obey him, whose heart is that of a bond servant of his own independent will. Obedience assures the believer of a long, successful, and prosperous life.

[9] *Strong's Exhaustive Concordance of the Bible, NT,* 5219.

> *Hear, my son, and receive my sayings, and the years of your life will be many.*
>
> **—Proverbs 4:10 NKJV**

> *If you are willing and obedient, You shall eat the good of the land; but if you refuse and rebel, you shall be devoured by the sword; for the mouth of the Lord has spoken.*
>
> **—Isaiah 1:19–20 NKJV**

> *If they obey and serve Him, They shall spend their days in prosperity, And their years in pleasures. But if they do not obey, They shall perish by the sword, And they shall die without knowledge.*
>
> **—Job 36:11–12 NKJV**

Defiance of the King, the Word of God, is not a good idea for the believer. There are many passages of scripture that point out the blessings that come with obedience and the curses that befall those who disobey God. Most notable is Deuteronomy 28:1–14, which promises blessings for obedience, while verses fifteen through sixty-eight detail the curses for disobedience. The somber message is that God doesn't tolerate disobedience. There is no middle ground. Each believer must choose between God's blessings or the curses that accompany disobedience, which are inclusive of rejection, retribution, captivity, and even death.

In 1 Samuel 15, Saul compounded the sin of disobedience with an outright lie and was rejected as king by God. He blamed his failure to obey God on the people. From this encounter, we also learn that partial obedience is disobedience.

> So Samuel said, "When you were little in your own eyes, were you not head of the tribes of Israel? And did not the Lord anoint you king over Israel? "Now the Lord sent you on a mission, and said, 'Go, and utterly destroy the sinners, the Amalekites, and fight against them until they are consumed.' "Why then did you not obey the voice of the Lord? Why did you swoop down on the spoil, and do evil in the sight of the Lord?" And Saul said to Samuel, "But I have obeyed the voice of the Lord,

> and gone on the mission on which the Lord sent me, and brought back Agag king of Amalek; I have utterly destroyed the Amalekies. (1 Samuel 15:17–20 NKJV)
>
> So Samuel said: "Has the Lord as great delight in burnt offerings and sacrifices, As in obeying the voice of the Lord? Behold, to obey is better than sacrifice, And to heed than the fat of rams. For rebellion is as the sin of witchcraft, And stubbornness is as iniquity and idolatry. Because you have rejected the word of the LORD, He also has rejected you from being king." (1 Samuel 15:22–23 NKJV)

Believers who do not obey God open themselves to his retribution: "Since it is a righteous thing with God to repay with tribulation" (2 Thessalonians 1:6a NKJV).

"Taking vengeance on those who do not know God, and on those who do not obey the gospel of our Lord Jesus Christ. These shall be punished with everlasting destruction from the presence of the Lord and from the glory of His power" (2 Thessalonians 8–9 NKJV).

God allowed his chosen people, first Israel by the Assyrians and then Judah by the Babylonians, to be taken captive because of their disobedience. Even today our disobedience to God, the Creator and Sustainer of the universe, opens the door to his wrath, judgment, and eternal separation.

> *Therefore put to death your members which are on the earth: fornication, uncleanness, passion, evil desire, and covetousness, which is idolatry. Because of these things the wrath of God is coming upon the sons of disobedience.*
>
> **—Colossians 3:5–6 NKJV**

> *For if the word spoken through angels proved steadfast, and every transgression and disobedience received a just reward, how shall we escape if we neglect so great a salvation, which at the first began to be spoken by the Lord, and was confirmed to us by those who heard Him.*
>
> **—Hebrews 2:2-3 NKJV**

As we obey the principles of the kingdom of heaven, we become kingdom compliant by learning obedience as Jesus did during his earthly ministry through the things that we suffer (Hebrews 5:8 NKJV). Adversity produces maturity for completion; we become the fulfillment of our divine assignment. The apostle Peter said, "We ought to obey God rather than men" (Acts 5:29 NKJV).

As I stated earlier, our flesh doesn't want to obey. But as we feed our spirit more and more of the Word of God, as we memorize and meditate upon God's Word, we begin to learn obedience by doing what the word says should be done in any situation. I believe we learn as we suffer for the word's sake. Our steadfast faith, even in the midst of our suffering, teaches us obedience.

Our acts of obedience become driven by our faith, which is pleasing to God, and we begin to experience blessings in life—happiness. We begin to be led and guided by the Holy Spirit, thereby avoiding evil. We have divine security, safety, and protection. We are free from anxiety and worry. We reflect the love of God at all times, and we bear much fruit that remains for the kingdom. We become epistles that are alive, known, and read by people. We have the assurance of salvation and eternal life, and we are guaranteed entrance into heaven and the greatness in the kingdom of heaven. These are the rewards of obedience.

The revelation behind obedience to the Word of God as a foundation of the kingdom of heaven becomes even clearer when applied to the Christian lifestyle. In order to please God, we must exercise faith—total trust in God. And sincere faith that leads to obedience to the Word of God is empowered by the Holy Spirit and put to the test.

> *But God be thanked that though you were slaves of sin, yet you obeyed from the heart that form of doctrine to which you were delivered. And having been set free from sin, you became slaves of righteousness.*
>
> **—Romans 6:17–18 NKJV**

> *Since you have purified your souls in obeying the truth through the Spirit in sincere love of the brethren, love one another fervently with a pure heart.*
>
> **—1 Peter 1:22 NKJV**

> *Therefore I have reason to glory in Christ Jesus in the things which pertain to God. For I will not dare to speak of any of those things which Christ has not accomplished through me, in word and deed, to make the Gentiles obedient – in mighty signs and wonders, by the power of the Spirit of God.*
>
> **Romans 15:17–19 NKJV**

As believers, citizens of the kingdom of heaven, obedience to Christ not only should be our example to the world but it should also be our duty as his representatives on earth. We ourselves have been built on the foundation of the apostles and prophets, Jesus Christ himself being the cornerstone (Ephesians 2:20 NKJV).

In Jesus, we are built together to live with God in the Holy Spirit. As we are submissive to Jesus Christ, we do what he did and say what he said: "O My Father, if it is possible, let this cup pass from Me; nevertheless, not as I will, but as You will … the spirit indeed is willing, but the flesh is weak" (Matthew 26:39–41 NKJV).

> Let this mind be in you which was also in Christ Jesus, who, being in the form of God, did not consider it robbery to be equal with God, but made Himself of no reputation, taking the form of a bondservant, *and* coming in the likeness of men. And being found in appearance as a man, He humbled Himself and became obedient to *the point of* death, even the death of the cross. Therefore God also has highly exalted Him and given Him the name which is above every name. (Philippians 2:5–9 NKJV)

Obedience is indeed a foundation of the kingdom of heaven. Just as we—our relationship to God through Jesus Christ—have been built on the foundation of the apostles and prophets, the kingdom of God on earth has been built upon the saints: "For indeed, the kingdom of God is within you" (Luke 17:21 NKJV). Therefore, not only is Jesus Christ the cornerstone, the foundation of the kingdom of heaven, but he is also the foundation of the kingdom of God on earth.

Obedience is a Holy Spirit wavelength that transmits the frequency of heaven to earth.

THE KINGDOM OF HEAVEN IS ESTABLISHED UPON REPENTANCE—REFORMATION OF LIFE

> *In those days John the Baptist came preaching in the wilderness of Judea, and saying, "Repent, for the kingdom of heaven is at hand!" For this is he who was spoken of by the prophet Isaiah, saying: "The voice of one crying in the wilderness: 'Prepare the way of the Lord; Make His paths straight.'"*
>
> **—Matthew 3:1–3 NKJV**

> *But when he saw many of the Pharisees and Sadducees coming to his baptism, he said to them, "Brood of vipers! Who warned you to flee from the wrath to come?" Therefore bear fruits worthy of repentance.*
>
> **—Matthew 3:7–8 NKJV**

The Father's good pleasure is to give us the kingdom of heaven—God's way of being and doing righteous acts while on earth, based on the New Testament, which is a stronger covenant established upon grace, not law, which makes it a better promise of which Jesus is the Guarantor (Hebrews 7:22, 8:6 NKJV).

But the Pharisees and the Sadducees never came to the knowledge of and true meaning of repentance. Their hearts were hardened like stone against the teaching and preaching of the Gospel of the kingdom and seared as with a hot iron. The Pharisees separated themselves from those people who did not observe their man-made laws and supported the scribes and rabbis in their interpretation of the Law of Moses; they were legalistic and hypocritical. The Sadducees were the societal elite and were advocates of the Law of Moses but denied any human interpretation thereof. They supported the Roman government under which they enjoyed a privileged status.

Clearly, legalism and hypocrisy are the language of Pharisees and Sadducees—those who speak the Word of God and hold others accountable but are unwilling to hold themselves accountable to the same Word of God because their hearts are far from Him. Jesus said, "These people draw near to Me with their mouth, and honor Me with their lips, but their heart is far from Me. And in vain they worship Me, teaching as doctrines the commandments of men" (Matthew 15:8–9 NKJV).

John the Baptist referred to these two sects of Jewish society as a "brood of vipers." John's mandate was to "prepare the way of the Lord"—to soften their hearts, to remove the blinders from their eyes, and to renew their religious mindsets, preparing them to receive the grace of the coming Messiah. John's message: "Repent, for the kingdom of heaven is at hand!" (Matthew 3:2 NKJV).

The Greek word rendered *repent* is the verb *metanoeo.* It means to think differently or afterward—that is, to reconsider, feel compunction: repent for guilt, reformation, reversal of another's decision: repentance.[10] In present truth terms, it means to change one's mind and to feel remorse, to repent. It signifies a turning away from sin, which is what John the Baptist preached.

Today we are living in unprecedented times—times of uncertainty driven by fear, hate, anxiety, doubt, unbelief, and terrorism—all at the hands of men. As saints of God, we must always stay front and center in alignment with the principles of the kingdom, the Word of God. Like John the Baptist, we must turn the hearts of the disobedient to the wisdom of the just.

The anointing and mantle of John the Baptist, which encompasses that of the prophet Elijah, await us—the kingdom remnant the Father has prepared to bring divine restoration to the body of Christ for such a time as this. Like John the Baptist, we must turn the heart of our nation's attention back to the Lord and pray that believers will realize their hope in Christ—that their hearts are changed on the inside first in order to control and have dominion over what takes place on the outside. We are equipped for service and empowerment from the inside out.

> *And he will turn many of the children of Israel to the Lord their God. He will also go before Him in the spirit and power of Elijah, 'to turn the hearts of the fathers to the children,' and the disobedient to the wisdom of the just, to make ready a people prepared for the Lord.*
>
> **—Luke 1:16–17 NKJV**

---

[10] *Strong's Exhaustive Concordance of the Bible, NT,* 3340 and 3341.

> *For all the prophets and the law prophesied until John. And if you are willing to receive it, he is Elijah who is to come. He who has ears to hear, let him hear!*
>
> **—Matthew 11:13–15 NKJV**

Like Elijah, we must beckon people to sit up and take notice of the work of the Lord. Elijah's mantle caused people to repent of their wicked ways and turn back to God. His anointing gave people hope for their future and caused them to see that their righteous God was working on their behalf. It made them ready on the inside to receive change on the outside. This, too, is our mandate, especially within the body of Christ—the church—of which Jesus Christ is the head.

Elijah means the Lord is my God!

> *Behold, I will send you Elijah the prophet before the coming of the great and dreadful day of the Lord.*
>
> **—Malachi 4:5 NKJV**

Many people still don't believe Jesus is coming back to the earth to receive those who are "in Christ." It's a very familiar mindset that seems to be the worldview of far too many people, including some believers. Even some Christians have said, "We've been saying this for years, and Jesus hasn't returned yet." This mindset has led many believers to backslide, thinking that Jesus isn't coming anytime soon, and they might as well "live a little." The mindset here is that they will eventually get their lives back right with the Lord before his return. We all probably know someone who had that mindset and is no longer with us, and one would be hard-pressed to say they repented before they died because of the state of their life immediately prior to their death. Yet God judges the heart.

> Where is the promise of His coming? For since the fathers fell asleep, all things continue as they were from the beginning of creation ... But, beloved, do not forget this one thing, that with the Lord one day is as a thousand years, and a thousand years as one day. The Lord is not slack concerning His promise, as

> some count slackness, but is longsuffering toward us, not willing that any should perish but that all should come to repentance. (2 Peter 3:4, 8–9 NKJV)

> Or do you despise the riches of His goodness, forbearance, and longsuffering, not knowing that the goodness of God leads you to repentance? But in accordance with your hardness and your impenitent heart you are treasuring up for yourself wrath in the day of wrath and revelation of the righteous judgment of God. (Romans 2:4–5 NKJV)

Repentance is necessary because it hastens the "Day of the Lord," and because the goodness of God himself actually leads to repentance (Romans 2:4 NKJV). To boot, repentance has its origins entrenched in the Trinity—the Father, the Son, and the Holy Spirit. The apostle Peter, in defense of his ministry to the Gentiles while in Jerusalem, let the church brethren know he was led by the Holy Spirit to minister to the Gentiles, as they had accused him, saying, "You went in to uncircumcised men and ate with them!" (Acts 11:3 NKJV).

As Peter explained the vision of the great sheet let down from heaven by four corners filled with four-footed animals, wild beasts, creeping things, and birds of the air—creatures that were considered common or unclean for a Jew to eat under the law—he heard a voice from heaven say, "Rise, Peter; kill and eat" (Acts 11:7 NKJV). Peter's reply was based upon his religious zeal strictly to adhere to the Law of Moses. But he heard the voice of God from heaven say, "What God has cleansed you must not call common" (Acts 11:9 NKJV).

> Then I remembered the word of the Lord, how He said, "John indeed baptized with water, but you shall be baptized with the Holy Spirit. If therefore God gave them the same gift as He gave us when we believed on the Lord Jesus Christ, who was I that I could withstand God?" When they heard these things they became silent; and they glorified God, saying, "Then God has

> also granted to the Gentiles repentance to life." (Acts 11:16–18 NKJV)
>
> The God of our fathers raised up Jesus whom you murdered by hanging on a tree. Him God has exalted to His right hand to be Prince and Savior, to give repentance to Israel and forgiveness of sins. And we are His witnesses to these things, and so also is the Holy Spirit whom God has given to those who obey Him. (Acts 5:30–32 NKJV)

Long-suffering is one thing that leads to repentance; God's goodness is another. But conviction of sin leads to repentance, and this is the one thing that many people fear. Let's face it: People don't like to put themselves in that vein, because they don't like to willfully admit they've committed a sin. They would rather take a chance on "getting away with it," essentially living a lie, because to those who fit this mold the very mention of the word *repent* means they're dirty, sinful, outside the will of God, and unworthy. And it doesn't help when these people are bombarded by self-righteous saints telling them they're going to hell if they don't repent.

When Philip the evangelist witnessed to the Samaritans, he preached the things concerning the kingdom and the name of Jesus—the king and his kingdom and both men and women were baptized, among them a sorcerer named Simon. This man claimed to be great, and the people were somewhat afraid of him because they thought, "This man is the great power of God" (Acts 8:10 NKJV). But as Philip ministered concerning the kingdom and the name of Jesus, Simon also believed and was baptized. But when he saw the apostles lay hands on the people, and they received the Holy Spirit, he offered them money. Imagine that. He literally thought the Holy Spirit could be purchased as another item in his bag of tricks to hold people spellbound and to make himself even greater (Acts 8:5–25 NKJV).

Sadly, there are saints who think they can purchase their way into heaven and live life eternally with the king. The Word of God, however, lets us know there is nothing, not even money, we can exchange for our soul (Matthew 16:26 NKJV). One can be saved and still possess an evil heart. This is partly how the goodness of God leads to repentance.

> *But Peter said to him, "Your money perish with you, because you thought that the gift of God could be purchased with money! You have neither part nor portion in this matter, for your heart is not right in the sight of God. Repent therefore of this your wickedness, and pray God if perhaps the thought of your heart may be forgiven you.*
>
> **—Acts 8:20–22 NKJV**

I believe godly sorrow and contrition are signs of true repentance. A heart of contrition, penitence, remorse should be clearly visible in the life of a believer who has repented and turned away from a lifestyle of sin. The New Testament kingdom of grace is available through repentance, which makes repentance a foundation of the kingdom of heaven. We can come boldly before the throne of grace to obtain mercy and find grace to help in our time of need (Hebrews 4:16 NKJV). We can confess our sins and ask our heavenly Father to forgive us for our sins, knowing he is faithful and righteous to forgive us for our sins and to cleanse us from all unrighteousness (1 John 1:9 NKJV).

The kingdom of heaven is all about a good king who possesses an ever-increasing kingdom, and whose desire is to give good gifts to his loyal subjects. The eyes of the Lord run throughout the entire earth to show himself strong to those whose hearts are loyal to him (2 Chronicles 16:9 NKJV). It amazes me how so many believers have allowed the accuser of the brethren to harden their hearts to the One who loves them unconditionally and has an open-door policy for their return.

> Now I rejoice, not that you were made sorry, but that your sorrow led to repentance. For you were made sorry in a godly manner, that you might suffer loss from us in nothing. For godly sorrow produces repentance leading to salvation, not to be regretted; but the sorrow of the world produces death. For observe this very thing, that you sorrowed in a godly manner: What diligence it produced in you, what clearing of yourselves, what

> indignation, what fear, what vehement desire, what zeal, what vindication! In all things you proved yourselves to be clear in this matter. (2 Corinthians 7:9–11 NKJV)

> Repent therefore and be converted, that your sins may be blotted out, so that times of refreshing may come from the presence of the Lord. (Acts 3:19 NKJV)

This is the opportune time for the body of Christ to love one another, make true repentance from the heart a reality, and become the living organism fit to function and carry out our kingdom mandate. One billion souls await our faithfulness to "occupy till I come" (Luke 19:13 KJV) so that "The kingdoms of this world have become the kingdoms of our Lord and of His Christ, and He shall reign forever and ever" (Revelation 11:15 NKJV)! Repentance is a foundation of the kingdom.

Repentance is a Holy Spirit wavelength that transmits the frequency of heaven to earth.

THE KINGDOM OF HEAVEN IS ESTABLISHED UPON PATIENCE—COMPLETE, LACKING NOTHING

"Patience has rewards attached to it." This was a Holy Spirit revelation to me over ten years ago. I live in South Carolina. Here, our summers are very hot. After a long season of hot weather, I get anxious for that first bite of crisp fall air. I feel like there ought to be something I can do to help with the transition. But anything I could possibly come up with would probably rival rain makers for stupidity. So I resign myself to endure the heat and humidity of South Carolina's extended summer days. Then one morning I awake to the first crisp bite of fall. What a relief. Windows and doors are opened, extending an invitation to the refreshing breeze. Cooling systems are turned off and utility bills are temporarily lowered. The sound of birds chirping and squirrels racing up and down South Carolina pines can be heard all day long. These joys of fall are the reward of my patience.

On such a fall morning as I sat on my back porch immersed in the crisp morning air, meditating on patience, the Holy Spirit revealed to me that patience has rewards attached to it. Having mused over that revelation for a long while, I thought back to times of my life when I was impatient and wondered what rewards I had missed. I certainly had my share of regrets for not being patient. The Holy Spirit revealed to me that day the advantage kingdom citizens have through patience. What kingdom citizens are waiting for will eventually show up if we adhere to the laws that govern patience. Patience teaches us how to legally possess those things we desire without the stress and losses that come with being impatient.

I can't help wondering how many rewards people miss on a daily basis because of their impatience. I believe our desire to immediately fulfill the lusts of our flesh keeps us from experiencing patience's rewards.

It costs to be patient. It costs in terms of bringing fleshly lusts under spiritual subjection because our flesh wants no part of that. It only wants immediate gratification. When the flesh is allowed to go unchecked, the end result is wantonness with no limitations.

King David, the master psalmist, understood patience. Patience worked for David because he used it to his benefit. Patience brought David from the shepherd's field to the king's palace. This was his reward from patience for enduring the adversity, self-sacrifice, and suffering that befell him on his journey of transition and transformation to become king. Patience was the key to David's avoidance of self-destruction so that he could achieve his destiny.

David was anointed to be king over Israel by Samuel while he was yet a teenager. Obviously, at that age, he was not ready to govern a nation. Training for his God-ordained purpose would require a process of development, maturity, grace, and time. David would have to mature. His character would have to be developed. He would have to learn through God's mentorship and his own mistakes, which occurred most often when he was impatient and sought immediate gratification.

But David eventually learned to trust God and patiently wait for his deliverance. David wanted to give up many times. Had he done so, he would have relinquished his God-ordained purpose to become Israel's king. In the Epistle to the Hebrews, the writer reminds Christians who get weary and want to defect from their faith that success in living the Christian life is attained through faith and patience.

> But beloved, we are confident of better things concerning you, yes, things that accompany salvation, though we speak in this manner. For God is not unjust to forget your work and labor of love which you have shown toward His name, in that you have ministered to the saints, and do minister. And we desire that each one of you show the same diligence to the full assurance of hope until the end, that you do not become sluggish, but imitate those who through faith and patience inherit the promises. (Hebrews 6:9–12 NKJV)

David could have forfeited his life's reward had he not embraced patience. Even when he had two separate opportunities to kill King Saul, which could have hastened his ascension to the throne, he would not stretch forth his hand against the Lord's anointed (1 Samuel 26:11 NKJV).

Like David, we must also learn to trust God, understanding that God may not answer our requests immediately. But he will never fail to ultimately answer when we trust him and patiently wait on him.

> *I waited patiently for the Lord; and He inclined to me, and heard my cry. He also brought me up out of a horrible pit, out of the miry clay, and set my feet upon a rock, and established my steps.*
>
> **—Psalm 40:1–2 NKJV**

Patience is defined as "the capacity, habit, or fact of being patient," which is inclusive of "bearing pains or trials calmly or without complaint."[11] How many people habitually endure trials and pain without complaining? I would say, "Probably not many." I would venture to say that few people, saved or unsaved, endure trials and pain without complaining. Yet this is the sacrifice God requires of us in order to reap the rewards he's ordained for our lives. David had to do it, and so do we.

---

[11] *Merriam-Webster's Collegiate Dictionary: Eleventh Edition*, sv "patience."

Apostles James and Peter had very strong advice for believers concerning patience and trials. James tells us that trials produce patience, while Peter tells us not to be surprised concerning the suffering we must endure during trials:

> My brethren, count it all joy when you fall into various trials, knowing that the testing of your faith produces patience. But let patience have its perfect work, that you may be perfect and complete, lacking nothing. (James 1:2–4 NKJV)

> Beloved, do not think it strange concerning the fiery trial which is to try you, as though some strange thing happened to you; but rejoice to the extent that you partake of Christ's sufferings, that when His glory is revealed, you may also be glad with exceeding joy. (1 Peter 4:12–13 NKJV)

Notice that James uses the word *when*, not *if*. He stresses the fact that trials and tests of faith will occur, and this is God's way of developing spiritual maturity and abundance for the believer. But we must endure the trials by trusting God and not getting discouraged as we go through this process.

Peter tells us that we should focus on the joy of being a partner in Christ's suffering rather than on the trial itself. Like James, Peter stresses the fact that trials for believers are not strange things. They will come, and believers should expect them; however, we can rejoice in the fact that we are partakers in Christ's suffering.

The Greek word for *patience* is *hupomone*, taken from *hupomeno*, which means cheerful, hopeful endurance, constancy—enduring patience, patient continuance (waiting). It also means to stay under; to undergo or bear trials, have fortitude, persevere.[12]

Patience is a necessity for believers to successfully live as citizens of the kingdom of heaven here on earth. Patience is imperative not only to do God's will but also to receive God's promises. To receive God's

---

[12] *Strong's Exhaustive Concordance of the Bible, NT*, 5281, 5278.

best, his goodness, we must undergo or bear trials with fortitude and perseverance.

> *For ye have need of patience, that after ye have done the will of God, ye might receive the promise.*
>
> **—Hebrews 10:36 KJV**

> *Wait on the Lord; be of good courage, and He shall strengthen your heart; wait, I say, on the Lord!*
>
> **—Psalm 27:14 NKJV**

Yes, patience has its rewards. Be of good courage. God is true to his word. His promises always arrive on time, in his time. This is the reward of patience and why patience is a foundation of the kingdom of heaven. Wait on the Lord!

Patience is a Holy Spirit wavelength that transmits the frequency of heaven to earth.

Saints of God, this is our time—the body of Christ—to heal and recover. And love, faith, grace, humility, forgiveness, obedience, repentance, and patience make up heaven's foundation; a complete incorporate foundation from which we can build ourselves on our most holy faith by praying in the Holy Spirit and by embracing this opportunity to examine ourselves to make sure we are in the faith and compliant with the principles of the kingdom of heaven.

The solid foundation of God's kingdom stands firm. And anyone who makes Jesus Lord and Savior of their life can stand firm in his kingdom by embracing the foundation and invoking each component of the foundation—the superior materials that have been afforded us to live life more abundantly in this ever-increasing kingdom upheld by the word of his power. "Where the word of a king is, there is power; and who may say to him, 'What are you doing?'" (Ecclesiastes 8:4 NKJV).

"For if these things abound, *we will be* neither barren nor unfruitful in the knowledge of our Lord Jesus Christ" (2 Peter 1:8 NKJV).

As we stand on the firm foundation of the kingdom of God and abide its principles, we stay tuned-in to the frequency of heaven.

CHAPTER 3

On Earth as It Is in Heaven

Your kingdom come. Your will be done on earth as it is in heaven.
—Matthew 6:10 NKJV

In this portion of the Lord's Prayer, Jesus signifies his Father's will for a colony on earth where his will in heaven is reproduced and lived out by man, whom he made in his image and likeness. Our life on earth, then, should be one of submission to the authority, dominion, and sovereignty of God—one of obedience as bond servants to the king of the universe.

I cannot fathom the depth of Jesus's Gethsemane experiences. Most saints are familiar with Jesus's agony in the garden near Jerusalem, but not many remember that Gethsemane was also the place of Jesus's betrayal. As a matter of fact, Gethsemane was a place often visited by Jesus. "When Jesus had spoken these words, He went out with His disciples over the Brook Kidron, where there was a garden, which He and His disciples entered. And Judas, who betrayed Him, also knew the place; for Jesus often met there with His disciples" (John 18:1–2 NKJV).

I am awed by the fact that although Jesus suffered in agony until his sweat became like "great drops of blood" (Luke 22:44 NKJV), he maintained his integrity and stood on his own words of allegiance to his Father. He had been severely beaten by Roman soldiers, mocked, slapped, and spat on. He endured excruciating pain on the cross at Calvary, as he who knew no sin (2 Corinthians 5:21 NKJV) took in his body the sins of the entire world—past, present, and future. Prior to his giving up his spirit, Jesus made sure that Mary, his mother, would be taken care of by the apostle whom he loved (John 19:26–27 NKJV). At the ninth hour, Jesus cried out in a loud voice, "My God, My God, why have You forsaken Me?" (Mark 15:34 NKJV). He then asked his Father to forgive those who crucified him (Luke 23:34 NKJV), becoming obedient even to his death (Philippians 2:8 NKJV).

What loyalty, what faithfulness, what integrity. Jesus fulfilled his earthly mandate by keeping his promise to his Father. "Previously saying, 'Sacrifice and offering, burnt offerings, and offerings for sin You did not desire, nor had pleasure in them' (which are offered according to the law), then He said, 'Behold, I have come to do Your will, O God'" (Hebrews 10:8–9 NKJV).

Jesus knew He would have to fulfill his passion without his disciples. And he told them so, predicting Peter's denial, yet Peter and the other eleven disciples declared, "'Even if I have to die with You, I will not deny You!' And so said all the disciples" (Matthew 26:35 NKJV).

As a student of the law, Jesus understood the words of Zechariah the prophet: "Strike the Shepherd, and the sheep will be scattered" (Zechariah 13:7 NKJV). Knowing his disciples would forsake him prior to his crucifixion couldn't have been of any consolation to Jesus. "But all this was done that the Scriptures of the prophets might be fulfilled. Then all the disciples forsook Him and fled" (Matthew 26:56 NKJV).

Believers often forget that Jesus is the Son of God and the Son of man. Although equality with God was his right, he did not consider it robbery to be equal with God. Nevertheless, by an act of his will, he took on the form of a bond servant and made himself of no reputation, being fashioned in the likeness of men (Philippians 2:6–7 NKJV). That means Jesus had to walk by faith in God's Word and be led and guided by the Holy Spirit.

Yet Jesus took his disciples with him to the garden of Gethsemane on the night of his betrayal. Peter, James, and John, his top lieutenants, accompanied him to the place where he prayed three times that God would "let this cup pass from Me" (Matthew 26:39 NKJV). The story is told that Jesus became sorrowful and deeply distressed.

What occurred next, and what Jesus said, is a powerful revelation as to the distinct nature of the spirit and soul and flesh, and he exposes the power of each. We know we are tripartite beings—spirit, soul, and body.

Man is a spirit, created in God's own image and likeness. God is spirit (John 4:24 NKJV). Therefore, we are spirits that come from God, and we inhabit a body of flesh. Because we are spirit man, we can inhabit two realms at the same time, heaven and earth. Our spirit is eternal and can inhabit all spiritual realms or dimensions; our earthly body makes us legal inhabitants of earth and binds us in time. So we really do have access to heaven and earth. And for those of us who are born again, we possess the same authority in both realms that Jesus possesses: "All authority has been given to Me in heaven and on earth" (Matthew 28:18 NKJV).

But we still have a problem. As we know, the spirit and the flesh are contrary to one another, making it impossible to do the things we wish (Galatians 5:17 NKJV). God created man with an independent will. And that will lies within the soul, which along with spirit and flesh makes us tripartite beings. The soul is inclusive of our mind, will, emotions, and intellect. Our spirit can only have access to the natural world through our soul. The soul allows our spirit and our body to communicate, to draw energy from it.

In this way, the soul simply aligns itself with the dominant part, which means it can be persuaded. We can choose to be for God or to go against God. If our spirit is the dominant part, our soul will align itself with our spirit, essentially forcing our body to comply. If our body is the dominant part, our soul will align itself with our body, essentially forcing our spirit to comply. The spirit of man is always willing to comply with the Word of God but runs into opposition because of the flesh body in which it dwells. The apostle Paul explains it this way:

> For I know that in me (that is, in my flesh) nothing good dwells; for to will is present with me, but how to perform

> what is good I do not find. For the good that I will to do, I do not do; but the evil I will not to do, that I practice. Now if I do what I will not to do, it is no longer I who do it, but sin that dwells in me. I find then a law, that evil is present with me, the one who wills to do good. For I delight in the law of God according to the inward man. But I see another law in my members, warring against the law of my mind, and bringing me into captivity to the law of sin which is in my members … So then, with the mind I myself serve the law of God, but with the flesh the law of sin. (Romans 7:18–23, 25b NKJV)

Jesus first prays from a mentality of victory. He admits his agony, but he prays for God's will. "My soul is exceedingly sorrowful, even to death … O My Father, if it is possible, let this cup pass from Me; nevertheless, not as I will, but as You will" (Matthew 26:38–39 NKJV). With this statement, Jesus consciously submits himself to the will of the Father in spite of the deep sorrow he experienced in his soul.

Even while submerged in agony, his soul exceedingly sorrowful, Jesus prayed more earnestly for a third time: "Father, if it is Your will, take this cup away from Me; nevertheless not My will, but Yours, be done. Then an angel appeared to Him from heaven, strengthening Him" (Luke 22:42–43 NKJV).

Obviously, God intervened and sent an angel from heaven to strengthen Jesus. Why did Jesus need to be strengthened? And in what area?

I would submit to you that Jesus needed to be strengthened in two areas: his soul and his body.

Remember, Jesus is the Son of man. His flesh did not want to go to the cross to be crucified, and so it cried out through Jesus's soul in hopes that his soul would agree to abort the mission of Jesus dying on the cross for the remission of the sins of the world past, present, and future.

> *Watch and pray, lest you enter into temptation. The spirit is willing, but the flesh is weak.*
>
> **—Matthew 26:41 NKJV**

Jesus literally puts his flesh on notice. He knew that temptation takes place through the flesh. And he tells Peter, James, and John to "watch and pray" (Matthew 26:41 NKJV). The Greek rendition of the word *watch* in this text is *gregoreuo*, which means to keep awake—be vigilant, be watchful.[13]

Jesus's appeal to himself and to his disciples was to stay alert, vigilant, and awake because of the subtle, selfish desires of the flesh. As an ordained minister of thirty years, I know the subtle, selfish desires of the flesh, but I've also learned that I have to be vigilant and alert through my spirit to detect it. I believe Jesus raised the alarm to warn his disciples to make sure they were consciously praying, keeping their spirit engaged and watching for any movement away from their inner being's will to obey God. The spirit is always willing; but the flesh is weak (Matthew 26:41 NKJV).

But even Jesus's most astute apostles could not remain awake. "Why do you sleep? Rise and pray, lest you enter into temptation" (Luke 22:46 NKJV). Jesus's plea to his disciples was to "stay here and watch with me" (Matthew 26:38 NKJV).

After his first prayer, Jesus returned and found them asleep. "What? Could you not watch with me one hour?" (Matthew 26:40 NKJV). Prior to the second prayer, in which Jesus's sweat became like great drops of blood, I believe that the Father sent an angel to strengthen Jesus's spirit so that his soul—his mind, will, emotions, and intellect—would be drawn into alignment with his spirit, which was willing. The spirit and the soul had to win the day, causing Jesus's body to submit to the will of his spirit. After his second prayer, Jesus found the disciples asleep again, noting that their eyes were heavy (Matthew 26:43 NKJV).

Even after Jesus's third prayer, he came and found them asleep. "Are you still sleeping and resting? Behold, the hour is at hand, and the Son Man is being betrayed into the hands of sinners" (Matthew 26:45 NKJV). What if the disciples had remained awake, alert, vigilant, and watchful in prayer rather than falling asleep? Would the Father have had to send an angel to strengthen Jesus? I really don't know, but it certainly would seem that their prayers and encouragement may have served the same purpose as the angel had they remained awake and in

[13] *Strong's Exhaustive Concordance of the Bible, NT*, 1127.

prayer. I submit that the thought is most worthy of consideration, since temptation through our flesh is an everyday occurrence. Satan tempts us in the same manner he tempted Jesus–through the weakness of our flesh. Satan is the tempter, the accuser of the brethren (Revelation 12:10 NKJV). He is a thief and his nature is to steal, and to kill, and to destroy (John 10:10 NKJV). Each day believers must "submit to God. Resist the devil and he will flee from you" (James 4:7 NKJV). We must stay alert and watchful so that we do not enter into temptation. Jesus implores believers to watch and pray. As we do so, we will not give place to the devil's temptations; instead we will be confident, knowing, "I can do all things through Christ who strengthens me" (Philippians 4:13 NKJV).

I believe we are just as vulnerable as Jesus was concerning his passion. As we take up our cross and follow Christ, Satan unleashes various kinds of temptations upon us attempting to hijack, stall, or overthrow our divine assignment and destiny. Like Jesus, we must be passionate with regard to our divine assignment. We must watch and pray, keeping our spirit and soul attached and in alignment with the will of God so that we will not forfeit our liberty or our ability to glorify God. We stand by faith and in humility before God so that whenever temptation arises we are conscious that God, through his Spirit, resides in us. His presence makes the way of escape for us from Satan's temptations.

> *Therefore let him who thinks he stands take heed lest he fall. No temptation has overtaken you except such as is common to man; but God is faithful, who will not allow you to be tempted beyond what you are able, but with the temptation will also make the way of escape, that you may be able to bear it.*
>
> **—1 Corinthians 10:12–13 NKJV**

> *For if God did not spare the angels who sinned, but cast them down to hell and delivered them into chains of darkness, to be reserved for judgment … then the Lord knows how to deliver the godly out of temptations and to reserve the unjust under punishment for the day of judgment.*
>
> **—2 Peter 2:4, 9 NKJV**

THY KINGDOM COME: CHANGING MINDSETS FROM RELIGION TO KINGDOM

From time to time, I reflect upon the magnitude of Jesus's commission to teach and preach the Gospel of the kingdom to the entire world. I can even visualize Jesus going from town to town in different regions teaching and preaching the Gospel of the kingdom.

I think about the challenges he faced not only from unbelievers but also from various factions of the religious order—Pharisees, Sadducees, scribes, teachers of the law, even the chief priests and the high priest. These were people who tried to stop Jesus from teaching the Gospel of the kingdom. This they could not do; however, they found many intimidating ways to stall the process. Their hope was to bring to nothing Jesus's teaching by threatening those who believed in him, by making light of the effectiveness of Jesus's ministry, by imposing restrictions to keep him from teaching in their villages and synagogues, and by threatening legal repercussions against him.

In the book of Acts and the other New Testament epistles, we find the apostles being persecuted in much the same way. Many were even martyred for the sake of the gospel. Nevertheless, they were committed to teaching and preaching the Gospel of the kingdom. They did not allow persecutions or their personal conditions to distract them from their mission.

The apostle Paul describes the many tribulations he faced as he continued teaching the Gospel of the kingdom (2 Corinthians 11:22–31 NKJV). Even after Paul had been stoned in Lystra for preaching the Gospel and healing a crippled man, he went forth, "confirming the souls of the disciples, and exhorting them to continue in the faith, and that we must through much tribulation enter into the kingdom of God" (Acts 14:22 KJV).

Paul was mission driven. What if believers today possessed this level of loyalty and commitment to teach and preach the Gospel of the kingdom? Even when Paul was faced with the possibility of afflictions, bonds, and death, he remained steadfastly committed to his mandate to teach and preach the Gospel of the kingdom to the Gentiles at all costs:

> We are hard-pressed on every side, yet not crushed; we are perplexed, but not in despair; persecuted, but not forsaken; struck down, but not destroyed – always carrying about in the body the dying of the Lord Jesus that the life of Jesus also may be manifested in our body. For we who live are always delivered to death for Jesus' sake, that the life of Jesus also may be manifested in our mortal flesh. So then death is working in us, but life in you. (2 Corinthians 4:8–12 NKJV)

> And see, now I go bound in the spirit to Jerusalem, not knowing the things that will happen to me there, except that the Holy Spirit testifies in every city, saying that chains and tribulations await me. But none of these things move me; nor do I count my life dear to myself, so that I may finish my race with joy, and the ministry which I received from the Lord Jesus, to testify to the gospel of the grace of God. (Acts 20:22–24 NKJV)

These testimonies of loyalty and commitment to Jesus and the Gospel of the kingdom can be very frightening to the half-hearted believer—the lukewarm saint who is neither hot for God nor cold toward God (Revelation 3:16 NKJV). The uncommitted believer doesn't believe he or she should suffer for Christ's sake. Many will promote the mission of preaching the Gospel to all people of the world as long as it doesn't interfere with their comfort, pose a threat to their livelihood, or jeopardize their lavish and maybe even wanton lifestyle. But Paul was consistent through all of these challenges and fulfilled his divine purpose. "I have fought the good fight, I have finished the race, I have kept the faith" (2 Timothy 4:7 NKJV).

Most of us come woefully short in comparison to Paul's level of commitment, although we possess the same spiritual qualities or virtues that prepare us for the same level of commitment that Paul possessed. And like Paul, we are anointed to transform earthbound mindsets, atmospheres, and environments to be conformed to the mindsets, atmospheres, and environment of heaven.

It is our heavenly Father who develops us and prepares us to walk in the same intense level of commitment as the apostle Paul to fulfill our divine purpose. What the Father needs from those who are his is their surrender and availability to allow him to teach, train, and educate them in the government of the kingdom. It is our Father who empowers us with the prevailing grace and anointing of Jesus's governmental authority.

This is how believers will affect world kingdoms for Christ. There will be adversaries to overcome, and personal sacrifices will have to be made. But if we keep the faith, our heavenly Father will be with us to help us finish our course, just as he was with Paul.

THE PITFALLS OF RELIGION

The body of Jesus Christ will be the overcoming, victorious church. The pitfalls of religion that currently divide the church, keeping it operating far below its level of authority, must be shattered, scattered, and eradicated. As we see, this will not be a quick or easy task; however, the defeat of this spirit of religion is imminent.

The rebellious spirit of religion, with its opposition to kingdom advancement through revelatory knowledge rather than man's wisdom, must be forced to submit to the power and demonstration of the Holy Spirit to teach, train, and equip believers to understand and activate the kingdom life on the earth. Unless this self-righteous spirit is dealt with through supernatural means, it will continue to cause division and splits in the church. Jesus said, "Every kingdom divided against itself is brought to desolation" (Matthew 12:25 NKJV). The church—body of Christ—cannot become the prevailing grace and power of God's demonstration on the earth unless or until we, the body, are unified. "Is Christ divided?" (1 Corinthians 1:13 NKJV). Neither can we be!

The Holy Spirit said to me, "Don't teach and preach the Gospel of the kingdom and depend upon this world's evil systems to take care of you."

As we look back on 2020 and 2021, two of the most tumultuous, angst-ridden years in American history, we see very clearly that the body of Christ—namely, evangelicals—placed their confidence not in God, but in spiritual counterfeits. Many stockpiled gold and other financial resources, including food and assault weapons. They relied on charismatic personalities of great influence. They talked the walk, but they did not walk the talk.

They outwardly acknowledged God as their sustainer and deliverer, while inwardly they sought to insure their future—their superior way of life built on wealth, power, and an opulent lifestyle, even at the expense of human life. They prioritized their political party and their investment accounts; they built underground bunkers, reinforced shelters to secure and protect its inhabitants against falling bombs. Their religious mindset persisted as they taught and preached "the kingdom" while not relying on God as their first option, which implies they were not truly living a faith lifestyle. "But the just shall live by his faith" (Habakkuk 2:4b NKJV). "For we walk by faith, not by sight" (2 Corinthians 5:7 NKJV). "But seek first the kingdom of God and His righteousness, and all these things shall be added to you" (Matthew 6:33 NKJV).

Obedience to God grows out of a heart for God. Our perspective of God, how we see him, has a profound bearing on whether or not we will instinctively look to him in times of adversity. Is he still the Sovereign Creator of the universe? And were all things made by him—the heavens and the earth and the fullness thereof—the world and all who live in it? Do we see the fullness of his unrivaled power, or do we seek imaginary solutions and other gods?

The church has lost its "awe" of God. And I am convinced that in 2022 the Father is doing a work of reuniting and reinvigorating the body of Christ for kingdom compliance—his way of doing and being righteous in the earth by grace through faith in Jesus Christ and our living first and foremost as citizens of the kingdom of heaven, adhering to its principles, the Word of God.

> *You answer us in righteousness, with awe-inspiring works, God of our salvation … Those who live far away are awed by Your signs.*
>
> **—Psalm 65:5, 8**

Our hearts must be overwhelmed by God. God is simply amazing. And as David implies, words fail to tell the whole of it. "For there is not a word on my tongue, but behold, O Lord, You know it altogether ... Such knowledge is too wonderful for me; It is high, I cannot attain it" (Psalm 139:4, 6 NKJV).

Like David, the body of Christ must move beyond human descriptions of God and instead seek intimacy with him through a personal relationship built upon faith and obedience, even in the midst of our struggles and adversity. Personally, my experiences with struggle and adversity have produced spiritual maturity because I learned obedience by the things I suffered, which things have perfected me for completion of my divine assignment, just as it was with Jesus (Hebrews 5:8–9 NKJV).

Being equipped to carry out our divine assignment requires spiritual growth, which often involves great struggle. My wife and I have had to surrender to God's plan for our lives and struggle with the prophetic word of God spoken over our lives concerning our kingdom assignment. Like Peter and the other apostles, my wife and I literally left all to follow Jesus. We left house, land, brothers and sisters, father, etc. for Jesus's sake and the gospel's. We were willing to surrender our lives to God and endure the struggles that led to growth in our faith in order to see the blessing of God manifested. We were willing to suffer for the sake of Christ, the author of our kingdom assignment, and for the Gospel, "which is manifest evidence of the righteous judgment of God, that you may be counted worthy of the kingdom of God, for which you also suffer" (2 Thessalonians 1:5 NKJV).

I believe the body of Christ is on the verge of a great spiritual awakening that will reverse this current generation's retreat from Christlike values and godly character that have led to the church's current crisis. The COVID-19 pandemic simply exposed the depth to which Satan crept in subtly and lulled believers to sleep. While we should have been on the battlefields reaping the harvest of souls teaching and preaching the Gospel of the kingdom, many were enjoying extravagant lifestyles. King David probably would not have sinned against the Lord with Bathsheba or murdered her husband, Uriah, if he had been on the battlefield, which was his custom during the time this sin took place (2 Samuel 11:1 NKJV).

Nevertheless, we owe a great debt of gratitude to the Lord for sustaining us during 2020 and 2021 when so many churches, businesses, and ministries—mega and small—closed permanently. Yet the Father has preserved a remnant of faith warriors whom he has raised to feed the body of Christ by demonstrations of the Holy Spirit and power that will usher the Ekklesia into kingdom compliance. Their time and anointing are being poured out like oil to promote this very end.

I pray that the pressures of 2020 and 2021 have stripped the Ekklesia of life's nonessentials, allowing us to recover the priority of intimate friendship with God. This doesn't mean we do not enjoy life and all it offers in a righteous way, for the Father has given us richly all things to enjoy (1 Timothy 6:17). But we must not allow money and other material things to possess us. We must possess them, for we live in the world, but we are not of the world (John 17:15–16 NKJV). "And those who use this world as not misusing it. For the form of this world is passing away" (1 Corinthians 7:31 NKJV).

The church is the vital force within our society, empowered by God through Jesus Christ, to lead men and women, boys and girls to salvation. In order for it to become a functioning organism of new wine in new wineskins, however, the saints must become bond servants, yielding themselves in surrender to obey and serve God of their own independent will. We must come up higher by raising our spiritual rank and allowing ourselves to be led by the Holy Spirit, our guide into all things truth (Romans 8:14 NKJV and John 16:13 NKJV).

All who desire to please the Lord Jesus, our commanding officer, should seek to live a committed Holy Spirit–led life. To do so means we have died to our own ways and have given the Lord the unconditional right to choose for us, as he leads and guides us into all truth.

There is a price the saints must pay if we are to experience perpetually the Lord's best. We cannot *overcome* unless there is something to overcome. The reward we receive for putting the Lord first is the prize that is beyond comparison as we forget what's past and reach toward what lies ahead. We must press toward the prize of the upward call of God in Christ Jesus (Philippians 3:13, 14). Saints must realize that the Lord greatly desires to introduce his body to his true kingdom, the kingdom of their hearts, through a Holy Spirit–led life and walk.

The kingdom of God is a realm in which everything moves in divine order and purpose. There is much that is available to us that we have yet to appropriate, as we tend to settle for less than the Lord's best provision, which is a mentality of poverty manifested through religion.

During this time of the saints' transition from the church—religious bondage—into the kingdom—freedom built upon grace and truth—the Father has raised the spiritual rank of his kingdom remnant saints into the realm of kingdom compliance—identification with and obedience to our Lord and his word—for "as He is, so are we in this world" (1 John 4:17 NKJV). The goal is to advance the kingdom of God on earth.

Saints of God, this is our time to heal, and love is the foundation from which we can build ourselves on our most holy faith by praying in the Holy Spirit (Jude 20 NKJV) and by embracing this opportunity for the body of Christ to examine herself to make sure she is in the faith and compliant with the principles of the kingdom of heaven.

This is an opportune time for the body of Christ to make true repentance from the heart a reality and become the living organism fit to function and carry out our kingdom mandate. One billion souls await our faithfulness to "occupy till I come" (Luke 19:13 KJV) so that "The kingdoms of this world have become the kingdoms of our Lord and of His Christ, and He shall reign forever and ever!" (Revelation 11:15 NKJV).

As we offer peoples of the world, saved and unsaved, credible evidence of who Jesus is, no longer bound by religion, we can invite them to "come and see" God's awesome deeds for themselves, and they will rush into the arms of Jesus, prioritizing his kingdom and living from a never exhausted economy of "more than enough." This is how we will attract and retain young people, leading them to Christ, in a skeptical age in which social media is the main platform of communication and learning. What a revival we have in store! What a privilege to live in such a time!

THE JOY OF THE KINGDOM

Like the scribes and Pharisees of Jesus's day, many Christians possess a religious mindset, a mindset bent on tradition, legalism, and the commandments of men. "Hypocrites! Well did Isaiah prophesy about you, saying: 'These people draw near to Me with their mouth, and honor Me with their lips, but their heart is far from Me. And in vain they worship Me, teaching as doctrines the commandments of men'" (Matthew 15:7-9 NJV). This mentality exposes attitudes of pride, arrogance, self-sufficiency, and self-righteousness that are opposed to total dependence on God and his sufficiency. And like the Pharisees, a religious mindset attempts to please God through works of the flesh. It focuses on outward appearances. This is actually a carnal mind.

Jesus possessed a kingdom mindset, one in which heaven's government—its laws, principles, systems, and keys by which it operates—is revealed and accepted by what God knows and believes to be the truth. The kingdom mindset is one of complete, absolute, uncompromising trust in God. The kingdom mindset understands that the King is all-sufficient and therefore is pleased to give the citizens of his kingdom the best of heaven manifested on earth. Joy is a kingdom manifestation, a major component of its culture.

The first Adam lost the original kingdom of God on the earth because of his disobedience. The second Adam, Jesus, came to earth to restore his Father's kingdom through his own obedience. If Jesus had to learn obedience through his suffering, where does that leave believers? The servant is never greater than his lord (John 13:16 NKJV).

Jesus went about teaching in synagogues and preaching the Gospel of the kingdom (Mark 4:23 NKJV); therefore we must pattern our teaching after him. He did not come preaching a religion. This is the main reason the religious sects of Jesus's day were always astonished by his preaching and wanted him killed. The kingdom message is empowered by the authority of the King, the supernatural power of God.

Kingdom authority is the authority of God's Word. God authorized Jesus, giving Jesus his authority to speak on his behalf. We, too, need to understand the authority we possess as the King's ambassadors on earth. God is with us! And religion can't do anything about it. In fact, what religion does is keep believers from experiencing the King's best for their life on earth.

Let me reiterate: the kingdom of God and the Gospel thereof is

God's way of living righteous—his rule in heaven carried out on the earth by those who are born again. As soon as one is born again, the kingdom of heaven takes up residence in his spirit. The problem we face is that old mindsets still exist, primarily due to lack of spiritual maturity.

Spiritual maturity is a process of growth over a period of time through consistent prayer, study, fasting, meditation of the Word of God, and application of that which is learned. It's about spending quality time in God's presence so that we are weaned off milk and become of full age by reason of use. When we abide in the presence of God, his presence becomes a gym where our inner being consistently works out, building strong spiritual muscles so that our senses are exercised to discern between good and evil (Hebrews 5:14 NKJV).

Many people have tried in vain to put new revelations into a religious mindset. It is impossible to do so because the person who possesses a religious mindset does not have revelatory knowledge of the Word of God; therefore he or she cannot broker a change. A lack of Holy Spirit knowledge of the Word of God is one of the reasons religious mentalities still exist among those who are born again, and yet it is prevalent throughout the church.

Again, the kingdom of God is not a religion. It is not a forced set of rules, doctrines, or legalistic rituals that people can add to the Gospel or change whenever it pleases them. The kingdom of God is a living, functional organism within the spirit of those who are born again. It is a lifestyle. The religious mindset loves to give its own opinion, but the kingdom mindset simply obeys the king's command, trusting the king's faithfulness to his word.

Paul warns us not to be conformed to the world's way of living which is evil, bent on lies, fear, terror, greed, and power in rebellion against God. He urges us sincerely to learn how to live a lifestyle acceptable and pleasing to God by renewing our minds and receiving deliverance from the evils of the world (Romans 12:2 NKJV).

This requires a transformation of the mind, which is an inward job. When a person is born again by grace through faith in Jesus Christ, God delivers them from the power of darkness and translates them into his kingdom (Colossians 1:13 NKJV). But the realization of that translation may never be affected in the mindset of those born-again believers who remain spiritual babies for lack of growth in revelatory knowledge of God's Word.

If we are going to truly reflect God's glory in the earth by expanding his kingdom, we must settle it in our minds to seek, pursue, study, explore, learn, meditate, and appropriate God's Word from a kingdom perspective.

Paul urges believers not to live futile or worthless lifestyles but that they should learn Christ by changing their mindset from the lusts of the world and be renewed in the spirit of their mind, adapting to the character of Jesus. This is the "new man" kingdom mindset, which is acceptable to God, having been created in his righteousness by the power of the Holy Spirit (Ephesians 4:17, 20–24 NKJV).

In order for believers to lead the lost to salvation by the multitudes and expand the kingdom of God on earth, we must make a conscious and committed decision to renew our minds from religion to kingdom. We cannot straddle the fence and expect to be the end-time remnant army of saints the church is to become prior to Jesus's return. Our lack of commitment to God's kingdom—to learn its principles and live them from a heart of love, faith, and total trust in God—has not only robbed us of our God-given authority in the earth but also has kept us from realizing God's promises of a full, varied, and prosperous life.

Our lack of commitment has labeled us as lukewarm Christians and has placed us in danger of being rejected by God. And we should never lose the light of the Gospel. It is time for a new attitude in the body of Christ, an attitude of change that commits us to God as faithful and wise stewards in service to him through Jesus Christ. We have the mind of Christ. Now we must use it to reap the harvest of the world and bring glory to God by expanding his kingdom on earth.

Like Jesus, we must be about our Father's business, possessing the mind of the kingdom. We must turn from a religious mindset to a kingdom mindset—the same mindset Jesus had during his life on earth. And he invites us to allow that same mindset to be ours as well (Philippians 2:5 NKJV), "for the kingdom of God is not eating and drinking, but righteousness and peace and joy in the Holy Spirit" (Romans 14:17 NKJV).

THY WILL BE DONE: THE MAKING OF A BOND SERVANT

It baffles me to this day that some pastors teach their congregants that saints don't have to suffer. I can remember a prophet, who was my pastor, telling me that. There are two kinds of suffering that fall into the general context of what I'm attempting to convey here. One is suffering for Christ's sake and the sake of the Gospel, and the other is suffering for wrongdoing.

To suffer, as related to Christ and the Gospel, is the same Greek word for *passion*, which is *pascho*, meaning to experience a sensation or impression usually painful—suffer, vex.[14] There is a connection between those who suffer for Christ's sake and those who are chosen vessels of the Lord. Jesus said to Ananias concerning Saul, whom Ananias was to minister to so that Saul would receive his sight, "Go, for he is a chosen vessel of Mine to bear My name before Gentiles, kings, and the children of Israel. For I will show him how many things he must suffer for My name's sake" (Acts 9:15–16 NKJV).

It seems to me that Jesus chooses those who will suffer for his name's sake to be vessels of his, to bear his name among believers and unbelievers alike, even dignitaries. Paul said that if we suffer with Christ, we will also be glorified together (Romans 9:17 NKJV). "For to you it has been granted on behalf of Christ, not only to believe in Him, but also to suffer for His sake" (Philippians 1:29 NKJV).

Suffer, as used in the scripture above, is the Greek word *sumpempo*, which means to experience pain jointly or of the same kind; specifically persecution—sympathize; suffer with.[15]

> *"Therefore I endure all things for the elect's sake, that they may also obtain the salvation which is in Christ Jesus with eternal glory … If we suffer, we shall also reign with him: if we deny him, he also will deny us."*
>
> **—2 Timothy 2:10, 12, KJV**

Clearly, there are rewards for those who suffer for Christ's sake and the sake of the gospel. And conversely, there are penalties for those who

[14] *Strong's Exhaustive Concordance of the Bible, NT,* 3958.

[15] *Strong's Exhaustive Concordance of the Bible, NT,* 4841.

suffer for a wrong done. "For what credit is it if, when you are beaten for your faults, you take it patiently? But when you do good and suffer, if you take it patiently, this is commendable before God. For to this you were called, because Christ also suffered for us, leaving us an example, that you should follow His steps" (1 Peter 2:20–21 NKJV).

Many saints find themselves bound by unnecessary suffering. This is the religious mindset. Some suffer mentally, which is even more intense than some physical suffering because of justified or unjustified concerns over matters that leave them filled with mental anguish. They are always disturbed, and many display ungodly attitudes. This is undue agony, unlike Jesus's suffering in the garden of Gethsemane because of his passion.

Saints who don't suffer for Christ's sake and the sake of the Gospel generally respond to suffering in the wrong way. They tend to despise suffering, and they tend to take it lightly or for granted. Others get weary and give up; they end up treating it too seriously. But the correct response to suffering for the believer is to be exercised by it, to receive instruction from it. The apostle Peter says, "For this is commendable, if because of conscience toward God one endures grief, suffering wrongly" (1 Peter 2:19 NKJV).

As believers, we are to commit our suffering to God, knowing that he is faithful to work all things together for our good (Romans 8:28 NKJV) and for his glory. As a matter of fact, the apostle James tells us to "count it all joy when you fall into various trials" (James 1:2 NKJV). Jesus learned from the things in which he suffered (Hebrews 5:8 NKJV). All these affirmations relative to suffering for the sake of Christ and for the preaching and teaching of the Gospel must have significant purposes.

So why does God permit his children—those who are His chosen vessels—to suffer? For what purpose? First of all, a good God only produces good results. One purpose, then, is to produce lasting fruit that will confirm us as true disciples (John 15:8 NKJV); another is to shut the mouth of the accuser (Job 1:9–12 NKJV); another is to bring glory to God (1 Peter 2:21 NKJV); another is to conform us to Jesus's image (Romans 8:29 NKJV); a fifth purpose is to teach believers how to depend on God (Psalm 20:7 NKJV); a sixth purpose is to refine the life of the believer and bring him into abundance (Psalm 66:10–12 NKJV); and yet a seventh purpose is to create a platform for ministry of the Gospel of the kingdom to others (2 Corinthians 1:3–7 NKJV).

The scriptures below are the sum total of what suffering for the sake of Christ and for the Gospel of the kingdom is about, and why we, too, must suffer. Christ Jesus is our example!

> *Therefore let those who suffer according to the will of God commit their souls to Him in doing good, as to a faithful Creator.*
>
> **—1 Peter 4:19 NKJV**

> *But may the God of all grace, who called us to His eternal glory by Christ Jesus, after you have suffered a while, perfect, establish, strengthen, and settle you. To Him be the glory and the dominion forever and ever. Amen.*
>
> **—1 Peter 5:10–11 NKJV**

ON EARTH AS IT IS IN HEAVEN

The Ekklesia is the mature governing body of Christ on earth to bring heaven—its constitution and its culture—to earth. We have a mandate as ambassadors for Christ to release heaven upon the earth. The Ekklesia, the governing body of believers who come together in unity to legislate the kingdom of God on the earth according to the Word of God, has as its mandate to live the constitution of the kingdom of God on the earth. While the church is focused on heaven, the Ekklesia is focused on our mandate to be fruitful and multiply and replenish and subdue the earth in order to have dominion over all of God's creatures (Genesis 1:26–30 NKJV).

There is a church mindset, and there is a kingdom mindset. "And He said to them, 'To you it has been given to know the mystery of the kingdom of God'" (Mark 4:11 NKJV).

Sadly, the church mindset is still one based on religiosity—living under the Old Testament, the traditions of the elders, and legalism—touch not, taste not, handle not:

> Therefore, if you died with Christ to the elementary principles of the world, why, as if you were living in the

> world, do you subject yourself to legalistic rules? 'Do not touch! Do not taste! Do not handle!' These all are to perish with use and are aligned with the commandments and doctrines of men. These things have indeed a show of wisdom in self-imposed worship and humility and neglecting of the body, but are worthless against the indulgence of the flesh. (Colossians 2:20–23 MEV)

In the above scripture verses, it is clearly stated that none of the legalistic rules and doctrines of men have any true merit toward our salvation through faith in Jesus Christ. Rules and doctrines of men only have a show of wisdom—in this case, trying to live righteous before God through works of the flesh instead of by the power of an endless life through Jesus Christ—but are powerless to bring the lusts of the flesh, which will perish with use, under subjection of the Holy Spirit. As I so often say in my ministry of the Gospel of the kingdom to the body of Christ, "Y'all work too hard!"

Living the life of the kingdom of God on earth was never meant to be "hard." Living the kingdom life on earth brings the days of heaven to us here on earth. "That your days may be multiplied, and the days of your children, in the land which the Lord sware unto your fathers to give them, as the days of heaven upon the earth" (Deuteronomy 11:21 KJV).

Consider Job 36:11 MEV: "If they obey and serve Him, they will spend their days in prosperity and their years in pleasures."

Also consider Isaiah 1:19 MEV: "If you are willing and obedient, you shall eat the good of the land."

The church mindset is so heavily focused on getting to heaven that it doesn't care very much for the above verses because they, through our willing and obedient service to God, dictate our life of abundance as opposed to a life of poverty. The church mindset is focused on going to heaven, where there will be no more pain, crying, or death. The church mindset relegates those believers who adhere to it as orphans and slaves governed by rules, tradition, legalism, and a spirit of bondage—all because they are trying to live the life of Christ through the power of their flesh and not by the power of the Holy Spirit and the grace of God afforded us through our faith in Jesus's finished work on the cross at Cavalry.

The kingdom mindset is focused on our influence on the earth. We understand we are sons and daughters, heirs of God, and joint heirs with Christ. We are governed by the Holy Spirit, who gives us the life of Jesus living in our spirit. We have the spirit of adoption, and we are Holy Spirit led:

> For as many as are led by the Spirit of God, these are the sons of God. For you have not received the spirit of slavery again to fear. But you have received the Spirit of adoption, by whom we cry, "Abba, Father." The Spirit Himself bears witness with our spirits that we are the children of God, and if children, then heirs: heirs of God and joint-heirs with Christ, if indeed we suffer with Him, that we may also be glorified with Him. (Romans 8:14–17 MEV)

In order to have influence, kings know that kingdoms are always reached from the top to the bottom. The church, on the other hand, starts from the bottom and tries to reach the top, but that doesn't work. The church is focused on events and numbers, keeping people attending. Many churches in the United States have large numbers, but they don't necessarily have any influence among the elite, the power brokers who through Congress legislate according to their personal ambitions and status. We need the Ekklesia. We need kingdom senators and representatives in Congress who will not take bribes or compromise for self-promotion and self-aggrandizement but will legislate based upon the "present truth" of the Word of God. We need believers who are thinking and acting like ambassadors for Christ in God's stead (2 Corinthians 5:20 NKJV).

Prior to Adam's and Eve's fall in the Garden of Eden, God's will was done on earth as it was in heaven. Their job was to duplicate heaven on the earth, causing the earth to be filled with the same glory as the kingdom of heaven. The first Adam lost this kingdom colony, but the second Adam, Jesus, restored that kingdom to those of us who believe—the heirs of salvation. And at the end of Jesus's earthly ministry, he gave his disciples the mandate to preach the Gospel of the kingdom as a witness to all nations (Matthew 24:14 NKJV). As present-day disciples, we are to do the same: "For the earth will be filled with the knowledge of the glory of the Lord, as the waters cover the seas" (Habakkuk 2:14 MEV).

The body of Christ needs to learn what God's will is according to the constitution of the kingdom, the Word of God, which instructs us as to how things are done from a heavenly perspective. Paul said, "Imitate me, just as I also imitate Christ" (1 Corinthians 11:1 NKJV). I think the body of Christ, the Ekklesia, needs to meditate on that. God's will, his plans and purposes for our lives, will lead us more abundantly into the enjoyment of a life that Jesus died for us to have (John 10:10b NKJV)—all things richly to enjoy (1 Timothy 6:17 NKJV)—as we submit ourselves in complete loyalty and devotion to him as bond servants, who of our own independence will choose to serve him and say, "Your kingdom come. Your will be done on earth as it is in heaven" (Matthew 6:10 NKJV).

Doing things on earth as they are done in heaven can be realized only by those who possess a mindset based upon an eternal perspective of the kingdom of God. It is from an eternal perspective that we stay tuned-in to the frequency of heaven!

CHAPTER 4

We Are Not of the World

I have given them Your word; and the world has hated them because they are not of the world, just as I am not of the world. I do not pray that You should take them out of the world, but that You should keep them from the evil one. Sanctify them by Your truth. Your word is truth. As You sent Me into the world, I also have sent them into the world. And for their sakes I sanctify Myself, that they also may be sanctified by the truth.

—John 17:14–15, 17–19 NKJV

How many believers, worldwide, experience the same problems and vices as nonbelievers because, for whatever reason(s), they became alienated from the truth, the Word of God, which sanctifies them, consecrates them, and separates them for God's use on the earth?

For too many believers, alienation from the truth—trying to live life on earth apart from the Holy Spirit—resulted in them backsliding. My take on this is that they were not willing or simply did not grow spiritually to the point of being led by the Holy Spirit (Romans 8:14 NKJV), who guides the believer into all truth (John 16:13 NKJV).

Without the comfort and power of the Holy Spirit, they hit the "real world," and the burden of religion, tradition, and legalism compounded by their fleshly lusts became too heavy to bear. So they opted for what seemed to be an easier, more self-indulgent lifestyle. And before they knew it, Satan had crept in, unaware to them, and their spiritual senses became dull (Hebrews 5:11 NKJV). The eyes of their mind became blind (2 Corinthians 4:4 NKJV) to the subtle, deceptive ways of their adversary, the devil. The apostle Paul sums up their dilemma best: "This happened because false brothers were secretly brought in, who sneaked in to spy out our liberty, which we have in Christ Jesus, that they might bring us into bondage" (Galatians 2:4 MEV).

In many cases, it can take years before a backslider returns to his or her first love, if at all. Meanwhile, their sinful experiences are real and graphic. "The backslider in heart shall be filled with his own ways" (Proverbs 14:14 KJV), which means that every backslider will relate to the worldly lifestyle that will ensue when their heart is turned away from God.

Today popular culture is bent on independent expression, alternative lifestyles, same-sex marriage, greed, love of self, and hating and abusing those who have a different opinion from their own. Nevertheless, backsliders need to be assured that no matter how deep they've fallen into sin they can repent, ask for God's forgiveness, and be received back into his family. "Return, you backsliding children, and I will heal your backslidings. Indeed we come to You, for You are the Lord our God" (Jeremiah 3:22 NKJV).

The apostle Paul warns believers that perilous times will come. And the question still looms large as to how we, the saints, can live in a world where these perils occur and not be of the world. Paul urges us to turn away from those people who embrace these perilous times as a normal act of living on the earth by following carefully his doctrine and manner of life, purpose, faith, endurance, love, perseverance, persecutions, and affliction, which happened to him in his life on earth as well: "What persecutions I endured. And out of them all the Lord delivered me … But you must continue in the things which you have learned and been assured of, knowing from whom you have learned them … that the man of God may be complete, thoroughly equipped for every good work" (2 Timothy 3:11b, 14, 17 NKJV).

> *But know this, that in the last days perilous times will come: For men will be lovers of themselves, lovers of money, boasters, proud, blasphemers, disobedient to parents, unthankful, unholy, [3]unloving, unforgiving, slanderers, without self-control, brutal, despisers of good,[4] traitors, headstrong, haughty, lovers of pleasure rather than lovers of God, [5]having a form of godliness but denying its power. And from such people turn away!*
>
> **—2 Timothy 3:1–5 NKJV**

Indeed, perilous times have befallen us. The apostle Paul has described our current societal dilemma in the above scripture. The Greek word for *perilous* is *chalepos*, which means to reduce the strength of; be difficult—that is, dangerous, furious; to lower as into a void; strike down.[16]

Because saints live in the world, we have use of the world just like anybody else. How can we have life more abundantly (John 10:10b NKJV) and enjoy the things that the Father has given us richly to enjoy (1 Timothy 6:17b NKJV) while not allowing the perils that take place in the world to reduce our strength or lower us into a void where we are struck down by the perils of evil rather than raised in the strength of Jesus, living as if we are not of the world, through the power of the Holy Spirit?

I believe the short answer to this question is that believers must think from an eternal perspective rather than from a natural perspective. The spiritual always supersedes the physical. "By faith we understand that the worlds were framed by the word of God, so that the things which are seen were not made of things which are visible" (Hebrews 11:3 NKJV).

Believe it or not, there is also a simple answer, and it, too, comes from scripture: "And those who use this world as not misusing it, for the form of this world is passing away" (1 Corinthians 7:31 NKJV). Add to this verse: "And the world is passing away, and the lust of it; but he who does the will of God abides forever" (1 John 2:17 NKJV).

Each of the two previous verses of scripture presents to the believer a powerful theme. In the former, we can use and enjoy the things of the world as long as we do not misuse or abuse them. And in the latter, as we do the will of God, the lusts of this world become less meaningful,

[16] *Strong's Exhaustive Concordance of the Bible, NT*, 5467, 5465.

since the world as we now know it, along with the lusts thereof, are passing away.

The Greek word used for *abuse* is *katachraomai*, which means to overuse—that is, misuse; abuse, in the sense of opposition.[17] Abuse is actually opposed to what is good or right by reason of misuse or overuse in a wrong way.

Abuse is the improper usage or treatment of a thing, often to unfairly or improperly gain benefit. Abuse can come in many forms, such as physical or verbal maltreatment, injury, assault, violation, rape, unjust practices, crimes, or other types of aggression. To these descriptions, one can also add the Kantian notion of the wrongness of using another human being as means to an end rather than as ends in themselves. Some sources describe abuse as "socially constructed," which means there may be more or less recognition of the suffering of a victim at different times and societies.

In Christ, abuse is not necessary; therefore it is not condoned. Each believer will stand before the judgment seat of Christ to receive the things done in the body, whether good or bad (2 Corinthians 5:10 NKJV). The truth is, believers can live in the world and not be of it or controlled by it through abuse or misuse; however, this posture requires saints to grow up in spiritual maturity, having their spiritual senses exercised to discern both good and evil (Hebrews 5:14 NKJV).

The way to achieving this is by consciously surrendering our lives to follow and learn Jesus Christ through the power of the Holy Spirit, not through our own strength or self-willed righteousness. We must put off the old man, the nature of our flesh, and put on the new man—the nature of God through the renewing of our mind.

> But you have not so learned Christ, if indeed you have heard Him and have been taught by Him, as the truth is in Jesus: that you put off, concerning your former conduct, the old man which grows corrupt according to the deceitful lusts, and be renewed in the spirit of your mind, and that you put on the new man which was created according to God, in true righteousness and

[17] *Strong's Exhaustive Concordance of the Bible, NT,* 2710, 2596.

> holiness ... nor give place to the devil. And do not grieve the Holy Spirit of God, by whom you were sealed for the day of redemption. (Ephesians 4:20–24, 27, 30 NKJV)

I feel it is safe to say, in light of the revelation we've just received, that we can live in this world and not be of it as we surrender our lives to God and are filled with his spirit. As we are filled with the Holy Spirit, we are controlled by him. Being filled with him is our assurance of a successful life on earth as a Christian. And because being filled is a repeated experience of renewing of the spirit of our mind with the Word of God, we are Holy Spirit conscious not to abuse or misuse the things of the world. Instead, we enjoy them to the full, in moderation, *epieikes*—mild; gentle, moderation, patient, and appropriate as superimposed in time, place, order, etc.[18] "Rejoice in the Lord always: and again I say, Rejoice. Let your moderation be known unto all men. The Lord is at hand" (Philippians 4:4–5 KJV).

USE—DON'T ABUSE

We live in a physical world that God created as a colony of his heavenly kingdom. We legally inhabit earth because we have a physical body, and our real identity, our spirit, is bound therein. Yet we are not of this world and are constantly being reminded in scripture that we should not make friends with the "evil systems" of the world. "Do you not know that friendship with the world is enmity with God? Whoever therefore wants to be a friend of the world makes himself an enemy of God" (James 4:4 NKJV).

Since Satan is the prince of this world (John 12:31 NKJV), he has corrupted it with his very own nature—a murderer from the beginning and the father of lies (John 8:44 NKJV), who is an accuser of the brethren (Revelation 12:10 NKJV). He comes only to steal, kill, and destroy (John 10:10a NKJV), and his tactics are always the same: to imitate, deceive, and take advantage of us through the lust of our flesh, the lust of our eyes, and our pride of life, which is not of the Father but is of the world

[18] *Strong's Exhaustive Concordance of the Bible, NT,* 1933, 1909.

(1 John 2:16 NKJV). As the Word of God says, "Lest Satan should take advantage of us; for we are not ignorant of his devices" (2 Corinthians 2:11 NKJV).

Why, then, do we act as if we are ignorant of Satan's devices, especially since throughout the Bible we do not lack information or intelligence as to who and what he is? From Genesis to Revelation, we are told how Satan appeals to us through deception; he deceives us into thinking there is a better way than God's way. Through powerful images in our minds, he paints pictures of how pleasant sin is; he promotes the self-benefit of bitterness, hatred, and revenge; he advocates the love of money over God and power over love among fellow men. He reminds us often that we've failed to "live right" and therefore are not going to heaven. Satan wants people, especially believers, to buy into this lie. Sadly, too many of us do.

Satan is a slanderer. The word *slander* is the Hebrew word rendered *dibbah*, which means defaming, evil report, infamy.[19] The Greek rendition of *slander* is *diabolos*: a traducer; Satan; false accuser, devil, slanderer.[20] He uses the evil tactic of slander to defame God to people—to keep people defaming and falsely accusing one another and to accuse people before God with an evil report.

Satan is a tempter who presents to us plausible reasons and advantages for sinning that appeal to us. "Stolen waters are sweet, and bread eaten in secret is pleasant" (Proverbs 9:17 KJV).

The apostle Paul said, "For this reason, when I could no longer endure it, I sent to know your faith, lest by some means the tempter had tempted you, and our labor might be in vain" (1 Thessalonians 3:5 NKJV).

As the god of this age, Satan foments the secular worldviews of religious systems that are contrary to biblical truth. He influences unrighteous political systems and advocates absolute power. He promotes injustice, abuse of power and authority, and oppression. Greed, fear, and terror are among his classic trademarks. Paul taught, "But even if our gospel is veiled, it is veiled to those who are perishing, whose minds the god of the age has blinded, who do not believe, lest

---

[19] *Strong's Exhaustive Concordance of the Bible, OT*, 1681.

[20] *Strong's Exhaustive Concordance of the Bible, NT*, 1228.

the light of the gospel of the glory of Christ, who is the image of God, should shine on them" (2 Corinthians 4:3–4 NKJV).

As the prince of the power of the air (Ephesians 2:2 NKJV), Satan is chief commander of the army of fallen angels, who took sides with him in his rebellion against God, whose earthy mandate is to conspire with him to tempt, deceive, and corrupt the minds of men by any evil means possible. But God! We have victory over Satan through the finished work of Jesus Christ on the cross at Cavalry. "And they overcame him by the blood of the Lamb and by the word of their testimony, and they did not love their lives to the death" (Revelation 12:11 NKJV).

When Jesus died on the cross, Satan thought he had won. What the devil didn't know is that Jesus's death would shatter and scatter as dust in the wind all his plans and expectations. Jesus's precious blood, the purchased price for our redemption, is still available by grace through faith to all who will receive him as Savior. "But thanks be to God, who gives us the victory through our Lord Jesus Christ" (1 Corinthians 15:57 NKJV).

As saints, we have already won. Therefore, we do not have to live as if we belong to the world. We do not. We simply live in the world, as in sojourning. Our true citizenship is heaven. We must learn to live heaven's principles on the earth and not be overcome by the evil systems thereof. "The just shall live by faith" (Romans 1:17 NKJV) isn't a phrase or slogan we simply toss around as a good testimony to impress one another to think we are faith giants totally dependent upon Abba Daddy as our source of all things good. No! It is the principle by which we stand in kingdom compliance with the King, who knows those who are his true subjects and grants to them the benefits of his kingdom. We use the things of the world, but we do not abuse them, for we know they are passing away. This is our position as true sons and daughters of God. "If then you were raised with Christ, seek those things which are above, where Christ is, sitting at the right hand of God. Set your mind on things above, not on things on the earth. For you died, and your life is hidden with Christ in God. When Christ who is our life appears, then you also will appear with Him in glory" (Colossians 3:1–4 NKJV).

"We live in the world" means we get to use and enjoy, in moderation, the things of the world. "But we are not of the world" simply means we don't abuse or misuse the things of the world to our own demise.

LIVE IN THIS WORLD BY THE POWER OF GOD

I once had an old freezer on my back porch that reminded me of some Christians I knew. It would run loud and shake violently at times, but it would not freeze. It had all the signs of a freezer, but it did not have the ability to freeze, similar to those believers I knew who always had a form of godliness, but always denied its power. "And from such people turn away!" (2 Timothy 3:5 NKJV).

I had to come to that same conclusion as it relates to that old freezer. I had to turn away from it. In short, get rid of it! Needless to say, there was something wrong with it. First and foremost, it was really old, and its parts had become worn after battling years of seasonal elements. It struggled to run, signifying that the motor was almost gone. Add to that, it had a leak and would no longer hold the Freon required for freezing.

I was faced with a decision: I could have the old freezer repaired and hope it would freeze again without the shaking and loud noise, or I could solve the problem altogether by purchasing a new freezer. It was a situation involving my level of trust at the time. It would cost less to repair the old freezer, but there would be no guarantee how long the repair would sustain the freezer, and I would have no warranty. If the freezer broke again, I would be facing yet another repair bill.

On the other hand, I could purchase a new energy-efficient freezer with an extended warranty that would cost more than I could afford at the time but would last for years and save me money. If I needed to repair the freezer, it would not cost me any out-of-pocket money. It was a matter of immediate cost versus long-term savings. I chose the latter.

My new freezer did not run loud. As a matter of fact, I couldn't hear it running at all. It did not shake. It produced no frost and had greater storage capacity. And it had full power to freeze. What a great decision! It reminded me of what happens when the saints allow their minds to be renewed by the Word of God with the Holy Spirit revelation.

An interesting analogy this is: the comparison of a new cost-efficient freezer under warranty for many years and the renewed mind of the believer. The Holy Spirit revealed to me a parallel between my old freezer and those who are born again but have never had their minds renewed through revelatory knowledge of the Word of God. Yes, they are saved, but they cannot express the benefits of their salvation on earth. They generally relegate salvation to "going to heaven when I die" and never come to the knowledge that salvation is far more than "not going to hell." So they never enjoy salvation on earth, never coming to the knowledge that salvation is a two-realm reality: physical and eternal.

The Greek word for *salvation* is *soteria*, which means rescue or safety, deliver, health, defender; deliverer—that is, God or Christ; savior.[21] The Hebrew word is *yeshuwah*, meaning something saved—that is, deliverance; hence, aid, victory, prosperity; health, help, welfare, make whole.[22]

By these definitions, not only is salvation something we need so we will go to heaven and not go to hell but it's also what we need here on earth—now! In heaven, we will not need deliverance, health, prosperity, rescue, welfare, or safety. We need these components of life here on earth. The heavenly part is already taken care of. So on earth is where we need to be made whole through our Savior Jesus Christ. Life after we die, our oneness with God in his presence, is our eternal state. The physical and the eternal work together, giving us days of heaven on earth, and after that we will find eternal life.

Saved people who cannot express the benefits of their salvation here on earth are a lot like my old freezer. In short, they have little to no spiritual power. And much of their earthly life is relegated to living in poverty, poor health, ignorance, working hard for God, and little to no personal or societal accomplishment.

Many of these saints relegate the power of God to goose bumps and emotional spasms. They run loud, shake violently, yet they possess little to no real power to carry out kingdom mandates, which require revealed knowledge of the word. It's like trying to yoke an ox with a donkey. There is little to no spiritual growth. Old mindsets must be renewed by the Word of God in the power of the Holy Spirit.

Like my old freezer, no matter how old it was or what it could no longer do, no matter how loud it was or how violently it shook, it was still called a freezer. But like these powerless believers, it was relegated to its age, limited capacity, and inability to hold the fluorocarbons needed

---

[21] *Strong's Exhaustive Concordance of the Bible, NT*, 4991.

[22] *Strong's Exhaustive Concordance of the Bible, OT*, 3444.

to produce cold air and the lack of an energy-efficient motor to power and channel the cold air. But the kingdom of God is about power: "For the kingdom of God is not in word but in power" (1 Corinthians 4:20 NKJV).

Let's talk about the real power of God. The Holy Spirit impressed upon my spirit that knowledge of scripture and demonstration of the Holy Spirit and power work together.

When questioning Jesus relative to the resurrection, the Sadducees tried unsuccessfully to trap him. They actually tested Jesus's knowledge of scripture. They did not believe in the resurrection of the dead and set forth to prove it, using Jesus himself. Jesus, however, broke their little setup with one very powerful statement: "You are mistaken, not knowing the Scriptures nor the power of God" (Matthew 22:29 NKJV).

The Greek word for *power* in the previous verse is *dunamis*, which means force, miraculous power, strength, abundance, ability, and mighty work. It is taken from *dunamai*, which means to be able and to be of power; to be possible.[23] Therefore, God's power or ability is the hallmark of miraculous power performed on earth in and through believers as the Holy Spirit wills.

Jesus equated knowledge of scripture with the power of God. In light of this revelation, any attempt to manifest the power of God without a revealed knowledge of scripture can lead to a spirit of error. Paul taught that the Gospel of Christ is the power of God (Romans 1:16 NKJV), and one cannot know the Gospel of Christ without knowledge of the scriptures.

As I look back over my own life, I can say that much of my lack of knowledge of scripture can be traced to traditions perpetuated and handed down through generations from other ministers who probably meant well but could barely read, let alone understand the scriptures. I can remember some preachers who could not read. But because they knew how to yield to the Holy Spirit for revelation of the word, they were able to experience the power and demonstrations that confirmed the word preached (Mark 16:20 NKJV).

We must never fail to remember that knowledge increases. And Paul teaches us to "be filled with the knowledge of His will in all wisdom and

[23] *Strong's Exhaustive Concordance of the Bible, NT*, 1410.

spiritual understanding; that you may walk worthy of the Lord, fully pleasing Him, being fruitful in every good work and increasing in the knowledge of God" (Colossians 1:9–10 NKJV). The angel of the Lord said to Daniel, concerning the sealing of the book, "But you, Daniel, shut up the words, and seal the book until the time of the end; many shall run to and fro, and knowledge shall increase" (Daniel 12:4 NKJV).

I think we are living in the time of the end, and knowledge continues to increase. As the unsaved increase in knowledge and technology through the world's evil systems, believers should be increasing in the knowledge of God and his word, receiving heaven's technology of "witty inventions" (Proverbs 8:12 KJV) and "knowledge and discretion" (Proverbs 8:12 NKJV). We can no longer be spiritually blind, lagging behind the people of the world, who through unrighteous means become wiser, shrewd, in their generation than the sons of light (Luke 16:8 NKJV).

This is a sad indictment against believers because the Word of God declares that we are children of light: "For you were once darkness, but now you are light in the Lord. Walk as children of light" (Ephesians 5:8 NKJV).

To walk as children of light requires a transformation of the mind through revelatory knowledge of the Word of God. Jesus gives us our best and most potent example of how powerful the Word of God is, fully backed by Holy Spirit power.

At Jesus's baptism in the Jordan River by John the Baptist, the Holy Spirit descended in bodily form upon him like a dove. God then spoke from heaven saying, "You are My beloved Son; in You I am well pleased" (Luke 3:22 NKJV).

I am awed by the fact that God both confirmed and affirmed Jesus prior to his tests by the devil in the wilderness. God's confidence toward Jesus lay in the fact that God knew Jesus himself knew he was the word made flesh (John 1:14 NKJV). Jesus knew he was equal with God but made himself of no reputation, coming in the likeness of men and taking on the form of a bond servant (Philippians 2:6–7 NKJV), which means he had to yield to and rely upon the power of the Holy Spirit.

Jesus was filled with the Holy Spirit as soon as the Holy Spirit descended upon him following his baptism, and immediately the Holy

Spirit led him into the wilderness to be tempted by the devil. But after Jesus defeated the devil with the Word of God by the power of the Holy Spirit, he returned in the power of the spirit (Luke 4:1–4 NKJV).

After Jesus received the Holy Spirit, the spirit led him into a desolate, lonely place for the express purpose of testing his knowledge of scripture and whether or not he would use and stand firm on the word. It baffles me that many believers who have been saved for decades still have not come to the knowledge that the devil can only be defeated with the Word of God spoken out of their mouths by faith and by the power of the Holy Spirit, who resides in their spirit. But in order to live in this spiritual dimension, the word must become their first priority and their final authority, and the word must be spoken by faith consistently.

I can imagine that over the course of his forty-day fast Jesus prayed, read, and studied the Old Testament scroll and meditated on God's Word. After the forty days of Jesus's temptation by the devil in the wilderness were ended, Jesus was physically at his weakest. He was hungry. This was the opportune time for the devil to play his ace card, tempting Jesus in the three areas he uses to seduce people, which temptations also describe his nature: "The lust of the flesh; the lust of the eyes; and the pride of life" (1 John 2:16 NKJV).

But because Jesus was full of the Word of God (power) and possessed it in his heart (spirit), he could stand against the devil's temptation by speaking the Word of God in the power of the spirit. I grew up listening to the old saint's testimony: "No Word, no power; little Word, little power." If Jesus had not had knowledge of scripture, and if he had not been filled with the Holy Spirit, he would not have possessed the power required to defeat the devil. As believers, we must consistently strengthen our inner being with the Word of God.

> *How God anointed Jesus of Nazareth with the Holy Spirit and with power, who went about doing good and healing all who were oppressed by the devil, for God was with Him.*
>
> **—Acts 10:38 NKJV**

> *And they were astonished at his doctrine, for His word was with power.*
>
> **—Luke 4:32 KJV**

> *And it came to pass on a certain day, as he was teaching … and the power of the Lord was present to heal them.*
>
> **—Luke 5:17 KJV**

Clearly, as believers, we cannot possess the power of God without a working knowledge of scripture and how it is to be applied. Neither can we take for granted the power of the Holy Spirit working in us and through us, enabling us with miraculous ability and power to do mighty deeds in the name of Jesus.

Like my old freezer, there are still many believers who do a whole lot of shaking but with little to no real power. As saints, we must learn how to plug in to the real power. We must renew our minds through Holy Spirit revelation of the Word of God and boldly decree it as we talk the walk and walk the talk; there is much more to the power of God besides shaking, quaking, and goose bumps.

The purchase of my new freezer was like a transition from one mindset to another. Instead of all those shaking, rattling noises my old freezer made, I now have a peaceful environment for a quiet, serene time of fellowship and communion in the presence of God. This is the environment in which I receive revelatory knowledge of scripture given by the Holy Spirit and learn how to effectively appropriate it so that the power of God is manifested in my life—to the glory of God and for the edification of the saints. God gets the glory, not me.

> *But we have this treasure in earthen vessels, that the excellence of the power may be of God and not of us.*
>
> **—2 Corinthians 4:7 NKJV**

> *That your faith should not be in the wisdom of men but in the power of God.*
>
> **—1 Corinthians 2:5 NKJV**

God's transcendent power—this treasure—signifies the weakness of our humanity. We are compared to ordinary clay pots that reveal the excellence of the power contained therein. And so our faith should be in the power of God and not the intelligence of man. We live in the world by the power of God, his Word, the truth that sanctifies us and sets us apart for his use—to model life as it is in heaven—but we are not of the world. We use and enjoy the things of this world, but we don't abuse or misuse them through the corruption of our lustful flesh:

> As His divine power has given to us all things that pertain to life and godliness, through the knowledge of Him who called us by glory and virtue, by which have been given to us exceedingly great and precious promises, that through these you may be partakers of the divine nature, having escaped the corruption that is in the world through lust. (2 Peter 1:3–4 NKJV)

We grow in Christ and experience God's divine power on earth by way of his exceedingly great and precious promises, which gives us all things to enjoy in accordance with a lifestyle of godly character through our knowledge of God. As we do so, we partake of his divine nature, which removes us from the corrupt systems of the world drawn to us through the lust of our flesh, in which lies no good thing.

As we grow in knowledge of God and Jesus, we partake of his divine nature and power, displaying them on earth as commissioned kingdom-compliant servant-leaders. This is how we stay tuned-in to the frequency of heaven.

CHAPTER 5

Dual Citizenship and How to Prioritize the Kingdom of Heaven

You're no longer wandering exiles. This kingdom of faith is now your home country. You're no longer strangers or outsiders. You belong here, with as much right to the name Christian as anyone.

—Ephesians 2:19 Message

In obedience to God, Abram became a man without a country. He obeyed God's command to leave his country and journey to a land that God would show him—a land that God would establish as a great nation—and there God would make his name great. In that land, God would make Abram a blessing. God also promised to bless those who bless Abram and curse those who cursed Abram. And the final promise is absolutely mind-blowing. God promised that all the families of the earth would be blessed through Abram. And Abram obeyed (Genesis 12:1–5 NKJV).

What must Abram have been thinking? The command by God to leave his country and his family and Abram's obedience to his word would probably have sounded like a death sentence to most of us. I would venture so far as to say many believers have never come to grips with the fact that God will ask us to give up something we currently have in order for us to acquire something better in our future.

I wonder what influenced Abram to obey God's command. Could it have been that God promised him that he'd be a great nation? Maybe it was a promise with national implications. God essentially promised Abram that through him and his descendants all the world would be blessed. Could this imply the expectancy of a heavenly kingdom on earth?

This command by God and Abram's obedience to it signifies the initiation of a covenant. After Abram left Haran with Sarai, his wife, and Lot, his brother's son, they traveled through parts of Canaan, but there was a famine is the land, and Abram led his family to Egypt, where God protected them from the Egyptian pharaoh because of Sarai. God also strengthened Abram with 318 trained servants who were born in his own house to rescue Lot from the four enemy kings who captured him out of Sodom. Upon Abram's return from the defeat of the four kings, God led him into an encounter with Melchizedek, king of Salem, priest of God Most High (Genesis 14:18 NKJV).

Melchizedek took communion with Abram prior to blessing him. And Abram gave to Melchizedek a tithe of all his goods. This communion symbolized God as Abram's One, True Source, his Provider. For when the king of Sodom tried to offer a bribe to Abram, which would have allowed Abram to keep the spoils of the battle, he would not take it, saying, "I have raised my hand to the Lord, God Most High, the Possessor of heaven and earth, that I will take nothing, from a thread to a sandal strap, and that I will not take anything that is yours, lest you should say, 'I have made Abram rich'" (Genesis 14:22–23 NKJV).

After Abram's firm stance against the king of Sodom, by which he established God as his Source, God then promised to childless Abram that one born from his own body would be his heir, and that his descendants would number more than the stars in the sky. Abram believed in the Lord, and he accounted it to Abram for righteousness (Genesis 15:6 NKJV).

Grab hold of the noble and generous Spirit of God. His reward to

Abram for his faithful obedience is magnanimous. How magnanimous? In essence, when God told Abram that his descendants would number more than the stars in the sky, he made Abram heir to the world (Genesis 4:13 NKJV).

What is even more gracious is that God made a covenant with Abram based upon his faith and obedience. And the reward for his faith and obedience expanded even further. God changed Abram's name to reflect his new identity. I think it is safe to say one of the rewards of living by faith and obeying God is a new name and a new identity.

> I am Almighty God; walk before Me and be blameless. And I will make My covenant between Me and you, and will multiply you exceedingly … As for Me, behold, My covenant is with you, and you shall be a father of many nations. No longer shall your name be called Abram, but your name shall be Abraham; for I have made you a father of many nations. I will make you exceedingly fruitful; and I will make nations of you, and kings shall come from you. And I will establish My covenant between Me and you and your descendants after you in their generations, for an everlasting covenant, to be God to you and your descendants after you. (Genesis 17:1–2, 4–7 NKJV)

God changed Abram's name to Abraham—from exalted father to father of many nations. What a promotion! God really does share his glory with those who are his. Because Abraham believed God, he could obey him, even to the point of offering his own son Isaac on the altar as a sacrifice, because he believed God when he told him, "In Isaac your seed shall be called" (Genesis 21:12 NKJV).

This level of faith and obedience shown by Abraham is even more incredible when we factor in Isaac being Abraham's son of promise. Abraham was seventy-five years old when he left Haran at God's command. A full twenty-five years were required for the fulfillment of God's promise to him and Sarah. Finally, at age one hundred, Abraham realized his promised seed, only to be commanded to offer him as a sacrifice while Isaac was just a lad. Abraham did this by faith. "By faith Abraham, when he was tested, offered up Isaac, and he who had received the promises offered up his only begotten son, of whom it was said, 'In Isaac your seed shall be called,' concluding that God was able to raise him up, even from the dead, from which he also received him in a figurative sense" (Hebrews 11:17–19 NKJV).

So why did God command Abraham to leave his own country? What was God's purpose, and why did he choose Abraham? I believe a very significant answer to these questions is that God did not want to destroy life on earth again, as he had done with the Great Flood of Noah's time, because of the rebellious hearts and perverse acts of the people. Things seemed to be headed in that direction again after the flood, as the sons of Noah and their families conspired against God to build a tower whose top would reach the heavens. This tower, which emerged from their vain imaginations, would be a symbol of their sinful pride and rebellion against God. They said, "Let us make a name for ourselves" (Genesis 11:4 NKJV).

God was not willing to appease humankind, his creation, by allowing their misguided efforts at self-glorification to share the power and glory that belongs only to him. So he confounded their language so they could no longer communicate with each other, which led to their abandonment of this evil imagination. God's judgment against them was to confuse their language and scatter them throughout the face of the earth:

> But the Lord came down to see the city and the tower which the sons of men had built. And the Lord said, "Indeed the people are one and they all have one language, and this is what they begin to do; now nothing that they propose to do will be withheld from them. Come, Let Us go down and there confuse their language, that they may not understand one another's speech. So the Lord scattered them abroad from there over the face of all the earth, and they ceased building the city. (Genesis 11:5–8 NKJV)

If God had not intervened in the selfish affairs of man, there would be no restraint to him to do whatever he imagined. That in itself tells us how powerful our imagination is to the fulfillment of our desires, whether good or evil. There is an old adage that says, "If you can perceive it, you can achieve it." But there is something else that also stands out in the above context of scripture. Notice that God wasn't interested in the tower alone. He came down to see the "city" too. After God's judgment on all the family lines, scattering them over the face of the earth, they ceased building the city. God's concern surpasses the tower and focuses on the city. Why?

I believe the answer can be found in the definition of the word city. According to the law of first mention, the Hebrew word for *city* is *ayar*, taken from *uwr [oor],* which means a place guarded by waking or a watch; an encampment or post. Through the idea of opening the eyes, it means to wake up, lift up self; to master, raise up, and stir up self. To be bare—be made naked.[24]

If God had allowed the descendants of Noah to continue building the tower, making a name for themselves and defying him, their Creator, nothing they imagined to do would be withheld from them. All their evil creations and concoctions would have been guarded within an encampment, sort of like a military outpost. Their primary focus would have been solely on themselves—to master their evil ways and to think highly of themselves from an evil perspective. In that state, they would have been naked, unashamed of their evil lifestyles, which would become more and more evil. An extension of cities would lead to nations. God did not create man to build evil nations; he created man to be a part of his family, who would steward a colony called earth after the pattern of heaven.

The prophet Jeremiah can shed a little light on why God judged the families of Noah's sons: "The heart is deceitful above all things, and desperately wicked; Who can know it? I, the Lord, search the heart, I test the mind, even to give every man according to his ways, according to the fruit of his doings" (Jeremiah 17:9–10 NKJV).

Let's return to Abraham's story. God needed someone who would give up his pagan beliefs, sever ties with those in his country who

[24] *Strong's Exhaustive Concordance of the Bible, OT,* 5892, 5782.

adhered to pagan beliefs, and leave his status of a wealthy landowner in order to create a new nation of people who would worship him only. And so Abraham's story marks the founding of Israel as a people and their move toward a land of their own—their own country.

We know Abraham was indeed looking for a new country, as he had the opportunity to return to his previous country and chose not to. He confessed that he was a stranger and a pilgrim on earth. Because of his great faith, Abraham became a friend of God and the father of faith:

> By faith Abraham obeyed when he was called to go out to the place which he would receive as an inheritance. And he went out, not knowing where he was going. By faith he dwelt in the land of promise as in a foreign country, dwelling in tents with Isaac and Jacob, the heirs with him of the same promise; for he waited for the city which has foundations, whose builder and maker is God. (Hebrews 11:8–10 NKJV)

> For those who say such things declare plainly that they seek a homeland. And truly if they had called to mind that country from which they had come out, they would have had opportunity to return. But now they desire a better, that is, a heavenly country. Therefore God is not ashamed to be called their God, for He has prepared a city for them. (Hebrews 11:14–16 NKJV)

> For here we have no continuing city, but we seek the one to come. (Hebrews 13:14 NKJV)

Clearly Abraham believed God concerning being made the father of many nations, and he consistently showed this by his many acts of faith. Abraham looked for a better country, one modeled after heaven, with God as its king. And even though he did not get to that country himself, he paved the way for his descendants, and they became citizens of that country.

Through our faith in Jesus, we, too, have entered that same country, which has foundations on earth as it is in heaven, but whose builder and maker is God. As believers, our primary citizenship is heaven, described as that continuing city established by God. Though we live on earth, because of our faith in Jesus Christ, we are registered as citizens of heaven. We are the church of the firstborn, registered in heaven to the Judge of all, even those Old Testament saints who were faithful are at home in heaven because they were made perfect by Jesus's finished work at Calvary.

> *But you have come to Mount Zion and to the city of the living God, the heavenly Jerusalem, to an innumerable company of angels, to the general assembly and church of the firstborn who are registered in heaven to God the Judge of all, to the spirits of just men made perfect, to Jesus the Mediator of the new covenant, and to the blood of sprinkling that speaks better things than that of Abel.*
>
> **—Hebrews 12:22–24 NKJV**

> *Now, therefore, you are no longer strangers and foreigners, but fellow citizens with the saints and members of the household of God, having been built on the foundation of the apostles and prophets, Jesus Christ Himself being the chief cornerstone.*
>
> **—Ephesians 2:19–20 NKJV**

AS SAINTS, WE ARE BI-DIMENSIONAL

We have active dual citizenship in two realms: heaven and earth. God created heaven and earth to exist together as one; however, heaven trumps earth. That's why Jesus taught his disciples to pray, "Thy kingdom come. Thy will be done in earth, as it is in heaven" (Matthew 6:10 KJV). As believers, we must prioritize our citizenship in the kingdom of heaven. But first, let's take a look at what citizenship actually means.

In the Bible, the Greek word for *citizen* is *sumpolites*, taken from *sun*, which means a native of the same town—that is, coreligionist (fellow-Christian); union; with or together by association, companionship, process, resemblance, possession, instrumentality, completeness.[25]

[25] *Strong's Exhaustive Concordance of the Bible, NT*, 4847, 4862.

According to Wikipedia, citizenship is the status of a person recognized under the law of a country and/or local jurisdiction of belonging to thereof. In international law, it is membership to a sovereign state. Each state is free to determine the conditions under which it will recognize persons as its citizens, and the conditions under which that status will be withdrawn. Recognition by a state as a citizen generally carries with it recognition of civil, political, and social rights, which are not afforded to noncitizens. In general, the basic rights normally regarded as arising from citizenship are the right to a passport, the right to leave and return to the country, or countries, of citizenship, the right to live in that country, and the right to work there.

Dual citizenship is a legal status in which a person is concurrently regarded as a citizen of more than one country under the laws of those countries. Conceptually, citizenship is focused on the internal political life of the country, and nationality is a matter of international dealings. There is no international convention which determines the nationality or citizenship status of a person. This is defined exclusively by national laws, which can vary and conflict with each other. Different countries use different and not necessarily mutually exclusive criteria for citizenship. Technically, each nation makes a claim that a particular person is considered its national. A person holding dual citizenship is generally entitled to the rights of citizenship in each country whose citizenship they are holding.

On earth, the conditions under which a country will recognize persons as citizens is laid out in that country's constitution, which establishes and recognizes certain rights—civil, political, and social—that are not afforded to noncitizens. And in many countries, the wealth of that country determines the benefits to its citizens.

In heaven, the condition under which it recognizes its citizens is laid out in the Bible, which is by faith in Jesus Christ. The moment a person accepts Jesus as Savior and Lord, he or she becomes a member of the royal family of God: "Fellow citizens with the saints and members of the household of God" (Ephesians 2:19 NKJV). As the Greek definition of citizen notes, we become in union together with God and all those Old Testament saints and New Testament saints who have died in faith. We are fellow Christians bonded together through association—faith in Jesus Christ. Through him, we have companionship, process, resemblance, possession, instrumentality, and completeness.

As citizens of the kingdom of heaven, our benefits are proportionate to the wealth, power, authority, and influence of the King. And that really says it all when we compare the benefits of our dual citizenship. Since the earth is the Lord's and all that is in it (Psalm 24:1 NKJV), and since all the money belongs to God (Haggai 2:8 NKJV), and since we are his heirs, what is his belongs to us (Romans 8:17 NKJV; Galatians 4:7 NKJV).

Likewise, what is ours belongs to him. That's what covenant means. And covenant is the basis, the foundation, of our heavenly citizenship. Just ask Abraham, Paul, and Jesus. "And if you are Christ's, then you are Abraham's seed, and heirs according to the promise" (Galatians 3:29 NKJV).

Our earthly citizenship pales in comparison to our heavenly citizenship. But our earthly citizenship is so much more when we prioritize our heavenly citizenship, even as we live as citizens of our earthly country. We really can have the best of both worlds.

How do we become like Jesus, who lived in two dimensions while he was on earth? And how do we prioritize our heavenly citizenship as he did?

While on earth, Jesus told Nicodemus that he was also in heaven. "No one has ascended to heaven but He who came down from heaven, that is, the Son of man who is in heaven" (John 3:13 NKJV). Jesus is Son of God and Son of man. In this context, Jesus refers to his earthly citizenship as Son of man who is in heaven.

I would say there is a supernatural extension, a spiritual cord from heaven suspended between heaven and earth that each believer can attach themselves to—something like a ladder or escalator that reaches from earth to heaven. Like Jesus, we possess all power that the Father gives us in heaven and in earth (Matthew 28:18 NKJV). This verse sheds light on the spiritual "ladder" that transferred Jesus from earth to heaven and vice versa: "You shall see heaven open, and the angels of God ascending and descending upon the Son of Man" (John 1:51). Here again, Son of man means that Jesus was on earth:

> Then he dreamed, and behold, a ladder was set up on the earth, and its top reached to heaven; and there the angels of God were ascending and descending on it. And behold, the Lord stood above it and said: I am the Lord God of Abraham your father and the God of Isaac; the land on which you lie I will give to you and your descendants … Then Jacob awoke from his sleep and said, "Surely the Lord is in this place, and I did not know it." And he was afraid and said, "How awesome is this place! This is none other than the house of God, and this is the gate of heaven!" (Genesis 28:12–13, 16–17 NKJV)

The spiritual ladder has substance. Jacob awoke from his dream and realized he'd had a spiritual experience in two realms—heaven and earth. "Surely the Lord is in this place … this is none other than the house of God" (Genesis 28:16 NKJV) is symbolic of his earthly reality. And "This is the gate of heaven" (Genesis 28:17 NKJV) is symbolic of his heavenly reality, as the Lord stood above the ladder and spoke to Jacob. Jacob's response—"How awesome is this place" (Genesis 28:17 NKJV)—describes both heaven and earth. The earth is awesome because heaven is awesome. In the mind of God, heaven and earth are the same place.

The prophet Jeremiah wrote, "For I know the thoughts that I think toward you, saith the Lord, thoughts of peace, and not of evil, to give you an expected end" (Jeremiah 29:11 KJV).

The word *expected* in Hebrew is *tiqvah*, which literally means a cord (as an attachment); the thing that I long for. The word *end* is the Hebrew word *achariyth*, which means the future.[26]

I love that definition and description of "expected end". What I expect is the thing that I long for, the desire of my heart, manifested in my future because the Father's thoughts toward me, his son, his heir, are of peace continuously. What that alludes to is heaven's transfer of the Father's thoughts of peace to accompany what I desire, since I desire only good things out of right motives. Remember, "Blessed be the God and Father of our Lord Jesus Christ, who has blessed us with every spiritual blessing in the heavenly places in Christ" (Ephesians 1:3 NKJV).

---

[26] *Strong's Exhaustive Concordance of the Bible, OT,* 8615, 319.

As citizens of the kingdom of heaven, we have access to every kind of spiritual blessing—all that we need pertaining to life and godliness (2 Peter 1:3 NKJV)—which comes to us from the unseen realm of spiritual realities in which saints of God live and receive grace through our faith in Jesus Christ.

In order for believers to live their best life as dual citizens of heaven and earth, they must view the world from an eternal perspective. In other words, they must always be God conscious. We can do this since our spirit is already in heaven. "But God, who is rich in mercy, because of His great love with which He loved us, even when we were dead in trespasses, made us alive together with Christ (by grace you have been saved), and raised us up together, and made us sit together in the heavenly places in Christ Jesus" (Ephesians 2:4–6 NKJV).

We know through scripture that Jesus constantly lived in both realms. He was bi-dimensional. But we know that his heavenly realm superseded his earthly realm. Jesus stayed tuned-in to the frequency of heaven. Whatever he did on earth was a directive from heaven. Jesus said nothing but what he heard his Father in heaven say; he did nothing but what he saw his Father in heaven do (John 12:49 NKJV; John 5:19 NKJV).

In order to realize the best of our dual citizenship in heaven and on earth, we, too, must stay tuned-in to the frequency of heaven so that we will possess and walk in the full benefits of each. This is a supernatural reality illuminated in the life of the mature believer who understands that the spirit dimension is the only instrument that can blend both realms to release the best that each has to offer.

Our life on earth should not be inferior to life in heaven—that is, accomplishing heaven's best here on earth. As believers, we should not harbor the escapism mentality. We can do the will of God on earth and enjoy all of earth's pleasures as well without diminishing our Christian lifestyle. God wants our earthly lives to reflect heaven's best. But we cannot enjoy the best of our dual citizenship unless we prioritize the kingdom of heaven. The kingdom of God exists both in heaven and on earth at the same time! It exists in both places simultaneously so there is to be no difference in where the will of God is executed. The kingdom of God cannot be divided; therefore heaven and earth are one kingdom. If a kingdom is divided against itself, that kingdom cannot stand (Mark 3:24 NKJV).

PRIORITIZING THE KINGDOM OF HEAVEN

One of the most potent verses of scripture in the Bible for the believer is Matthew 6:33 NKJV: "But seek first the kingdom of God and His righteousness, and all these things shall be added to you."

I still remember the moment that verse became real to me back in July 2000. I was attending a weekday service in Jesup, Georgia taught by an apostle from Chicago. I had never heard the word of God expounded with such revelatory knowledge. As he ministered from Matthew 6:33, a light came on in my head and I received revelatory knowledge of that scripture via the Holy Spirit. I had been an ordained minister since 1992, and that was the first time Matthew 6:33 came alive in my spirit. It is a promise from God. If we seek his way of doing and being righteous in the earth, he promises that all our basic needs would be met or added, bestowed on.

Suddenly I received a revelation of what it means to prioritize the kingdom of God and his righteousness and be at peace, resting in the fact that he would add the basic necessities of life to me—that I didn't have to waste time in a state of worry whenever a need arose, and I did not have the resources to take care of it. Matthew 6:33 is where the rubber meets the road, or where real faith meets reality.

Let's dissect Matthew 6:33 and find out how all the pieces fit into one whole. As one whole, I believe readers will not only receive a Holy Spirit revelation for themselves but also they will know the potency of this verse—that it is built upon complete, absolute, uncompromising trust in God. "And it is easier for heaven and earth to pass away than for one tittle [the smallest stroke in a Hebrew letter] to fail" (Luke 16:17 NKJV).

The word *but* should get our attention, but it generally does not. *But* is a conjunction that expresses antithesis, opposition, or adverse circumstance. It presents a contrast or exception; it is a part of speech that connects words, phrases, or clauses.

Matthew 6:33 is the antithesis of verses 19–32, which reflect Jesus's teaching on wealth. Verse 19 begins with "Do not …" (Matthew 6:19 NKJV), and verse 33 chimes in with "But …" (Matthew 6:33 NKJV). Clearly, what is taught by Jesus and written as Holy Scripture in verses 19–32 tells us what not to rely on, and verse 33 not only tells us what we should rely on but also the reward that comes with it.

Now let's deal with the word *seek*. It is the Greek word *zeteo*, which means to worship God.[27]

To worship God means to revere and adore him for who he is. The Hebrew word for *worship* is *shachah*, meaning to prostrate oneself in homage to God—bow down, crouch, make obeisance, do reverence.[28]

Instead of complying with verses 19–32, which describe worldly aspects of an evil heart, an evil eye, idolatry in the form of making money a god (mammon), and worry—things that unbelievers prioritize and seek after, which do not rely on complete, absolute, uncompromising trust in God, those who trust God are told to seek or worship, make obeisance and do reverence to God. And here's what gets most people: Jesus tells us to worship God first as a priority.

First is the Greek word *proton*, which means first in time, place, order or importance—before, at the beginning, chiefly, first of all.[29] I think it prudent that we also do a word study of the word *priority*, since its meaning is in alignment with "first of all."

Priority, in this context, means an item's relative importance. It is the quality of being earlier or coming first compared to another thing; the state of being prior.

Prioritization is the activity that arranges items or activities in order of importance relative to each other.

We're starting to get into the meat of Matthew 6:33. What the believer is to prioritize or place in order of importance relative to verses 19–32 is "the kingdom of God and His righteousness" (Matthew 6:33 NKJV). I've learned over the years that many believers, even those who profess to be "kingdom affiliated," really do not understand the kingdom of God. The major reason being, the kingdom of God is supernatural. "Now when He was asked by the Pharisees when the kingdom of God would come, He answered them and said, 'The kingdom of God does not come with observation; nor will they say, 'See here!' or 'See there!' For indeed, the kingdom of God is within you" (Luke 17:20–21 NKJV).

It is not a visible "kingdom" in the earth. The question concerning when the kingdom would come implies that it was not yet a physical

---

27 *Strong's Exhaustive Concordance of the Bible, NT*, 2212.
28 *Strong's Exhaustive Concordance of the Bible, OT*, 7812.
29 *Strong's Exhaustive Concordance of the Bible, NT*, 4412.

reality. It is an adherence to the kingdom of heaven, its principles, lived on the earth by our faith in Jesus and the power of the Holy Spirit—God's satellite on the earth who dwells or reside in the spirit of man.

> *Jesus answered, "My kingdom is not of this world. If My kingdom were of this world, My servants would fight, so that I should not be delivered to the Jews; but now My kingdom is not from here."*
>
> **—John 18:36 NKJV**

Here's something I'm sure many believers will have to chew on. The kingdom of God and his righteousness are one and the same. Notice what Jesus said in the above verse of scripture: "My kingdom" (John 18:36 NKJV). Jesus is righteous! He is Jehovah-Tsidkenu, the Lord our righteousness. That means that his kingdom is all righteous. "For He made Him who knew no sin to be sin for us, that we might become the righteousness of God in Him" (2 Corinthians 5:21 NKJV).

How could we be made the righteousness of God if Jesus were unrighteous? When we come to know Jesus through faith, he both declares and makes us righteous.

> Because He had done no violence, nor was any deceit in His mouth. Yet it pleased the Lord to bruise Him; He has put Him to grief. When You make His soul an offering for sin, He shall see His seed, He shall prolong His days, and the pleasure of the Lord shall prosper in His hand. He shall see the labor of His soul, and be satisfied. By His knowledge My righteous Servant shall justify many, for He shall bear their iniquities. (Isaiah 53:9b–11 NKJV)

> Therefore, as through one man's offense judgment came to all men, resulting in condemnation, even so through one Man's righteous act the free gift came to all men, resulting in justification of life. (Romans 5:18 NKJV)

His righteousness is trusting God's way of doing things—and doing them! "For I have come down from heaven, not to do My own will, but the will of Him who sent Me" (John 6:38 NKJV). Jesus lived thirty-three years on the earth, making obeisance and being righteous through his trust in God, his Father, and by the power of the Holy Spirit.

Righteousness is obedience to God by faith, trusting God and taking him at his word. This is what Jesus did. Before Jesus's physical life, Abraham, whom we discussed at length earlier in this chapter, was accounted as righteous because he believed God. "For what does the Scripture say? 'Abraham believed God, and it was accounted to him for righteousness'" (Romans 4:3 NKJV).

> But now the righteousness of God apart from the law is revealed, being witnessed by the Law and the Prophets, even the righteousness of God, through faith in Jesus Christ, to all and on all who believe. For there is no difference. (Romans 3:21–22 NKJV)

> Does this blessedness then come upon the circumcised only, or upon the uncircumcised also? For we say that faith was accounted to Abraham for righteousness. How then was it accounted? While he was circumcised, or uncircumcised? Not while circumcised, but while uncircumcised. And he received the sign of circumcision, a seal of the righteousness of the faith which he had while still uncircumcised, that he might be the father of all those who believe, though they are uncircumcised, that righteousness might be imputed to them also. (Romans 4:9–11 NKJV)

Please don't fight against God here. In Christ, there is no difference between Jews and Greeks. And there is no difference between faith in Jesus Christ and the righteousness of God. The requirement here is faith.

The Greek word that denotes *righteousness* is *dikaiosune*, taken from *dikaios*, and it means equitable in character or act; by implication—innocent, holy, just, righteous; justification; righteousness.[30]

[30] *Strong's Exhaustive Concordance of the Bible, NT*, 1342, 1343.

Latch on to the righteousness of God that is within you—his nature, his character, his way of doing and being right. His righteousness is within us. We are one with Father God and Jesus.

> And the glory which You gave Me I have given them, that they may be one just as We are one. I in them, and You in Me; that they may be made perfect in one, and that the world may know that You have sent Me, and have loved them as You have loved Me … And I have declared to them Your name, and will declare it, that the love with which You loved Me may be in them, and I in them. (John 17:22–23, 26 NKJV)

Whatever God instructs us to do on earth supersedes earth's natural laws. Why? Because God's instructions and the manifestations that follow our obedience to his instructions are supernatural.

As we surrender ourselves to him in obedience and avail ourselves for his use, we become channels through which we receive heaven's power on earth.

Matthew 6:33 really speaks of serving God with singleness of heart and purpose and prioritizing his kingdom. As we do so, we are freed from anxiety over lesser things, and the reward is outstanding. "And all these things shall be added to you" (Matthew 6:33 NKJV).

Jesus wasn't just referring to food, clothes, and shelter—basic needs—when he referred to all these things being added to us. "All these things" also include life. Food, clothes, and shelter are basic needs for our physical existence, but life goes beyond the physical—life is also eternal.

The Greek word used in our scripture context for *life* is *psuche*, which means heart, mind, and soul; breath of life, the natural life. It is the individual life, the living being. This life differs from *zoe*, which means life as a principle, life in the absolute sense, life as God has it, that which the Father has in himself, and which he gave to the Incarnate Son to have in himself (John 5:26), and which the Son manifested in the world (1 John 1:2). God holds our soul (*psuche*) in life (*zoe*).[31]

---

[31] *Expository Dictionary of New Testament Words: A Comprehensive Dictionary of the Original Greek Words with Their Precise Meanings for English Readers.*

Besides our food, clothing and shelter being added to us, we have life in life—our natural life in God himself, who is eternal. As we seek first the kingdom of God and his righteousness, we don't have to seek or prioritize food, clothing, shelter, jobs, or transportation because "all these things" are rewarded or "added" to us. Jesus taught that these are the things that unbelievers prioritize rather than seeking the kingdom of God.

> *Therefore do not be like them. For your Father knows the things you have need of before you ask Him. 9In this manner, therefore, pray: Our Father in heaven, hallowed be Your name. Your kingdom come. Your will be done On earth as it is in heaven.*
>
> **—Matthew 6:8–10 NKJV**

As we pray the Lord's "Kingdom" Prayer by faith and prioritize seeking his kingdom and righteousness, all basic needs for our natural life, which include our godly wants and desires also will be added. Added, as in given, not purchased—something added besides what exists already. Believers don't have to spend their lives scheming or hustling for the basics of life. They are provided as a gift, a bestowal—the reward for their priority in reverencing the Father in worship and thanksgiving.

The Greek word for *added* is *prostithemi*, which means to place additionally—that is, lay beside, annex, repeat; to give more, increase, and motion toward.[32] To proceed further—of repeating or continuing the action—the idea of supplementing an agreement already made; not that something had been added to the promise with a view to complete it, but that something had been given in addition to the promise.[33]

Let's put it all together now. This is my Holy Spirit revelation of Matthew 6:33: As we worship God, revere and adore him for who he is chiefly, first of all, his nature, character, his way of doing and being right, he will give us additionally more, repeating the action and supplementing the promise of life in life—our natural life lived as God knows life.

---

[32] *Strong's Exhaustive Concordance of the Bible, NT,* 4369.

[33] *Expository Dictionary of New Testament Words: A Comprehensive Dictionary of the Original Greek Words with Their Precise Meanings for English Readers.*

What a way to live!

As we prioritize the kingdom of heaven, duplicating God's righteousness here on earth, our minds are transformed from a natural perspective to an eternal perspective. In this "kingdom mental state," we have the capacity to view things in their true relations and according to their relative importance.

As believers, we have dual citizenship in heaven and on earth. We live on earth—in this world—but we are not of this world. Our true home and citizenship is in heaven. As we learn to prioritize seeking God's kingdom and his righteousness, the benefits of the kingdom of heaven are given to us besides or in addition to our basic needs on earth.

Stayed tuned-in to the frequency of heaven and never miss a beat—all the benefits of the kingdom, all the time! And remember: "It is your Father's good pleasure to give you the kingdom" (Luke 12:32 NKJV).

CHAPTER 6

The Word of God: The First Priority and the Final Authority

For the Word that God speaks is alive and full of power [making it active, operative, energizing, and effective]; it is sharper than any two-edged sword, penetrating to the dividing line of the breath of life (soul) and [the immortal] spirit, and of joints and marrow [of the deepest parts of our nature], exposing and sifting and analyzing and judging the very thoughts and purposes of the heart.

—Hebrews 4:12 AMP

The Word of God is alive. Jesus said, "The words that I speak to you are spirit, and they are life" (John 6:63b NKJV). The Word of God is so powerful that it can divide between soul and spirit. Both soul and spirit are invisible. Both soul and spirit reside in our inner being. But the only thing in existence sharp enough to divide something that closely related is the Word of God. The Word of God has the power to divide soul and spirit.

Nobody can even see how, with the natural eye, one can separate soul and spirit. Then the scripture goes on to say, "And is a discerner of the thoughts and intents of the heart" (Hebrews 4:12 KJV). When a believer makes the Word of God first priority as well as the final authority in his life, he or she gives the Holy Spirit authority to perform, in and through them, the Word of God in demonstrations and power.

Since God's Word is bound by an oath, he swore by himself that he will do what he said he will do—no if or but about it. God said, "I will hasten My Word to perform it" (Jeremiah 1:12 KJV). And since God cannot lie, why wouldn't every believer go to God's Word as their first choice in response to a bad situation? Why wouldn't we simply take God at his word as an act of our complete, absolute, uncompromising trust in him? Doing so would make his word, which is active and alert, the final authority, as God watches over his word to perform it.

> *God is not a man, that He should lie, Nor a son of man, that He should repent. Has He said, and will He not do? Or has He spoken, and will He not make it good?*
>
> **—Numbers 23:19 NKJV**

As believers, God's Word should mean everything to us simply because all things are upheld by the word of his power (Hebrews 1:3 NKJV), which means that God's Word has the power to sustain all things. If that were not proof enough, let's get even more personable. God and his word are one. "In the beginning was the Word, and the Word was with God, and the Word was God. He was in the beginning with God" (John 1:1–2 NKJV). Notice that the word is referred to by gender—"He." That means that he, the word, is alive.

Satan is so afraid of believers who live by faith in the Word of God, who have made the word their first priority and their final authority. Could it be that the devil knows the power of God's Word and what power and authority every believer would have if he or she lived each day making the word first place in their lives?

If the Word of God wasn't a significant force against Satan, why would he make it his first priority to snatch the word away from believers as soon as they receive it?

In Jesus's teaching on the parable of the sower, he makes his point as to the extent of the power of God's Word. Jesus uses four types of soil—the heart of believers—to teach to his disciples this spiritual truth, letting them know that if they did not understand this parable "How then will you understand all the parables?" (Mark 4:13 NKJV).

And like some who followed Jesus, many believers today have never gotten the depth of revelation pertaining to the power of God's Word, even though it is given to them to know the mystery of the kingdom of God (Mark 4:11 NKJV) "As servants of Christ and stewards of the mysteries of God" (1 Corinthians 4:1 NKJV).

> *But we speak the wisdom of God in a mystery, the hidden wisdom which God ordained before the ages for our glory, which none of the rulers of this age knew; for had they known, they would not have crucified the Lord of glory.*
>
> **—1 Corinthians 2:7–8 NKJV**

The devil wants no part of the living Word of God being the first place and the final authority in the believer's life, and he'll use whatever we allow him to use—fear and unbelief—to penetrate our minds and bombard us with everything but the Word of God. Much of what Satan can and cannot do, then, is really dependent upon us—our faith in the Word of God.

Let's take a deeper look into the four types of soil, symbolic of the heart of man. The heart of man is very fickle and deceitful above all things, and desperately wicked; who can know it (Jeremiah 17:9 NKJV)? In Jesus's explanation of the parable of the sower, he uses the word *immediately* to describe Satan's deep fear concerning saints receiving the Word of God:

> The sower sows the word. And these are the ones by the wayside where the word is sown. When they hear, Satan comes immediately and takes away the word that was sown in their hearts. These likewise are the ones sown on stony ground who, when they hear the word, immediately receive it with gladness; and they have no root in themselves, and so endure only for a time. Afterward, when tribulation or persecution arises for the word's sake, immediately they stumble. (Mark 4:14–17 NKJV)

Notice that Jesus uses the word *immediately* in three consecutive verses. *Immediately* means directly or at once.[34] The first use refers to how quickly Satan moves to snatch the word out of the heart of believers. But then Jesus says that some believers receive the word with gladness, immediately. Seems like they would want to keep it—accept for the fact that the word they received so gladly did not take root in their heart.

Matthew's version of this parable says that it is because those who received "the Word of the Kingdom" did not understand it, so the wicked one snatched it away before it could take root in the heart (Matthew 13:19 NKJV). This lets us know that a key to digesting and retaining the Word of God in one's heart is through understanding the word, having revelatory knowledge of it.

The parable of the sower is a reflection of what happens to those believers who allow Satan to snatch the Word of God out of their heart before it has taken root. When tribulation and persecution challenge their ability to stand on the word as first priority and final authority, they stumble. Their lack of understanding of the word never took root in their heart because they had no Holy Spirit revelation of it. And where there is no understanding of the word, there can be no consistent use or faith application of the word to their life situations.

When tribulation or persecution arises for the word's sake, immediately these types of believers will give up on the word because it never took root in their heart; the Word only endured for a short time. To these believers, the tribulation or persecution in their lives was bigger than the word they so gladly received. Sadly, too many believers fall into this category. Their hearts are stony ground.

TIME SPENT IN THE WORD

Too many times we allow natural things, the things of this world, to rob us of our priceless spiritual treasure—the Word of God. We become like Martha, who allowed the cares and troubles she encountered in the natural to steal her God consciousness. She became more physically conscious than spiritually conscious, which means she prioritized

[34] *Strong's Exhaustive Concordance of the Bible, NT,* 2112.

natural things and allowed them to rob her of priceless spiritual moments, like sitting at the feet of Jesus and hearing his teaching of the Word of God.

Today, in a similar manner, too many believers suffer from a lack of being God conscious. Our omnipresent God is present all the time, but we are not aware of his presence. We are more conscious of the physical things and situations that are around us—things that we tend to fall prey to when we should walk in total victory as overcomers. We forget that our faith in Jesus makes us overcomers of the evil systems of this world: "For whatever is born of God overcomes the world. And this is the victory that has overcome the world - our faith" (1 John 5:4 NKJV).

> *These things I have spoken to you, that in Me you may have peace. In the world you will have tribulation; but be of good cheer, I have overcome the world.*
>
> **—John 16:33 NKJV**

In Martha's case Jesus, the One who has overcome the world, was in her home teaching the Word of God, and yet she allowed "the cares of this world" to overshadow him. Martha was doing what I like to call busywork—the kind of work based on religion that Satan enjoys seeing believers get bogged down in—when she should have been doing what Mary was doing: listening to Jesus teach the Word of God.

Believers need to be more like Mary, who was God conscious. Her focus on Jesus's teaching of the Word of God drew her to him. If Mary had natural problems or concerns, and I'm sure she did, she did not allow those problems to become bigger than the presence of God through Jesus. She considered Jesus, not her problems.

What happened next in the context of that story is something that still happens too often among believers today. Martha became upset and took out her frustration in the form of a complaint against Mary, which she made to Jesus. "Lord, do You not care that my sister has left me to serve alone? Therefore tell her to help me" (Luke 10:40 NKJV).

Let's be honest: I believe there was a motive behind Martha's complaint to Jesus against her sister, Mary. The motive: jealousy and envy! Martha saw the closeness that Mary had developed with Jesus. She saw them laughing together, and she heard them discussing certain aspects of God's Word. There was intimacy between them, a bond of unity that Martha not only became jealous of but she also became envious toward her sister because of it.

Martha really wanted that closeness for herself, but she sought it through natural or fleshly means. It was all about works for Martha, which really boils down to religion, trying to win Jesus's approval by all the work she was doing "for the kingdom." Like many believers today, Martha could not see the "Christ" in Jesus; she only saw the man. Martha's state of mind, based on her flesh, opened the door to the spirits of jealousy and envy, and she was bitten by the "green-eyed monster."

Jealousy generally refers to the thoughts or feelings of insecurity, fear, and concern over a relative lack of possessions or safety. Jealousy can consist of one or more emotions, such as anger, resentment, inadequacy, helplessness, or disgust. In its original meaning, *jealousy* is distinct from *envy*, though the two terms have popularly become synonymous in the English language, with *jealousy* now also taking on the definition originally used for *envy* alone.

Envy is an emotion that occurs when a person lacks another's superior quality, achievement, or possession and either desires it or wishes that the other lacked it.

Having digested the above definitions, I feel it safe to say that Martha really liked Jesus, as in maybe she had a crush on him. And through natural thought and actions she tried to use her skills, talents, and maybe even her beauty to "seduce" Jesus—to draw Him to her. But Mary's eyes were single and full of purpose (Matthew 6:22– 23 KNJV). She could see the light, the anointing, on Jesus's life that drew her to sit at his feet and hear his words. Martha is of the mindset that if she did more work she could capture Jesus's attention; however, it seems that the more work she did the less attention Jesus paid to her. Martha felt that Jesus was ignoring her, and she became bitter. This root of bitterness (Hebrews 12:15 NKJV) opened the door for Satan to enter. Martha gave place to the devil, (Ephesians 4:27 NKJV), and she opened the door for the "green-eyed monster" to enter.

This goes to show how the distractions of the world can topple even lifelong believers, if prioritizing the Word of God is not a consistent act of commitment, our bond, our oneness with God through our relationship with Jesus and his word.

Jesus recognized the spirits of jealousy and envy operating in and through Martha and answered them firmly, tactfully, with love. "And Jesus answered and said to her, 'Martha, Martha, you are worried and troubled about many things. But one thing is needed, and Mary has chosen that good part, which will not be taken away from her'" (Luke 10:41–42 NKJV).

Notice that Jesus's answer focused on his word, to which he referred as "that good part" (Luke 10:42 NKJV). Well, a part is not a whole—in the natural; but in the spirit realm, "that good part" (Luke 10:42 NKJV) refers to all that God is. God is all good. So even if Mary, like her sister Martha, had eyes for Jesus through her flesh, her spirit was anchored in "that good part" (Luke 10:42 NKJV), which Jesus said would not be taken from her.

I believe what Jesus meant is, time spent with him in the word shall not be taken away. I like to say it like this: "Time spent in the Word is time spent with God, Jesus and Holy Spirit." Mary prioritized the word through relationship with Jesus from her inner being, her spirit. Therefore, spirit and life overcame her flesh. "That good part" (Luke 10:42 NKJV) is the one thing that is needful!

MAKE GOD'S WORD THE FIRST PRIORITY

When things go wrong in our lives, when we are confronted with bad news, what is the first thought that comes to mind? What are the first words we say? Are they, "Oh God, help me help me. What am I going to do?" Or do we have the presence of mind to be calm in the midst of the storm, knowing that we are anchored in God through faith in his word?

When we know the Word of God and abide in the Word, we become God-inside minded or Holy Spirit conscious, and the first words we say are in alignment with what God has already said concerning our situation—that is, "He will not be afraid of evil tidings; His heart is steadfast, trusting in the Lord" (Psalm 112:7 NKJV). "You will keep him in perfect peace, Whose mind is stayed on You, Because he trusts in

You" (Isaiah 26:3 NKJV). "Cast your burden on the Lord, and He shall sustain you; He shall never permit the righteous to be moved" (Psalm 55:22 NKJV).

When spoken in faith and adhered to, the Word of God will set us free from fear, worry, and anxiety. Instead, we will rest in the peace given to us by Jesus (John 14:27 NKJV). In doing so, we submit ourselves to God's Word, resist the devil, and he will flee from us (James 4:7 NKJV).

It is not enough to memorize and quote scripture, although that should be a part of our spiritual tool belt. Death and life are in the power of the tongue (Proverbs 18:21 NKJV), so when scripture is quoted as a proclamation or a decree from a heart of faith, it becomes a huge component toward how we acquire spiritual things into our natural hands. But we must understand that it is not enough just to know or quote what the word says. The word of God we speak must be reality to us. We must have a revelation of it via the Holy Spirit, and that revelation becomes more real, bigger than the problem or situation we face. We cannot increase the intensity of our faith in God without intensifying our trust in his word. Mixed with faith, the Word becomes what we need it to be.

The Word of God is eternal, which means it has supernatural life and power to manifest all the promises of God in our lives. That's why we should make the Word of God the final authority. Believers must learn to persevere in the word—make time each day to worship God through his word and allow the Holy Spirit to reveal the heart of God to us by making God's Word come alive as he teaches us what we should know.

The more of God's Word we know, and the more we prioritize his word in our everyday lives, the less we will allow the limitations of this physical world to hold us in bondage as hostages waiting for God to come pay our ransom and set us free. Jesus has already taken care of that! Everything God says in his written word is there for our example and benefit: "To the intent that we should not lust after evil things as they also lusted" (1 Corinthians 10:6 NKJV). "And they were written for our admonition, upon whom the ends of the ages have come" (1 Corinthians 10:11 NKJV), for he is an ever-increasing God.

Continuing in the Word of God and making it first place in our lives will secure and protect us against forfeiting the liberty we have in Christ Jesus.

The Word of God is a divine covenant filled with promises that God has said "Yes" to. They are promises of victory sworn to us and backed up by the precious blood of Jesus that will empower us to triumph in every place. God's Word is the anchor of our soul, and we can depend on him when we encounter life's storms sent by the devil to threaten us and try to shake our faith.

God's Word is an anchor to our soul—our mind, will, emotions, and intellect. When we know the Word of God and make it the top priority in our lives, it will keep our emotions in check in any situation.

The Greek word used for *anchor* is *agkura*, from *agkale*, which means to bend as an arm; to hook as an anchor.[35] God and his word are one. As we use the Word of God consistently as our first priority, it is as if God himself puts his arm around us and hooks us in faith and rest so that our soul won't be influenced by our flesh, and we won't give in to temptation. Let the Word of God "hook you up!"

As saints, the Word of God should be our first defense against bad things that happen or evil tidings that we hear. We should be conscious to speak God's Word in faith over our circumstances. Say what he says about them instead of what our circumstances say. The circumstance is reality, but the law of opposites says that where there is bad there is also good. Remember "that good part" that will not be taken from us. It is the Word of God that changes a bad reality into a good report.

As believers, we must spend time daily in the Word of God. This must become our number-one priority. God's Word is a creative force; it contains creative power. And when we get the word in our hearts, it will burst forth out of our mouths. As the scripture says, "He who believes in Me, as the Scripture has said, out of his heart will flow rivers of living water" (John 7:38 NKJV).

Make the Word of God first place and stay tuned-in to the frequency of heaven!

---

[35] *Strong's Exhaustive Concordance of the Bible, NT,* 43, 44, 45.

THE WORD OF GOD AS THE FINAL AUTHORITY

God is the Source! God's Word is the Source! By faith, believers must activate and stand firm on the promises of God, which are "in Him Yes and In Him Amen" (2 Corinthians 1:20 NKJV). It's the latter part of this scripture that many believers omit and therefore are never able to stand firm in a sustainable faith until the manifestation shows up in their lives. That part of scripture is our part—"to the glory of God through us" (2 Corinthians 1:20 NKJV). "For we walk by faith, not by sight" (2 Corinthians 5:7 NKJV).

God wants his glory displayed in the life of the believer. But in order for this to happen, we must agree with the promises God has made, which are in his Word. God's Word both confirms us, and it equips us.

> *Then Jesus said to those Jews who believed Him, "If you abide in My word, you are My disciples indeed. And you shall know the truth, and the truth shall make you free.*
>
> **—John 8:31–32 NKJV**

Notice that Jesus is not speaking to all the people who followed him and heard his teaching. He is speaking to a select group: "Those Jews who believed Him" (John 8:31 NKJV). This tells us that our faith must be engaged in the Word of God in order for God's promises to manifest in our lives. The remainder of that verse does not say only, "the truth shall make you free" (John 8:32 NKJV). That is the part of this verse that many people, saved and unsaved, quote. There is a prerequisite to the truth making you free. It is "and you shall know the truth" (John 8:32 NKJV). It is one thing to have the truth, but something else entirely to know the truth.

God desires for his sons and daughters to become disciples indeed of Jesus Christ. The Greek word used for *indeed* is *alethos*, which means truly and of a surety.[36] But let's take this word, *indeed*, a step further. Jesus uses it again a few verses later, but this time he expands the meaning of the word. "Therefore if the Son makes you free, you shall be free indeed" (John 8:36 NKJV).

---

[36] *Strong's Exhaustive Concordance of the Bible, NT*, 230.

The word *indeed*, as used in verse 36, is the Greek word *ontos*, which means to be free, verily, of a truth; eternal. This means that being a disciple of Jesus Christ indeed is a bi-dimensional state. The disciple indeed is truly, of a surety, actually free and eternally present in both the spiritual realm and the physical world.

But we're not done yet. We cannot omit the role the word *know* plays in revealing to us the deeper truth of discipleship. Remember that *know* is the prerequisite to the truth actually making you free. The Greek word *ginosko* is used to define *know*. It is a verb that signifies to be taking in knowledge, to come to know, recognize, understand, or to understand completely; to know in the sense of realizing a relation between the person knowing and the object known; in this respect, what is known is of value or importance to the one who knows, and hence the establishment of the relationship, especially of God's knowledge.

To know is an appreciation concerning the knowledge of God and his truth on the part of believers; such knowledge is obtained not by mere intellectual activity but by operation of the Holy Spirit consequent upon acceptance of Christ. It conveys the thought of connection or union, as between man and woman—to have divine knowledge. *Ginosko* frequently suggests inception or progress in knowledge, while *oida*, another Greek word for *know*, suggests fullness of knowledge.

From these definitions, we should see more clearly what Jesus means when he said to those who believed in him, "If you abide in My Word" (John 8:31 NKJV). This would imply that we don't have to have fullness of knowledge at the moment in order to be a disciple indeed, but we must initiate and progress in knowledge "that the God of our Lord Jesus Christ, the Father of glory, may give to you the spirit of wisdom and revelation in the knowledge of Him" (Ephesians 1:17 NKJV).

Knowledge of the Word of God is an ongoing requirement. This is why the Word of God must become the final authority in the life of the believer. And we can't make God's Word the final authority if we don't abide or continue in his word.

Meno is the Greek word used here for *abide*. It means to stay in a given place, state, relation, or expectancy; abide, continue, dwell, endure, be present, remain, stand, and tarry.

There are many believers who call themselves disciples of Jesus

Christ, but they are not disciples indeed because there is no evidence of their abiding in the Word of God. This is why we see so many of our Christian brothers and sisters living in bondage, and not living in the liberty provided for them through Jesus's finished work. The Word of God has to be the final authority in the life of the believer, whose desire is to always triumph in Christ in every place and please their commanding officer.

> *Now thanks be to God who always leads us in triumph in Christ, and through us diffuses the fragrance of His knowledge in every place … For we are not, as so many, peddling the word of God; but as of sincerity, but as from God, we speak in the sight of God in Christ.*
>
> **—2 Corinthians 2:14, 17 NKJV**

Mature believers should never have a plan B just in case the Word of God doesn't work. That is not a mentality of faith; it is a mentality of unbelief. God's Word cannot fail. "Heaven and earth will pass away, but My words will by no means pass away" (Matthew 24:35 NKJV). His word is spirit, life, and eternal. Jesus is the Apostle and High Priest of our confession (Hebrews 3:1 NKJV). His duty as High Priest is to bring to pass his word that we speak and stand on in faith. Our job is to say the same thing his word, his promises, and his covenant says.

When we believe God for something that we desire and attach his promises to it by faith, it may take some time before there is a manifestation of the thing for which we long. Nevertheless, when we make God's Word the final authority on the matter and are relentless in calling those things that do not exist as though they did (Romans 4:17 NKJV), he will give us the desires of our heart (Psalm 37:4 NKJV). What God does for those who are his is always worth the wait. But as it is written: "Eye has not seen, nor ear heard, nor have entered into the heart of man the things which God has prepared for those who love Him" (1 Corinthians 2:9 NKJV).

In order to make God's Word the final authority in our lives, we must saturate our mind, our spirit, with spiritual food—the Word of God. The Word of God is to our spirit what food is to our physical body. It provides nutrition that fuels our spirit with energy, passion, faith, and focus so that whenever we think about our problems or any negative situation we find ourselves in we remember first the word we've prayed, stood on, and made our final authority on the matter.

But making God's Word the final authority concerning any matter doesn't just happen. One can't do it by placing a Bible on their coffee table and never opening it. It won't happen just because someone rides around in their car with a Bible on their dashboard. It won't happen by reading scripture or even a chapter once or twice a month. To make the Word of God the final authority in one's life will require their commitment, discipline, and faith to continue or abide in the Word of God consistently, in a coherent manner. It really requires us to make a conscious decision to make God's Word the final authority—no alternative, no plan B. God is the Source!

Much has been said concerning whether or not the "major prophets" missed God in 2020 on the issue of Donald Trump having a second term as president of the United States. Sadly, this question has become a major contention within the body of Christ, threatening to further divide believers.

I, too, am a prophet of God, so I would never despise or write off a prophet who "missed it": "For we know in part and we prophesy in part" (1 Corinthians 13:9 NKJV). Whether or not some would admit it, we all are learning to prophesy (Corinthians 14:31). I do believe, however, it requires humility to admit when we "miss," and some have not been willing to do so. Instead, they continue to "pressure" God to make what they foretold come to pass.

If a prophet says, "God says," he or she should rest in faith that what he or she spoke will come to past. God can't be pressured. True faith rests. It doesn't struggle to produce results through pressure or works of the flesh through temper tantrums. In short, if God said it, there never should be a plan B. God's word is pure, and it is sure. God does not lie!

Believers should not teach and preach the Gospel of the kingdom, then turn around and depend on the evil systems of this world to take care of us. The kingdoms of this world are controlled by Satan, who is the accuser of the brethren (Revelation 12:10 NKJV), and the prince of this world (John 12:31 NKJV) will never sustain us in health, wealth, love, joy, peace, rest, humility, forgiveness, faith, grace, mercy, favor, prosperity, and success—all things good. Our trust must be in El Shaddai, Almighty God, who supplies "all your need according to His riches in glory by Christ Jesus" (Philippians 4:19 NKJV).

As tumultuous and angst ridden as 2020 was, and as difficult days loom ahead, believers must not place their confidence in spiritual counterfeits, stockpiled resources, including assault weapons of mass destruction and charismatic personalities of great influence, but in the Word of God. We must talk the walk and walk the talk. And that can only happen by making the Word of God our first priority and our final authority. "The just shall live by his faith" (Galatians 3:11 NKJV).

Obedience grows out of a sincere heart for God. Our perspective of God, how we see him, has a profound bearing on whether or not we will instinctively look to him in times of adversity. Is he still the Sovereign Creator of the universe? And were all things made by him—the heavens and the earth and the fullness thereof; the world and all who live in it? Do we see the fullness of his unrivaled power, or do we seek after imaginary solutions and other gods?

Speak the Word of God by faith with the authority of Jesus and dare to make it the final authority. As we do, we are surrounded by a spiritual shield that marks the boundaries of our lives, warning the devil that we are off-limits to him.

As we stand on the Word of faith consistently, making it our first priority and our final authority, we can authoritatively say to Satan, "In the name of Jesus, and according to God's Word, I don't belong to you. My family doesn't belong to you. My health doesn't belong to you. My wealth doesn't belong to you. My ministry doesn't belong to you. My business doesn't belong to you. I am a citizen of the kingdom of heaven, and I receive and enjoy all the benefits thereof. Now back off!"

> *Have faith in God. For assuredly, I say to you, whoever says to this mountain, "Be removed and be cast into the sea," and does not doubt in his heart, but believes that those things he says will be done, he will have whatever he says. Therefore I say to you, whatever things you ask when you pray, believe that you receive them, and you will have them.*
>
> **—Mark 11:22–24 NKJV**

It is the responsibility of the believer to bring heaven to earth by our spoken words, by the spirit of faith. "And since we have the same spirit of faith, according to what is written, 'I believed and therefore I spoke,' we also believe and therefore speak" (2 Corinthians 4:13 NKJV). We must get the Word of God in our heart so that it will flow in abundance out of our mouth.

The Word of God is our servant. We can send it to accomplish and prosper in that thing for which it is sent (Isaiah 55:8–11 NKJV). Believe and speak the Word of God, and our faith-filled words, God's promises, will produce bountiful results.

Make the Word of God the final authority and refuse to accept any alternative. And when trouble comes, we'll be ready. We will speak the Word of God in the name of Jesus with authority. Resist the devil, and he will flee.

There is no lack in God's kingdom, because the benefits of the kingdom are commensurate with the wealth, power, influence, and authority of the King of kings. I believe I receive.

Making the Word of God first place and final authority in our lives is a Holy Spirit wavelength that transmits the frequency of heaven to earth. Stay tuned-in!

CHAPTER 7

The Power of the Word Lies in Its Consistent Use

It is written, "Man shall not live by bread alone, but by every word that proceeds from the mouth of God."

—Matthew 4:4 NKJV

Of a surety, God upholds all things by the word of his power (Hebrews 3:1 NKJV). And Abba Father reminds us, "For I am the Lord, I do not change" (Malachi 3:6 NKJV).

My personal opinion is that believers do not use the Word of God to their advantage. Many do not realize the Word of God is our leverage; it lifts us above natural phenomenon. The Word of God, spoken out of the mouth of a believer by faith, actually becomes our servant. The Word of God is spirit, and it is life (John 6:63 NKJV). Whenever we speak or release the Word of God by faith over a situation, we actually do so as a command. We send it to work for us (leverage).

"He sent His word and healed them, and delivered them from their destructions" (Psalm 107:20 NKJV). David testifies that this word is evidence of how God delivered the Israelites out of Babylonian captivity. It is clear that some of the agitation and disruption which occurred during imprisonment and bondage was the result of Israel's own self-inflicted wound—sin against God's will. But because of his great mercy and love for his people, God answered their pleas for help. He not only healed them but he also delivered them from destroying themselves.

God never showed up in Babylon to heal and deliver his people. He sent his word, and the word acted as his servant to accomplish the task at hand. God's Word does not return to him void or without having accomplished or prospered in the thing for which it was sent (Isaiah 55:11 NKJV).

In the case of the centurion's servant, who was lying at home paralyzed and dreadfully tormented, Jesus sent his word to heal him. Believers should draw from this biblical context a powerful gold nugget—a Holy Spirit revelation—that backs the same revelation Jesus taught his disciples in the parable of the sower—how the devil comes immediately to snatch the word out of the heart of the person who gladly receives it in his or her heart. It was because the one who gladly received the word in his or her heart did not understand the word; he or she did not receive a revelation of it. And because he did not receive a revelation—a working knowledge of how to use and apply the Word of God—the word did not take root.

If we do not understand the Word of God, how can we apply it? And if the word isn't applied to life's situations, it has no effect for good. It's like owning a Bible and never opening it.

It was the faith and action of the centurion that moved Jesus to commend him for having great faith. The centurion, a man of authority in the Roman army, understood the fact that servants obey without opposition. The centurion believed that if Jesus sent his word as his servant to heal his servant, then his servant would be healed.

The centurion understood authority, a key component of the believer's leverage as "kingdom citizens" to influence and to rule as kings and priests unto God and as ambassadors for Christ. Sadly, many believers do not understand their authority through Christ Jesus. So many times we find ourselves playing the role of a servant to the evil systems of the world, when we should be ruling over these evil systems by our knowledge of and faith in the Word of God, making the world submissive to the eternal Word of God:

> The centurion answered and said, "Lord, I am not worthy that You should come under my roof. But only speak a word, and my servant will be healed. For I also am a man under authority, having soldiers under me. And I say to this one, 'Go,' and he goes; and to another, 'Come,' and he comes; and to my servant, 'Do this,' and he does it." When Jesus heard it, He marveled, and said to those who followed, "Assuredly, I say to you, I have not found such great faith, not even in Israel! … Then Jesus said to the centurion, "Go your way; and as you have believed, so let it be done for you." And his servant was healed that same hour. (Matthew 8:8–10, 13 NKJV)

I believe that Jesus's words became his servant because He consistently used his faith to activate his words. When God tested Jesus's loyalty in the wilderness during his forty-day fast, Jesus defeated Satan with the Word of God. In the first of the three temptations, Satan tempted Jesus through his flesh. Jesus was obviously hungry after forty days without food. Satan thought that Jesus's weakness through his flesh, for lack of food, was his opportunity to deceive him. So Satan tempted Jesus to perform an act of his faith that would appease his hunger by commanding that stones be made bread. Doing so would have meant that Jesus lusted for food for immediate self-gratification—that he had to have food at that very moment and could not wait to eat food prepared through natural processes.

Jesus answered Satan's deceptive ploy with the Word of God: "It is written, 'Man shall not live by bread alone, but by every word that proceeds from the mouth of God'" (Matthew 4:4 NKJV). Although man needs bread to live, his greater, expandable life is lived by every word that God has already spoken, which means that speaking the Word of God—what God has already said in his written word—must become a consistent practice. By faith, we must say the same things God has already said.

As we consistently speak the Word of God by faith, applying it to our daily situation, we become transformed in our minds toward truth. We keep Satan under our feet, and we live and enjoy the abundance of life. Believers who live like this have made the Word of God first place and final authority in their lives. Their total trust is in God, his word. They live in humility before God—complete, absolute, uncompromising trust, dependence on God.

The power of the Word of God is manifested by its consistent use. What one does every day, whether good or bad, becomes easier. It becomes habit. Why? Practice, practice, and more practice. If believers who are struggling in this life would read the word daily, Holy Spirit revelation of what they read would come to them sooner and more consistently. They would be spiritual powerhouses, and the fiery darts that Satan shoots at their heart, their mind, would not penetrate, because they wear the armor of God all the time—24-7.

And when the storms of life hit them square in the face they, like other spiritually mature believers, would possess a mindset of calm, peace, and rest. No longer would they be like the many saints who do not prioritize the Word of God to make it first place and final authority in their lives by reason of consistent use.

When we're going through a difficult time, we should feed on the Word of God as often as possible to starve the deceptive thoughts and schemes of Satan. Staying in the Word of God and using it—appropriating it by faith over our situation—will lead us to victory.

If believers would desire and pursue the Word of God, which grows and strengthens our inner being the same way we desire and pursue food that grows and strengthens our physical body, we all would be spiritual powerhouses. We would live! Like Jesus, we would live by every word that proceeds out of the mouth of the Lord. We would send the Word of God as our servant to accomplish and prosper in the thing to which it was sent. And it would obey!

No matter what Satan concocts to tempt and deceive us through the lust of the flesh, the lust of the eyes, and the pride of life, will not prosper. All these things are representative of the evils of this world. As saints, we are urged not to love these superficial, temporal things of the world. If anyone loves the world, the love of the Father is not in them. So the lust of the flesh, the lust of the eyes, and the pride of life is not of the Father but of the world (1 John 2:15–16 NKJV).

The Word of God remains the same. Jesus is the word made flesh (John 1:14 NKJV), and he is the same yesterday, today, and forever (Hebrews 13:8 NKJV). The Word is unchangeable and upholds all things—that includes upholding believers in times of trouble. The Word of God should be the foundation that every believer is built upon so that when the storms of life beat vehemently upon our lives we will not be washed away but stand firm, because we're built on the solid rock—Jesus Christ, the Word of God—and we use it consistently. It brings us safely through every storm. God has already spoken, and all things are upheld by the word of his power:

> Whoever comes to Me, and hears My sayings and does them, I will show you whom he is like: He is like a man building a house, who dug deep and laid the foundation on the rock. And when the flood arose, the stream beat vehemently against that house, and could not shake it, for it was founded on the rock. But he who heard and did nothing is like a man who built a house on the earth without a foundation, against which the stream beat vehemently; and immediately it fell. And the ruin of that house was great. (Luke 6:47–49 NKJV)

Notice that it was not so much the storm itself that caused the foolish man's—he who heard the word and did nothing—house to fall. It was his foundation. The same storm hit both houses. Believers who do not read and study the Word of God, building and strengthening their inner being, tend to be weak Christians who "fall for anything" because they have no foundation. The Word of God is a firm foundation, stronger than any physical thing. It will hold up under the pressures of life every time because the Word of God doesn't change. It is settled forever in heaven. Believers must say what heaven already has said. Heaven doesn't agree with torment and trouble, and neither should we.

IN CONSISTENCY LIES THE POWER

I first heard Gloria Copeland use that phrase years ago, and it has changed my life by empowering me with a ready, on-demand download of the specific Word of God that I need for any situation.

After I was delivered from my status as a backslider, I pledged to God that I would do his will and complete his divine assignment for my life with a spirit of excellence. I told God that I did not want to be a charlatan. I did not want to be a smooth-talking charismatic slickster who preyed on people for money, but I truly wanted to know him for myself. I wanted to learn and have divine revelation of the Word of God. So for several years I studied the Word of God every day for most of the day. It wasn't unusual for me to begin to study God's word in the morning and still be at my post studying into the evening. This was also the time that I began to memorize large portions of the word.

Consistency means firmness of constitution or character; substantiality; durability; persistency; of a regularly occurring, dependable nature.

I was consistent in the Word of God through study, but I did not get a revelation of the power of my consistency in the Word until I heard Gloria Copeland say, "In consistency lies the power." Through this phrase, she taught me the power contained in the Word of God and how to apply it to my life so that the power of that word would work for me as a benefit of my salvation, not when I got to heaven, but right here on earth. Wow! What a revelation.

Gloria says she received that phrase as a revelation from the Holy Spirit while listening to a teaching tape by Kenneth E. Hagin titled *You Can Have What You Say*. Suddenly the Lord spoke to her spirit: "In consistency lies the power."

She said, "That's when the revelation hit me: if I want to see God's promises manifest in my life, I can't just speak his word when I pray. I must talk faith all the time! I must say only what I want to come to pass. Faith speaks the answer."[37]—Gloria Copeland, *Nothing to Fear*

But before faith can speak the answer it must be acquired or obtained. All believers have been given a measure of faith, (Romans 12:3

[37] *Believer's Voice of Victory Magazine*, July 2014, 28–30.

NKJV), but that measure becomes expandable through continuously hearing the Word of God. "So then faith comes by hearing, and hearing by the word of God" (Romans 10:17 NKJV). Believers are "the just" who live by faith (Romans 1:17 NKJV); therefore our first priority should be spending quality time in the Word of God and hearing the word. Faith doesn't work without the word. The Word of God supplies believers with a continuous and sustainable faith that is required to please God and receive his blessings. The Word of God has the solution to every problem we will ever face.

> *But without faith it is impossible to please Him, for he who comes to God must believe that He is, and that He is a rewarder of those who diligently seek Him.*
>
> **—Hebrews 11:6 NKJV**

Our active faith pleases God, and he rewards us accordingly. We seek or worship him diligently—conscientiously, purposefully, and tirelessly—because our sustainable faith is a display of our trust in God.

As the Word of God gets into our heart in abundance, we become God-inside minded, Holy Spirit conscious, and word-conscious. The Word of God fuels our faith, and we begin to think like God does, for we have the mind of Christ (1 Corinthians 2:16 NKJV). As we consistently build our faith with the Word of God, we begin to think eternally. Our heart is full of the word, and we speak the Word of God. When evil tidings come, the first thing out of our mouth isn't "Oh God, what am I going to do?" We think and talk the word. It is an inside-the-heart transformation first that erupts in full measure out of our mouth. The first thing out of our mouth when confronted with evil tidings or bad situations should be what God has already said about bad news. God's Word says, "I will not be afraid of evil tidings; my heart is steadfast, trusting in You" (Psalm 112:7 NKJV).

> *A good man out of the good treasure of his heart brings forth good; and an evil man out of the evil treasure of his heart brings forth evil. For out of the abundance of the heart his mouth speaks.*
>
> **—Luke 6:45 NKJV**

> *But I say to you that for every idle word men may speak, they will give account of it in the day of judgment. For by your words you will be justified, and by your words you will be condemned.*
>
> **—Matthew 12:36–37 NKJV**

The first words we speak concerning a situation, bad or good, reveal what's really in our heart, because out of the abundance of the heart the mouth speaks. What is stored up in our heart will erupt out of our mouth. As believers, we cannot afford to spend each day speaking idle words—words of unbelief, fear, or doubt.

Why doesn't God want his sons and daughters to speak idle words? It is because our words have power. "Death and life are in the power of the tongue, and those who love it will eat its fruit" (Proverbs 18:21 NKJV). The Word of God is life, but an idle word is death because idle words are useless. They are inactive and have no assignment toward producing good works, because they are faithless.

The Greek word *argos* is used in the text above to define *idle*. It denotes inactive, idle, unfruitful, barren; to reduce to inactivity; metaphorically in the sense of ineffective, worthless, as of a word; of faith unaccompanied by works.[38]

When I was in college, my vocabulary professor would say, "Every word means something." Faithless and fear-filled words qualify as evil, and evil begets evil. "A wholesome tongue is a tree of life, but perverseness in it breaks the spirit" (Proverbs 15:4 NKJV).

As believers, we must grow up in the Word of God. We do that by making a conscious decision to put the word in our hearts on a daily basis. As we do so, our inner being is strengthened with the power of God's Word, and we speak it by faith, which activates the word to produce good works. We speak life because the Word of God is life, and as we speak life, we also dismiss death. Both life and death are governed by the words we speak. Words of life free us from death. "For the law of the Spirit of life in Christ Jesus has made me free from the law of sin and death" (Romans 8:2 NKJV).

Obviously, two laws are at work. And the thing about laws is that

---

[38] *Expository Dictionary of New Testament Words: A Comprehensive Dictionary of the Original Greek Words with Their Precise Meanings for English Readers.*

they work the same way every time for everybody. Our words dictate which law is activated. The Word of God spoken by faith activates the law of the spirit of life and freedom. Idle words activate the law of sin and death. Even if we don't consciously choose one or the other, the law of sin and death is activated by reason of forfeit—by failing to attend or participate, or by violation of the rules. We must choose life. And that means choosing the Word of God.

The supernatural power of the eternal Word of God that upholds all things is alive and powerful. When we consistently hear the Word of God, understand it, and receive it gladly in our heart, we unleash the creative power of God into our lives, and we emerge victorious.

Believers should never move away from the practices of the early church. The early church gives us an example of what consistent use of the Word of God looks like and the power that flows from it: "And they continued steadfastly in the apostles' doctrine and fellowship, in the breaking of bread, and in prayers ... So continuing daily with one accord in the temple ... praising God and having favor with all the people. And the Lord added to the church daily those who were being saved" (Acts 2:42, 46, 47 NKJV).

> *And daily in the temple, and in every house, they did not cease teaching and preaching Jesus as the Christ.*
>
> **—Acts 5:42 NKJV**

> *But we will give ourselves continually to prayer and to the ministry of the word ... Then the word of God spread, and the number of the disciples multiplied greatly.*
>
> **—Acts 6:4, 7 NKJV**

In order to be continually steadfast in our use of the Word of God, we must persevere in the word. The Greek word for *perseverance* is *proskarteresis*, from *proskartereo*, which means to be earnest toward a thing; to be constantly diligent, or in a place to attend assiduously all the exercises, or for a person to adhere closely to (as a servitor)—attend or give oneself continually to, continue in, instant in, wait on continually; persistency.[39]

[39] *Strong's Exhaustive Concordance of the Bible, NT*, 4343, 4342.

Through scripture, we can see this definition of *perseverance* in operation in the lives of the apostle Paul and in the life of the persistent widow. We can see that each person was consciously earnest toward their cause. And their perseverance, persistence, and continually giving themselves to their cause unleashed supernatural power.

> And he (Paul) went into the synagogue and spoke boldly for three months, reasoning and persuading concerning the things of the kingdom of God. But when some were hardened and did not believe, but spoke evil of the Way before the multitude, he departed from them and withdrew the disciples, reasoning daily in the school of Tyrannus. And this continued for two years, so that all who dwelt in Asia heard the word of the Lord Jesus, both Jews and Greeks. Now God worked unusual miracles by the hands of Paul, so that even handkerchiefs or aprons were brought from his body to the sick, and the diseases left them and the evil spirits went out of them. (Acts 19:8–12 NKJV)

If we look closely, we can see that "in consistency lies the power." Paul was so diligent, earnest toward teaching and preaching the Gospel of the kingdom that he would not allow those who spoke evil of the things of the kingdom of God to persuade him to give up. I believe this is a testimony to Paul's normal custom. He continually gave himself to study, speaking the Word of God by faith and witnessing the accompanying good works.

Many believers, especially church leaders, who get to the point where the people who they're leading are hardened and don't believe the Word of God simply quit. They give up. They don't persevere. Paul was conscientious in his endeavor to reach the world with the Word of God. It was his God-ordained assignment.

How do I know it was his God-ordained assignment? I feel certain of this because Paul didn't allow the evil speech and hardness of heart of those to whom he ministered to pressure him into defeat. He simply left them, took his disciples, and continued reasoning daily for two years in the school of Tyrannus. Consistency does not quit! It stays in vigorous pursuit of the intended target. Paul's target was to finish his assignment with joy, the ministry which he received from the Lord Jesus, and to testify to the Gospel of the grace of God (Acts 20:24 NKJV).

His consistent use of the Word of God manifested in supernatural power—demonstrations of the Holy Spirit and of power (1 Corinthians 2:4 NKJV). Diseases left the people, and evil spirits were forced to leave when Paul laid handkerchiefs from his body on the sick. Paul's consistent use of the Word of God manifested unusual miracles.

Let's look at a consistent use of the Word of God through persistence. To be persistent means obstinately refusing to give up or let go. It also means to be insistently repetitive—to be indefinitely continuous.

> Then He spoke a parable to them, that men always ought to pray and not lose heart, saying: "There was in a certain city a judge who did not fear God nor regard man. Now there was a widow in that city; and she came to him, saying 'Get justice for me from my adversary. And he would not for a while; but afterward he said within himself, 'Though I do not fear God nor regard man, yet because this widow troubles me I will avenge her, lest by her continual coming she weary me.' Then the Lord said, "Hear what the unjust judge said. And shall God not avenge His own elect who cry out day and night to Him though He bears long with them? I tell you that He will avenge them speedily. Nevertheless, when the Son of Man comes, will He really find faith on the earth?" (Luke 18:1–8 NKJV)

Wow! What persistence. What if every believer was as persistent in their pursuit of prioritizing God's Word as first place and final authority in their life through consistent use—reading, hearing, studying, speaking, and acting in faith repeatedly, over and over again, practice, practice, and more practice? What powerful and unusual miracles we would see?

The widow in this parable persisted in demanding that justice be given to her. What a daunting challenge she faced. She had to demand justice from a judge who was unconcerned about the needs of others or about their opinion of him. On top of that, she was vulnerable and somewhat helpless because of her social status as a widow. Her persistence was all she had. And she used it to the glory of God by obstinately refusing to give up or let go. She was insistently repetitive, and I believe her mind was settled to be relentless in her pursuit of justice.

Jesus said, "Hear what the unjust judge said" (Luke 18:8 NKJV). I believe this means that the widow's persistence caused a judge who wasn't concerned about anyone but himself nor about the opinions of others to grant her justice. Jesus wants all believers to know that God is a loving Father who cares about his sons and daughters, and he will not deny our steadfast faith, our diligence in consistently using the Word of God to unlock, breakthrough, and manifest the power that lies within. We have to use the Word of God consistently in all situations. The Word of God is our leverage. Thank God it is our victory through faith in Jesus Christ (1 Corinthians 15:57 NKJV).

We don't have to go through all that. We already know that God's promises in him are "yes" and in Him "amen" (2 Corinthians 1:20 NKJV). They are freely given from the heart of a loving Father who longs for us to have what we desire and what we expect. God will bring about justice for those who are his, like-minded in nature and character.

Abba Daddy will not delay his support and confirmation of those who are his when we use the Word of God consistently by our faith. We don't have to beg and plead with him to do so, like the widow had to do with the unreasonable judge. It is our Father's good pleasure to give us the kingdom (Luke 12:32 NKJV). He says, "Ask, and it will be given to you; seek, and you will find; knock, and it will be opened to you. For everyone who asks receives, and he who seeks finds, and to him who knocks it will be opened" (Matthew 7:7–8 NKJV).

Even so, when Jesus returns, will he really find us in faith? When Jesus returns, will he find the church, the body of Christ, in a sustainable faith, a faith that perseveres in prayer and loyalty in the things of the kingdom of God? Jesus's question leaves me to believe he is giving us a forewarning of what he might find upon his second coming because the word says that rampant sin will take place in the last days—perilous times shall come (2 Timothy 3:1 NKJV).

That time is now. Spiritual decline and persecution of the Way abound. Jesus is preparing the body to remain persistent and to persevere like the widow demonstrated. Through it all, believers are overcomers of the world. "For whatever is born of God overcomes the world. And this is the victory that has overcome the world—our faith" (1 John 5:4 NKJV).

"The secret of your future is hidden in your daily routine."[40] As believers, we must persist and persevere in feeding our inner being daily with the Word of God. As our hearts are filled with the word, we become God-inside minded and Holy Spirit conscious. Our victory is in our consistent use—our continual application by faith of the promises of God to whatever we long for.

Prioritize the Word of God as first place, and make it the final authority. The Word of God is the believer's authority, and in consistency lies the power. Use it!

Consistent use of the Word of God by faith is a Holy Spirit wavelength that transmits the frequency of heaven to earth. Stay tuned-in!

---

[40] Mike Murdock, *The Wisdom Library of Mike Murdock Volume 8* (Fort Worth, TX: Wisdom International, 2001), 190.

CHAPTER 8

The Word of God and Reality

It may be that the Lord will work for us. For nothing restrains the Lord from saving by many or by few.

—1 Samuel 14:6b NKJV

I remember being in situations in which it seemed God was somehow restrained—that the opposing forces of my best life were more powerful than God's ability to remove them and allow his blessings to flow into my life. Those were horrible times. I would talk openly to God and say, "God, you own everything, and you are no respecter of person. It really wouldn't be much for you to turn my negative situations around. You own all the gold and silver; it would only take a snap of your finger, and money would come to me in abundance." This was a common complaint of mine after May 29, 1998, the date I left my secular job to establish ministry full-time. I had no financial means of support and eventually lost my home, land and vehicle.

Sound familiar? From time to time, all of us have had a similar story. We felt that there was something restraining the Lord, keeping him from rescuing us. The devil would always bombard our minds with all the things we did wrong—how we weren't really serving the Lord with all our heart. He would remind us that we told a lie only a few minutes ago, or he'd really press the guilt button by reminding us that we were not tithing or giving offerings or attending church regularly. God forbid, he would remind us mercilessly of all our secret sins, our neglect to read and study the Word of God, and our lackluster prayer life.

In the end, we'd be broken, busted, and disgusted, feeling guilty, condemned, and unable to shake off the religious spirit through which the devil was operating. Then we'd say something like, "Well, Lord, you know my heart. If it's for me, it will be." We'd start to sing songs like, "What God Has for Me Is for Me" and "He's an On-Time God."

I suppose that rehearsing religious quotes and songs like these somehow made us feel a little less guilt. And so we simply continued with our vain prayers that basically were no more than wishful pleas, void of the promises of God and void of genuine faith when they were prayed. And when we got no "on-time" answer to our vain prayers, the reality of the dire consequences we were faced with hit so hard, we wondered to an even deeper degree why God didn't just intervene and make things right. We'd say, "Maybe God isn't strong enough, or maybe God won't help me, because I've been so bad."

Before we knew it, we were bogged down, steeped in unbelief, doubt, anxiety, worry, and stress, speaking idle words out of our mouths and calling our prayer partners to "touch and agree" with us for a breakthrough. We needed someone to "pray us through" our dilemma. Thank God for spiritual maturity!

The King James Version of the Bible says that "there is no restraint to the Lord to save by many or by few" (1 Samuel 6:14b). Could that verse of scripture imply there is nothing in existence that can restrain God? If so, what is it that many believers miss when it comes to God's willingness to bless us constantly? After all, blessings are the promises of God that he covenanted with Abraham and his seed, Christ Jesus (Galatians 3:16 NKJV). David wrote, "Blessed be the Lord, Who daily loads us with benefits, The God of our salvation!" (Psalm 68:19 NKJV).

First things first: let's examine a study of the word *restraint*. I believe this will shed light on the eternal fact that there is no restraint to the Lord.

The Hebrew word used for *restraint* is *ma'tsowr* from *atsar*, which means a hindrance; control—rule. To enclose; to hold back; also to maintain, rule, assemble—detain, restrain, retain, shut up, stop.[41]

The root word of *restraint* is *restrain*, which means to prevent from doing, exhibiting, or expressing something; to limit, restrict, or keep under control; to moderate or limit the force, effect, development, or full exercise of; to deprive of liberty; to place under arrest or restraint.[42]

Is anything too hard for God? This is a question that many believers struggle to answer. The first mention of this question in the Bible was posed by God himself, when he told Sarah that she would have a son:

> Now Abraham and Sarah were old, well advanced in age; and Sarah had passed the age of childbearing. Therefore Sarah laughed within herself, saying, "After I have grown old, shall I have pleasure, my lord being old also?" And the Lord said to Abraham, "Why did Sarah laugh, saying, 'Shall I surely bear a child, since I am old?' Is anything too hard for the Lord? At the appointed time I will return to you, according to the time of life, and Sarah shall have a son. (Genesis 18:11–14 NKJV)

God poses the question to Abraham in a way that literally answers the question for Sarah: "At the appointed time I will return to you … and Sarah shall have a son" (Genesis 18:14 NKJV). Notice that neither age nor time can restrain God. But there is something else God said that stands out: "At the appointed time" (Genesis 18:14 NKJV). I believe this is what believers have a problem with. Sometimes it is not a lack of faith or the praying of bogus prayers that cause our prayers to not be answered; it is our lack of patience to wait for God's appointed time. Remember, his promises are guaranteed!

Believers should have the faith displayed by Jeremiah, who said, "Ah, Lord God! Behold, You have made the heavens and the earth by Your great power and outstretched arm. There is nothing too hard for You" (Jeremiah 32:17 NKJV). Jeremiah makes a faith statement: "There is

---

41 *Strong's Exhaustive Concordance of the Bible, OT,* 4622, 6113.

42 *Merriam-Webster's Collegiate Dictionary: Eleventh Edition*, sv "restrain."

nothing too hard for You, Lord." Jeremiah seems to surmise that if God could make the heavens and the earth, then his power and outstretched arm had to be not only great but also unlimited and unrestrained.

Because of Jeremiah's display of unwavering faith, the Lord spoke back to Jeremiah, in verse 27, what Jeremiah prayed to him by faith in verse 17. "Then the word of the Lord came to Jeremiah, saying, 'Behold, I am the Lord, the God of all flesh. Is there anything too hard for Me?" (Jeremiah 32:27 NKJV). God wants to back our faith. And I believe he wanted Jeremiah to be sure he had faith to believe there is nothing too hard for God. God wanted Jeremiah to say this from a heart of faith, not trying to impress him with flattery.

Listen, God wants to do for us what He did for Jeremiah—that is, reward our faith. God knows genuine faith when he sees it. He knows genuine faith when he hears it. There is no amount of flattery that can sway God to move on our behalf. He moves because he hears and sees genuine faith—*pistis*, the faith of God, the truthfulness of God, what he knows and believes to be true.[43]

The expanse of God's outstretched arm is eternal. There is no place he is not, which means there is no place he cannot reach. God challenged Moses with a similar question. And like Moses, many believers today still have a great deal to learn about the miraculous power of God. God had to provide for Moses because he said he would. God told Moses, "I AM WHO I AM … say to the children of Israel, I AM has sent me to you" (Exodus 3:14 NKJV).

Like Moses, we question God's call on our lives. We ask God, "Who am I?" And when he tells us, we're frightened and offer excuses rather than faith. Our objections end up being a distrust of the One who called us. "Lord, I don't know if I can do this. Lord, if I do this, are you going to be with me? Are you going to be there when I need you? Are you sure you have the power to perform these things through me?" All these questions are ultimately questions about God—our trust, our faith in him, his Word.

Moses complained about the people; Moses complained about his own life. He said, "I am not able to bear all these people alone, because the burden is too heavy for me" (Numbers 11:14 NKJV). Yet God provided for Moses. God assured Moses that his outstretched arm

---

[43] *Strong's Exhaustive Concordance of the Bible, NT*, 4102.

could reach him wherever he was. "And the Lord said to Moses, 'Has the Lord's arm been shortened? Now you shall see whether what I say will happen to you or not'" (Numbers 11:23 NKJV).

Is God less able to deliver saints today as he did for the Old Testament heroes of faith? God wants us to look back at those heroes of faith and how he delivered them because he was with them. King Solomon's prayer is the perfect example of how we should live a life of gratitude to the one true living God, who chose us in him before the foundation of the world that we should be holy and blameless before him in love (Ephesians 1:4 NKJV):

> And so it was, when Solomon had finished praying all this prayer and supplication to the Lord, that he arose from before the altar of the Lord … Then he stood and blessed all the assembly of Israel with a loud voice, saying: "Blessed be the Lord, who has given rest to His people Israel, according to all that He promised. There has not failed one word of all His good promise, which He promised through His servant Moses. May the Lord our God be with us, as He was with our fathers. May He not leave us nor forsake us, that He may incline our hearts to Himself, to walk in all His ways, and to keep His commandments and His statutes and His judgments, which He commanded our fathers. And may these words of mine, with which I have made supplication before the Lord, be near the Lord our God day and night, that He may maintain the cause of His servant and the cause of His people Israel, as each day may require, that all the people of the earth may know that the Lord is God; there is no other. Let your heart therefore be loyal to the Lord our God, to walk in His statutes and keep His commandments, as at this day." (1 Kings 8:54–61 NKJV)

In many ways, today's believers are no different than Moses. We think only in terms of our own abilities, strength, and resources when we're challenged by the will of God, his divine assignment for our life.

Instead of offering God excuses as to why we cannot accept his divine mandate for our lives, we should trust in God's faithfulness to his own word. It is the same for us as it was for Joshua after Moses's death:

> Moses My servant is dead. Now therefore, arise, go over this Jordan, you and all this people, to the land which I am giving to them – the children of Israel. No man shall be able to stand before you all the days of your life; as I was with Moses, so I will be with you. I will not leave you nor forsake you. Have I not commanded you? Be strong and of good courage; do not be afraid, nor be dismayed, for the Lord your God is with you wherever you go. (Joshua 1:2, 5, 9 NKJV)

God is with us wherever we go. He alters our bad reality. Like the heroes of faith we just examined, we, too, must express confidence in God, which enables us through the power of the Holy Spirit to submit ourselves to his divine calling for our lives.

The prophet Isaiah received the word of the Lord concerning the Messiah's obedience to submit himself to the will of his Father. But first, God tells Isaiah the people have sold themselves because of their iniquities. In essence, God is saying he could not find one man who was not rebellious that he could call upon to submit to do his bidding on earth. That man would eventually be Jesus.

> *Why, when I came, was there no man? Why, when I called, was there none to answer? Is My hand shortened at all that it cannot redeem? Or have I no power to deliver? Indeed with My rebuke I dry up the sea, I make the rivers a wilderness; their fish stink because there is no water; and die of thirst. I clothe the heavens with blackness, and I make sackcloth their covering.*
>
> **—Isaiah 50:2–3 NKJV**

> *Behold, the Lord's hand is not shortened, that it cannot save; nor His ear heavy, that it cannot hear. But your iniquities have separated you from your God; and your sins have hidden His face from you, so that He will not hear.*
>
> **—Isaiah 59:1–2 NKJV**

Of a truth, there is nothing in existence that can restrain God; however, the above scriptures shed some light on why the prayers of Israel were not answered, when it seemed to them only a light or small thing for God to do so. God said, "When I came, there was no man; when I called there was no answer" (Isaiah 50:2 NKJV). He goes on to say, "Your iniquities have separated you from Your God; and your sins have hidden My face from you, so that I will not hear" (Isaiah 59:2 NKJV). Sin separates us from God. This was the reality of those living under Old Testament law. The penalty for sin is death. But Jesus conquered death on the cross at Calvary. And our faith in Jesus, who died to pay the penalty of man's sin, breaks the penalty for sin.

Yes, believers today live under a new covenant, a better covenant built upon better promises—the New Testament. The prophet Jeremiah foresaw this new covenant and foretold it. The writer of the Epistle to the Hebrews recounts what was prophesized in Jeremiah 31:31–34:

> For if that first covenant had been faultless, then no place would have been sought for a second. Because finding fault with them, He says: "Behold, the days are coming, says the Lord, when I will make a new covenant with the house of Israel and with the house of Judah – not according to the covenant that I made with their fathers in the day when I took them by the hand to lead them out of the land of Egypt; because they did not continue in My covenant, and I disregarded them, says the Lord. For this is the covenant that I will make with the house of Israel after those days, says the Lord: I will put My laws in their mind and write them on their hearts; and I will be their God, and they shall be My people. None of them shall teach his neighbor, and none his brother, saying, 'Know the Lord,' for all shall know Me, from the least of them to the greatest of them. For I will be merciful to their unrighteousness, and their sins and their lawless deeds I will remember no more." In that He says, "A new covenant," He has made the first obsolete. Now what is

> becoming obsolete and growing old is ready to vanish away. (Hebrews 8:7–13 NKJV)

The above passage sheds new light as to why believers today miss God's best, his promises. It is no longer because of sin, as it was for the children of Israel in the Old Testament. Our problem today isn't because of Old Testament law; it is because of our refusal through unbelief to accept the New Testament grace freely given to us by our faith in Jesus Christ. In the above passage, verse 12 says God is merciful to our unrighteousness, and our sins and our lawless deeds, he will not remember. That's New Testament grace. So if our sin is not the problem, what is?

The key to unlock this mystery is found in the word *covenant.* Too many believers today do not understand covenant and the benefits that are associated with it. In the Hebrew language, the word for *covenant* is *b^{e}riyth*, which means a cutting; a compact made by passing between pieces of flesh—a confederacy, covenant, league.[44] The Greek rendition of *covenant* is *diatheke*, which means a disposition—that is, a contract; a devisor will; covenant, testament; to put apart, dispose by assignment, compact, or bequest; make testator.[45]

Diatheke primarily signifies a disposition of property by will or otherwise. In its use in the Septuagint, it is the rendering of a Hebrew word meaning a covenant or agreement, from a verb signifying to cut or divide, in allusion to a sacrificial custom in connection with covenant-making—for example, Genesis 15:10, "divided" or "cut". In contradistinction to the English word *covenant* (a coming together), which signifies a mutual undertaking between two parties or more, each binding himself or herself to fulfill obligations, it does not in itself contain the idea of joint obligation. It mostly signifies an obligation undertaken by a single person. In Galatians 3:17, it is used as an alternative to a promise. God enjoined upon Abraham the rite of circumcision, but his promise to Abraham—here called a covenant—was not conditional upon the observance of circumcision, though a penalty was attached to its nonobservance.

---

[44] *Strong's Exhaustive Concordance of the Bible, OT,* 1285.

[45] *Strong's Exhaustive Concordance of the Bible, NT,* 1242, 1303.

The New Testament uses of *covenant* may be analyzed as a promise or undertaking, human or divine; a promise or undertaking on the part of God; an agreement, a mutual undertaking between God and Israel; the basis established by the death of Christ, on which the salvation of men is secured.[46]

The covenant God cut with Abraham is a better covenant because it was established by the death of Christ, on which the salvation of men is secured. It's called the new covenant, it's called the second covenant, and it's called the better covenant.

> *And for this reason He is the Mediator of the new covenant, by means of death, for the redemption of the transgressions under the first covenant, that those who are called may receive the promise of the eternal inheritance.*
>
> **—Hebrews 9:15 NKJV**

> *For if that first covenant had been faultless, then no place would have been sought for a second.*
>
> **—Hebrews 8:7 NKJV**

> *By so much more Jesus has become a surety of a better covenant.*
>
> **—Hebrews 7:22 NKJV**

Where is the distinction between the Old Testament covenant and the New Testament covenant? Clearly, there has to be one since the first covenant had faults, and the second covenant was a better covenant. May I suggest that the distinction can be made in that the first covenant was about fulfilling an obligation, while the second, new, better covenant is about receiving a free gift.

Believers must understand the grace of God that has been afforded or given to us as a free gift in the New Testament. This distinction concerning the two covenants still divides Christians today. The first covenant is about what one has to do to comply, and the new covenant is about faith in the covenant maker, who gave his Son to die for the salvation of all people.

Under the new, better covenant, we don't work to be accepted in his

[46] *Strong's Exhaustive Concordance of the Bible, NT.*

grace or to make ourselves righteous. We work because we are accepted in his grace, and we simply believe and receive righteousness as the gift that it is—faith in Jesus Christ.

Our sins have been forgiven; therefore we should not allow Satan to reduce our freedom to a life of guilt and sin consciousness. What we must do is hold fast to our confession of faith. As we do so, we will experience the grace of a better covenant by receiving the free gift, which is our inheritance. We will know without a doubt that the Lord's arm is not short, for there is no restraint to him to save by many or by few:

> Therefore, brethren, having boldness to enter the Holiest by the blood of Jesus, by a new and living way which He consecrated for us, through the veil that is, His flesh, and having a High Priest over the house of God, let us draw near with a true heart in full assurance of faith, having our hearts sprinkled from an evil conscience and our bodies washed with pure water. Let us hold fast the confession of our hope without wavering, for He who promised is faithful. (Hebrews 10:19–23 NKJV)

The body of Christ cannot continue to slip back into the religious, legalistic system of trying to please God through works in order to be accepted, justified, or even get their prayers answered. God's arm is not short! Nothing is too hard for God! There is no restraint to the Lord! Faith in Jesus Christ is the basis for acceptance with God in the new, second, better covenant.

Too many believers don't receive what they ask God for, because they don't adhere to the process—faith in the Word of God spoken consistently and acted upon as if they already possessed it while abiding the timing of God for its physical manifestation. They keep trying to earn it, not realizing that God will not allow them to earn it, because he gave it to them, his sons and daughters, as a free gift. All believers are required to do is believe, speak, act like it's so, and we will receive his rewards.

Never get caught up in trying to impress God or appease him or flatter him to get what we desire. Don't try to earn righteousness. We are accepted by God through faith in Jesus Christ. This should be our confidence.

> *Now this is the confidence that we have in Him, that if we ask anything according to His will, He hears us. And if we know that He hears us, whatever we ask, we know that we have the petitions that we have asked of Him.*
>
> **—1 John 5:14–15 NKJV**

Brother and Sister Christians, we will never get the things we long for trying to "force" God's hand or concluding that what we asked God for was too hard for Him to deliver. That self-righteous, legalistic, religious mindset only keeps us in a repeated cycle of failure. The only way to victory is through faith in the Word of God, the name of Jesus, and the Holy Spirit, which produces a pure heart, a clear conscience, peace of mind, and answered prayers. What a wonderful statement of faith. Nothing restrains the Lord! Not even our harsh realities.

FACTS DON'T CHANGE THE WORD OF GOD

Many years ago, I heard Kenneth Copeland make that statement on *The Believer's Voice of Victory* television broadcast, and it baffled me. "What does he mean?" I asked. "Facts are facts, and they don't change. A fact is reality. And what's real is real."

Obviously, I did not have a Holy Spirit revelation of what Brother Copeland was saying. He had released a five-star nugget to me that my spirit had yet to comprehend. But it sounded so cool to me. And I begin to say it over and over and over. Every time I'd get in a situation in which I was experiencing something bad, or I'd hear an evil tiding, I'd say, "Facts don't change the Word of God; the Word of God changes the facts. Praise God. I believe I receive."

Then one day it hit me: "The Word of God is the power of God to supernaturally change a physical reality." Since then, I have had many situations to occur in my life that were "bad" or not profitable for me or my family or my ministry; however, because I'd gotten that phrase in my heart and had found many occasions in scripture in which I found it to be true, this phrase would simply flow out of my spirit whenever I was confronted with a bad report or whenever something bad happened. Facts don't change the Word of God; the Word of God changes the facts. Thank you, Lord. I believe I receive.

I learned quickly to appropriate or apply the Word of God—the promises of God—to my current bad reality and to decree and declare the change that I desired. And I've seen many situations changed, turned around, because of my faith in commanding that the Word of God change my bad realities not for me only but also for people who I've prayed for over the years, and it is still happening today. That tells me the Word of God works with my confession of faith, in the name of Jesus, to effectually change my bad realities into good ones: "That the sharing of your faith may become effective by the acknowledgment of every good thing which is in you in Christ Jesus" (Philemon 6 NKJV).

> *In everything give thanks; for this is the will of God in Christ Jesus for you.*
>
> **—1 Thessalonians 5:18 NKJV**

> *For God is not unjust to forget your work and labor of love which you have shown toward His name, in that you have ministered to the saints, and do minister.*
>
> **—Hebrews 6:10 NKJV**

According to Wiktionary, a *fact* is something actual as opposed to invented; something that is real; something concrete used as a basis for further interpretation; an objective consensus on a fundamental reality that has been agreed upon by a substantial number of experts; and information about a particular subject, especially actual conditions and/or circumstances.

Each definition, respectively, deals with fact not fiction; fact as opposed to theory; facts before decision; facts as consensus; and facts as information.

Now let's look at the word *reality*. Wiktionary defines reality as the state of being actual or real; a real entity, event, or other fact; the entirety of all that is real; and an individual observer's own subjective perception of that which is real.

From the definitions given for *fact* and *reality*, I can surmise that both words are used interchangeably, though that may not be a fact.

I think most people, even believers, tend to talk about facts only from a natural or worldly perspective. Many never even consider that the only true facts that stand alone are the facts of the truth of the Word of God. The Word of God is not fiction; it is not theory; it is not based on a decision that any human made, only on God's truth—what he knows and believes to be true. It is not based on consensus nor is it simply information. The Word of God is eternal, and that makes all the difference.

Let's take a look in scripture where the Word of God changed the facts. I pray that readers who haven't already will receive a revelation as I did of the power of commanding the Word of God to change the facts—bad realities.

About eight or nine years ago, I was studying the Word of God, when my phone rang. It was one of my sisters, and I could tell by the tone of her voice that something was terribly wrong. She began to tell me that our older sister's husband had just had a heart attack. He was unconscious and not breathing, and that paramedics were on the way to their house.

Initially, this news hit me extremely hard. I knew this was a life-or-death situation. I quickly gathered myself. I had been quoting Psalm 112:7 NKJV for some time, and the Word of God brought calm and stilled me. The Word of God began to flow out of my heart and into my mouth. "He will not be afraid of evil tidings; His heart is steadfast, trusting in the Lord."

The sister who called me to inform me of what was happening was and is the leader of my ministry intercession team, so I knew I had agreement in prayer. Abba Daddy had the right person to call me. "Again I say to you that if two of you agree on earth concerning anything that they ask, it will be done for them by My Father in heaven. For where two or three are gathered together in My name, I am there in the midst of them" (Matthew 18:19–20 NKJV).

My sister and I agreed that our brother-in-law would not die but live and declare the works of the Lord (Psalm 118:17 NKJV). We agreed as touching the thing—in this case, our brother-in-law's life—that we wanted to be done for us by our Father in heaven. The King James Version of the Bible says, "Again I say unto you, that if two of you shall agree on earth as touching anything that they shall ask, it shall be done for them of My Father which is in heaven" (Matthew 18:19–20).

Many believers today generally misquote that scripture from the King James Version. They'll say, "If two of us touch and agree on anything we ask for it will be done for us." And to them that means they have to physically touch the person with whom they are agreeing. And while I understand what they mean, I believe it limits the expandable blessing because many of these same believers don't understand there is no distance in the spirit realm. They don't understand that when we agree in the spirit realm, we touch or attach ourselves to whatever we've agreed upon! And it shall be done for them of the Father, who is in heaven. We don't do the work; our heavenly Father does the work (John 14:10 NKJV): "For there is no restraint to the Lord to save by many or by few" (1 Samuel 14:6b KJV).

Many believers lack the faith to simply agree with the prayer for whatever they want without having someone physically touch them. Years ago, I had a couple leave my ministry because I could not physically go to the hospital where the husband was and lay hands on him in prayer. They held to the misconception of Matthew 18:19-20. If I was not there physically, how could I "touch and agree" with them? Religious mindsets such as this have kept many saints from receiving God's best. Prayer is a spiritual act, and there is no distance in the spirit realm.

Anyway, the key to what I want to get across here is that my sister and I agreed our brother-in-law would live and not die and declare the works of the Lord, in accordance with the Word of God. As we prayed in our Holy Spirit language, more and more of the Word of God pertaining to life began to flow out of our spirits. Praying in our Holy Spirit language allows the Holy Spirit to pray for us the will of God when we don't know how to pray as we ought:

> Likewise the Spirit also helps in our weaknesses. For we do not know what we should pray for as we ought, but the Spirit Himself makes intercession for us with groaning which cannot be uttered. Now He who searches the

> hearts knows what the mind of the Spirit is, because He makes intercession for the saints according to the will of God. And we know that all things work together for good to those who love God, to those who are the called according to His purpose. (Romans 8:26–28 NKJV)

It is our heavenly Father who does the work, who causes *all things*, not some things, to work for our spiritual good because we respond in faith to his word. We are confident there is nothing too hard for God. Nothing can happen to us that our heavenly Father can't change for our good, "for with God nothing will be impossible" (Luke 1:37 NKJV).

As my sister and I prayed over the phone, I could hear the ting in the background informing me that someone else was calling. I looked at my cell phone, and it was my sister, whose husband lay dying on the floor in their home.

I ended the call with my other sister, and before I could say anything my older sister began frantically telling me to pray. "I need you to pray right now. My husband is on the floor, and he's not breathing," she kept saying. "Breathe, AJ. Breathe."

Immediately, I began calling AJ's spirit back to his body. Like the apostle Paul, I commanded, "His life is in him" (Acts 20:10 NKJV). I commanded the blood to circulate in his body, "for the life of the flesh is in the blood" (Leviticus 17:11 NKJV). And I did what Moses did: I prayed to see God's glory manifested in AJ's life. "Now therefore, I pray, if I have found grace in Your sight, show me now Your way, that I may know You and that I may find grace in Your sight" (Exodus 33:13 NKJV).

"In the name of Jesus, I command AJ's spirit to return to his physical body right now." My sister was still frantic, but she had the presence of mind to agree with me as I prayed. I asked her after my initial prayer, "Is he breathing? Check and see whether or not he has a pulse." As she was checking, the paramedics arrived and began trying to resuscitate him. I continued to pray, "Father, your word says that if two of us agree as touching anything we ask you will do it for us. In Jesus's name, I call AJ's spirit back into his body. He shall not die, but live and declare the works of the Lord. Show us your glory, Father."

I asked again, "Is he breathing now?"

She answered, "No, he's still not breathing. Breathe, AJ. Breathe."

In that moment, it felt like time stood still. AJ had been lying unconscious for well over five minutes, maybe upward of ten minutes. But I kept praying. Then I heard my sister say, "They've got a pulse."

Immediately, I began to praise God. "Thank you, Lord. There is no restraint to you to save by many or by few." AJ was alive. And the paramedics rushed him to the hospital, where he made a remarkable recovery.

Today he is in his midsixties and praising God through his own ministry blog. "Facts don't change the Word of God; the Word of God changes the facts." The Word of God changed my brother-in-law's dead reality to life—a reality that he lives in to this day. Thank you, Abba Daddy. You're a good God and an awesome Father!

As I look at miracles in the Bible in which the dead were raised to life, I don't recall any of the apostles or prophets panicking as they ministered life to the dead. Paul did not panic after Eutychus, who was overcome by a deep sleep as Paul ministered, fell down from a third-story loft, and was pronounced dead. "But Paul went down, fell on him, and embracing him said, 'Do not trouble yourselves, for his life is in him … And they brought the young man in alive, and they were not a little comforted" (Acts 20:10, 12 NKJV).

The fact or reality was that Eutychus was dead. But God! Paul who had been ministering under the anointing of the Holy Spirit calmly proceeded to command Eutychus's spirit to return to his body. And God honored Paul's faith. God is not a respecter of fear; he is a respecter of faith.

In the case where Peter raised Dorcas from death to life, there was no panic on the apostle's part. The disciples who were in Joppa, where Dorcas lived, heard Peter was in Lydda, a nearby village, and they implored him not to delay to come to them.

> Then Peter arose and went with them. When he had come, they brought him to the upper room. And all the widows stood by him weeping, showing the tunics and garments which Dorcas had made while she was

> with them. But Peter put them all out, and knelt down and prayed. And turning to the body he said, "Tabitha, arise." And she opened her eyes, and when she saw Peter she sat up. Then he gave her his hand and lifted her up; and when he had called the saints and widows, he presented her alive. And it became known throughout all Joppa, and many believed on the Lord. (Acts 9:39–42 NKJV)

Let's face it: Calling those things that do not exist as though they did requires faith in God, his word, and Jesus, the word made flesh. But this is actually what we do when we, believers, proclaim the bad facts or realities in our lives don't change the Word of God; the Word of God changes the bad facts or realities. Before Peter could raise Dorcas to life, he had to get rid of all those who were not in faith. Remember, the widows stood by weeping, showing him the clothes that Dorcas had made while she was alive.

We can learn a lot when we compare Peter's calm approach to raising the dead to Jesus's. We'll see that Peter learned well from Jesus how to calmly remove those who are not in faith out of the immediate environment where the miracle is to take place. Nowhere in scripture do we see Jesus in a panic whenever it came to raising the dead to life. Jesus used his faith, knowing that his Father does the work (John 14:10 NKJV).

After Jesus had returned from Decapolis, where he cast out of a man the evil spirits that called themselves Legion, he was met by a great multitude. And Jairus, one of the rulers of the synagogue, fell at his feet, begging him to lay hands on his little daughter that she might be healed because she was near death.

Jesus started for Jairus's house, and on the way a woman who had suffered from an issue of blood for twelve years heard about him and mixed herself into the crowd and touched his garment: "For she said, 'If only I may touch His clothes, I shall be made well'" (Mark 5:28 NKJV).

This woman's faith was on the line. She wanted to be healed of her infirmity. No doctor could help her. But she heard about Jesus. And suddenly she had opportunity to act on her faith. She spoke out of her mouth, from her spirit, “If I can but touch the hem of His garment, I shall be made whole.” She acted on the word that she knew by faith, and she received her healing. “Daughter, your faith has made you well. Go in peace, and be healed of your affliction” (Mark 5:34 NKJV).

> While He was still speaking, some came from the ruler of the synagogue’s house who said, “Your daughter is dead. Why trouble the Teacher any further?” As soon as Jesus heard the word that was spoken, He said to the ruler of the synagogue, “Do not be afraid; only believe.” And He permitted no one to follow him except Peter, James and John the brother of James. Then He came to the house of the ruler of the synagogue, and saw a tumult and those who wept and wailed loudly. When He came in, He said to them, “Why make this commotion and weep? The child is not dead, but sleeping.” And they ridiculed Him. But when He had put them all outside, He took the father and the mother of the child, and those who were with Him, and entered where the child was lying. Then He took the child by the hand, and said to her, “Talitha, cumi,” which is translated, “Little girl, I say to you, arise.” Immediately the girl arose and walked, for she was twelve years of age. And they were overcome with great amazement. (Mark 5:35–42 NKJV)

Miracles take place in an atmosphere of faith. Peter learned from Jesus to remove those people who were not in faith so that immediately the environment was cleansed of unbelief. Again, there is no restraint to the Lord to save by many or by few. Jesus didn’t take all his disciples with him when he healed Jairus’s daughter, only his inner circle of disciples—those whom he knew had faith in him. Peter had already gotten the revelation that Jesus was the Christ and said, “You are the Christ, the Son of the living God” (Matthew 16:16 NKJV).

When Jesus heard Lazarus was dead, He did not panic. He was not even in a hurry to get to Lazarus. The glory of God was about to be displayed so that many people’s faith would arise, and they’d believe in

Jesus and hear his words concerning the kingdom of heaven as opposed to the kingdom of law, religion, and legalism.

Jesus waited on purpose to go to Lazarus and raise him from the dead. This four-day period between Lazarus's death and Jesus's resurrection of him was sure to be a conclusive act to the naysayers. So, when Jesus heard Lazarus was sick, he said, "This sickness is not unto death, but for the glory of God, that the Son of God may be glorified through it" (John 11:4 NKJV). Jesus said he would be glorified through Lazarus's sickness, death, and resurrection; many more people would believe and receive his teaching on the kingdom. And as Jesus is glorified, God the Father is glorified.

Jesus remained where he was for two more days after he heard Lazarus was sick. Is that not being calm? Even when Jesus informed his disciples that Lazarus was dead, he remained calm. Lazarus was dead. That was his current reality. Jesus said to his disciples, "And I am glad for your sakes that I was not there, that you may believe" (John 11:15 NKJV). Facts don't change the Word of God; the Word of God changes the facts.

When Jesus came to Bethany, Lazarus had already been in the tomb four days. Martha, one of the sisters of Lazarus, heard that Jesus was coming and went out to meet him. Martha represents those who are not in faith. Remember, whenever two touch as agreeing to anything, it is done of our Father who is in heaven. Jesus had to use his faith. He had to know who he was in and through his Father. Jesus needed someone from Lazarus's family to stand in agreement with him that Lazarus would be raised from the dead.

Martha sounded very religious. "Lord if You had been here, my brother would not have died. But even now I know that whatever You ask of God, God will give You. Jesus said to her, 'Your brother will rise again'" (John 11:21–23 NKJV). Many times the Holy Spirit will give us a rhema, and if we're not Holy Spirit conscious we'll miss it.

In our context, Jesus gave Martha a rhema—a prophetic word of revelation from God himself—"Your brother will rise again" (John 11:23 NKJV), and she missed it. She couldn't grasp it. Could it be that her personality was stronger than her relationship with the word made flesh? We'll see how Martha's lack of faith gave way to Mary's genuine faith. Could it be that Mary had the presence of the word in her inner spirit—that good part that Jesus refused to take from her?

> Martha said to Him, I know that he will rise again in the resurrection at the last day. Jesus said to her, "I am the resurrection and the life. He who believes in Me, though he may die, he shall live. And whoever lives and believes in Me shall never die. Do you believe this? She said to Him, "Yes, Lord, I believe that You are the Christ, the Son of God, who is to come into the world." (John 11:24–27 NKJV)

Martha says that she believes Jesus is the Christ. She did not say she believed he is the resurrection. Martha did not have faith in Jesus as "The Resurrection", and her reality remained the same.

Enter Mary, who sat at Jesus's feet and heard his words. When she ran to where Jesus was, she fell down at his feet. Mary worshipped Jesus—something Martha did not do. I believe Mary's worship is because of her relationship. Jesus needs her faith to agree with his faith that Lazarus will be raised from the dead. Mary's worship was a faith agreement with the word.

Notice in this next discourse that Martha still doesn't get it. But Jesus remains true to his nature! "Jesus said, 'Take away the stone.' Martha, the sister of him who was dead, said to Him, 'Lord, by this time there is a stench, for he has been dead four days.' Jesus said to her, 'Did I not say to you that if you would believe you would see the glory of God?'" (John 11:39–40 NKJV).

In the next verses, Jesus affirms his faith in who he is but prays to his Father because of the people—that they may believe. Their belief in Jesus and their obedience to his words would transform their mindsets from religion and legalism to kingdom—grace and truth. Remember, Lazarus's sickness, his death, and his resurrection would bring glory to Jesus.

> Jesus lifted up His eyes and said, "Father, I thank You that You have heard Me. And I know that You always hear Me, but because of the people who are standing by

> I said this, that they may believe that You sent Me. Now when He had said these things, He cried with a loud voice, "Lazarus, come forth! And he who had died came out bound hand and foot with graveclothes, and his face was wrapped with a cloth. Jesus said to them, "Loose him, and let him go." (John 11:41–44 NKJV)

Sitting at Jesus's feet and hearing his words made all the difference between whether or not Lazarus would remain dead or be raised from the dead. It's about relationship. God and his word are one. We can't have the one without the other.

It is the same for believers today. When we obey and serve God according to his word, we activate the promises of God. We glorify him, and his glory is seen in our lives so that our profiting may appear unto all (1 Timothy 4:15 NKJV).

Jesus was constantly faced with the reality of bad news. But he used his faith to heal, deliver, set free, to perform miracles, and to raise the dead. Like Jesus, we, too, must use our faith in the Word of God, which contains his promises to us, and know that it is our heavenly Father who does the work. Jesus said, "Most assuredly, I say to you, he who believes in Me, the works that I do he will do also; and greater works than these he will do, because I go to My Father" (John 14:12 NKJV).

We are here on earth, in Jesus's stead, to do the will of our heavenly Father, who called those things that are not as though they were. The Word of God is ours by covenant. As citizens of the kingdom of heaven, our benefits include the promises of God that are "yes" in him and "amen" in him. When we speak the Word of God that we know by faith—apply the Word of God to our bad situation or bad news—and trust our heavenly Father to do the work, we, too, can stand firm and calm even in turbulent times. We'll simply speak to the mountain and tell it to be removed. When we pray, we'll believe that we have received already what we asked for (Mark 11:22–24 NKJV), knowing that "facts don't change the Word of God; the Word of God changes the facts.

Calling things that do not exist as though they did (Romans 4:17 NKJV) is a Holy Spirit wavelength that transmits the frequency of heaven to earth. Stay tuned-in!

CHAPTER 9

Enjoy the Benefits of the Kingdom

Blessed be the Lord, Who daily loads us with benefits, The God of our salvation! Selah.

—Psalm 68:19 NKJV

Living the kingdom life is about enjoying the benefits of the kingdom, and the benefits of the kingdom are commensurate with the wealth and benevolence of the King. "For by Him all things were created that are in heaven and that are on earth, visible and invisible, whether thrones or dominions or principalities or powers. All things were created through Him and for Him. And He is before all things, and in Him all things consist … that in all things He may have preeminence" (Colossians 1:16–18 NKJV).

I'd say that's pretty clear. Our King, Savior and Lord, Jesus Christ, has preeminence in all things! As our King, Jesus's disposition is to do what's good; to show charitable kindness as a selfless gift or act. It is the King's nature to daily load the citizens of his kingdom with benefits that are inclusive in our salvation. These benefits are the promises that are "yes" and "amen" in him. We simply receive or take the benefits by faith, which brings glory to God. Indeed, God is a good God and an awesome Father!

Saints of God, citizens of the kingdom of heaven, need to learn the amazing power of gratitude—the state of being grateful, appreciative, and thankful. But many times believers find themselves disgruntled, displeased, and in a mental state of ingratitude. I think this is largely due to the fact that they're not satisfied with their lives. They think, "I should be further along in life by now," "I should be a millionaire by now," or "I should have substantially more than I have now." They become complainers instead of being joyful. What they are really saying is that they don't think that God has done enough for them; and their dissatisfaction is a result of their anger toward God.

The sad plight of many believers is that they trade the benefits of the kingdom for the hustle and bustle of the benefits their country affords them, as if the benefits the world affords them outweigh, supersede, or have greater value than the benefits of the kingdom. But there is a monumental difference between the two. The benefits of the kingdom are given; they are a free gift of the King. When believers live in the world as if they are of the world, they are forced to adhere to the evil systems of the world through their pursuit of what the world offers.

Instead of seeking first the kingdom of God and his righteous so that all things are added to them, they seek first the wealth of the world through work, credit, debt, and many other ungodly channels. Through these channels they give up their dignity and become slaves to an evil system, instead of citizens of the kingdom of God who enjoy to the full the prosperity and pleasures that are theirs because of the King's benevolence.

> *Therefore do not be like them. For your Father knows the things you have need of before you ask Him.*
>
> **—Matthew 6:8 NKJV**

Believers who find themselves in this worldly rut should seek the kingdom of God first. Remember, the word *seek* in that text means to worship. They must humble themselves in reverent worship to the Creator and Sustainer of the universe, Father Yahweh, first, and he will bring honor to them in the earth. His honor is his glory, which reflects the depth of his wisdom and riches bestowed upon his children. And in turn, bring glory to God.

> *By humility and the fear of the Lord Are riches and honor and life.*
>
> **—Proverbs 22:4 NKJV**

Our heavenly Father knows what we need before we ask, and he has already given us richly all things to enjoy (1 Timothy 6:17 NKJV). It is his good pleasure to give us the kingdom (Luke 12:32 NKJV). What we should ask Father is, "What shall I give you in return for all of your benefits to me?"

We should learn to love the Lord for who he is and what he has done. The Lord is gracious to us, and we should walk before him each day with an attitude of gratitude.

> *What shall I render to the Lord for all His benefits toward me? I will take up the cup of salvation, and call upon the name of the Lord. I will pay my vows to the Lord now in the presence of all His people.*
>
> **—Psalm 116:12–14 NKJV**

Believers need to live by faith, trusting God's faithfulness to his word, and live in obedience to his word. Our life before God should be an expression of our gratitude toward him through genuine praise and worship. We should be grateful to our heavenly Father now, reflecting his character in the presence of all people. Our gratitude is what we should render to the Lord for all his benefits toward us. In doing so, we get to enjoy life—to obtain his best life for us while we live in the world which, of course, is what the "blessing covenant" is all about.

What does it mean to enjoy the benefits of the kingdom of God?

The Greek word used for *enjoy* is *apolausis*, which denotes full enjoyment; completion.[47] It also means to take hold of, enjoy a thing; it suggests the advantage or pleasure to be obtained from a thing unto enjoyment; to enjoy the pleasures.

[47] *Strong's Exhaustive Concordance of the Bible, NT*, 619.

Enjoy means to receive pleasure or satisfaction from something; to have the use or benefit of something; to be satisfied or receive pleasure; appreciate, delight in, rejoice, relish.

King Solomon knew a thing or two about enjoyment of the benefits of a king since he was a king—the richest who ever lived! Solomon learned that life lived without regard for God is of no value; it is indeed vanity (emptiness), a lifestyle void of humility and gratitude toward God.

Jewish tradition alleges that Solomon wrote Song of Solomon in his youthful manhood, Proverbs in his middle years and Ecclesiastes in his golden years. I can agree with this since Ecclesiastes seems to express regret for his foolishness and wasted time, due to his pursuit of carnal and idolatrous things and people, especially his lust for women and his worship of idols (1 Kings 11 NKJV).

Anyone who begins writing a book with the words, "Vanity of vanities, all is vanity" (Ecclesiastesl:2 NKJV) has probably got some regrets he or she wants to resolve prior to their death. And I believe this was the case with King Solomon, since he concluded in the last chapter of Ecclesiastes that the "good life" is only attained by revering God.

He goes on to warn that those who fail or refuse to take God's will for their lives seriously, along with obeying his word, are doomed to live foolishly and in futility. Solomon asserts that life does not wait on the solution to all its problems; nevertheless, true meaning can be found by looking beyond the material things of the earth to the Great Shepherd of men's souls, who gives us enjoyment of the benefits of His kingdoms—heaven and earth—since "The kingdoms of this world have become the kingdoms of our Lord and of His Christ, and he shall reign forever and ever!" (Revelation 11:15 NKJV).

I'm sure we can learn a lot from Solomon, who "did it all," yet his wisdom remained with him.

> *So I became great and excelled more than all who were before me in Jerusalem. Also my wisdom remained with me. [10]Whatever my eyes desired I did not keep from them. I did not withhold my heart from any pleasure, For my heart rejoiced in all my labor; And this was my reward from all my labor.*
>
> **—Ecclesiastes 2:9–10 NKJV**

> *So I perceived that nothing is better than that a man should rejoice in his own works, for that is his heritage. For who can bring him to see what will happen after him?*
>
> **—Ecclesiastes 3:22 NKJV**

> *For who can eat, or who can have enjoyment, more than I?*
>
> **—Ecclesiastes 2:25 NKJV**

To the unregenerated mind, it would seem that Solomon sends mixed messages at times about life and the enjoyment thereof. He talks about the vanity of pursuing pleasure, the vanity of great accomplishments, and the vanity of hard labor, yet he says it is the gift of God. But believers, especially spiritually mature ones, have a revelation of what Solomon is referring to. And that is, God has predetermined our lives, the events of our lives and the conditions of our life; all our labors cannot change them. So instead of stressing over these limits, we should find the real joy and beauty that exist in and through our personal relationship with him. "He has made everything beautiful in its time … no one can find out the work that God does from beginning to end. I know that nothing is better for them than to rejoice, and to do good in their lives, and also that every man should eat and drink and enjoy the good of all his labor – it is the gift of God (Ecclesiastes 3:11–13 NKJV).

We will never fully understand the works of God or how God works. Only God knows all things from beginning to end. And as pertaining to our life, he knows the end from the beginning, declaring from ancient times things that are not yet done and assuring us that his counsel will stand, and he will do all his pleasure (Isaiah 46:10 NKJV).

God's counsel, His decisions for us and the world we live in, stand sure and complete. He has opened wide the door that will lead men to reverence and worship him, which is the basis for the proper approach to life and its enjoyment.

Like King Solomon, believers must learn to be content—not as in being satisfied with little or a poor lot in life but rather be content to know that God our Creator has everything under control. And no matter what happens in the world, how awful it becomes, nothing can keep true kingdom citizens from enjoying the benefits of the kingdom. We say like Solomon, "Nothing is better for a man than that he should eat and drink, and that his soul should enjoy good in his labor. This also, I saw, was from the hand of God" (Ecclesiastes 2:24 NKJV).

> *Here is what I have seen: It is good and fitting for one to eat and drink, and to enjoy the good of all his labor in which he toils under the sun all the days of his life which God gives him; for it is his heritage.*
>
> **—Ecclesiastes 5:18 NKJV**

God has purposefully blessed us already. As we walk in faith and obedience to his word, we enjoy the benefits of the kingdom. When believers fail or refuse to seek first the kingdom of God and his righteousness, they end up trying to help God bless them; or worse, they beg God for what is already available to them—all spiritual blessings in heavenly places in Christ (Ephesians 1:3 NKJV); all things that pertain to life and godliness (2 Peter 1:3 NKJV); richly all things to enjoy (1 Timothy 6:17 NKJV). We must understand that when we do things God's way we inherit the promises through faith and patience (Hebrews 6:12 NKJV). The covenant of blessings is sure, sworn by God himself.

The benefits of the kingdom of heaven are our heavenly Father's gifts to us—his children—those whom he knows to be his through surrender and willingness to allow the Holy Spirit to lead us into the wilderness of this evil world, where we defeat the devil with the Word of God; then we come out of the wilderness full of the Holy Spirit and power. "How God anointed Jesus of Nazareth with the Holy Spirit and with power, who went about doing good and healing all who were oppressed by the devil, for God was with Him" (Acts 10:38 NKJV).

Wherever we go, we should live a full and prosperous life, enjoying the benefits of the kingdom—the bountiful provision of beauty, welfare, health, prosperity, pleasure, security, and long life—so that all goes well for us.

HE DAILY LOADS US WITH BENEFITS

There is great joy in worshipping and praising God from a spirit of gratitude. This is one of those consistent qualities in my life that unleash the power of God, his spirit, as I meditate on the benefits of the kingdom

I'm daily loaded with. It's like each day Abba Daddy saturates me with a large quantity of his best gifts. Like me, many believers enjoy the daily "load" we carry.

> *Every good gift and every perfect gift is from above, and comes down from the Father of lights, with whom there is no variation or shadow of turning. Of His own will He brought us forth by the word of truth, that we might be a kind of first fruits of His creatures.*
>
> **—James 1:17–18 NKJV**

His good and perfect gifts are a display of his beneficence through which he pours out liberally, gratuitously and in kindness to those sons and daughters who trust him—a result of our complete, absolute, uncompromising trust in God. Trust in God and obedience to his word is God's process of raising our spiritual rank, our spiritual growth, so that we can produce fruit that remain. The result is that many people will believe in Christ Jesus because of our faithful life testimonies.

The Hebrew word used for *benefits* is *g^{e}muwl*, taken from its root word *gamal*, which means an act of good; service, benefit, that which he hath given, recompense, reward; to treat a person well, bestow on, deal bountifully with, do good, requite, yield.[48]

The Greek word is *charis* taken from *charizomai* and denotes the divine influence upon the heart, and its reflection in the life; gratitude; acceptable, favor, gift, grace, joy, liberality, pleasure, thankworthy; to grant as a favor, gratuitously, in kindness, pardon or rescue; deliver, forgive, freely give, grant.[49]

A *benefit* is an advantage; help or aid from something; beneficence; liberality.

All three definitions describe benefits as something freely given, a service; something done bountifully; something that treats people well; an advantage or aid; a bestowal of liberality. Notice that these are all 'acts of good' given in kindness. Since God's nature is only good, the benefits that he bestows upon his kingdom citizens can only be good; and since his kingdom is an everlasting kingdom and his dominion is

[48] *Strong's Exhaustive Concordance of the Bible, OT,* 1576, 1580.

[49] *Strong's Exhaustive Concordance of the Bible, NT,* 5485, 5483.

from generation to generation (Daniel 4:3 NKJV), the benefits of his kingdom are also everlasting to all generations.

In other words, the benefits of the kingdom of heaven continuously replicate themselves in greater measure, opening wide the doors of heavens treasury to its citizens for life and that more abundantly.

Psalm 103, verses 1 through 5, give believers an extraordinary illumination of the benefits that are available to every believer:

> Bless the Lord, O my soul; and all that is within me, bless His holy name! Bless the Lord, O my soul, and forget not all His benefits: Who forgives all your iniquities, who heals all your diseases, Who redeems your life from destruction, who crowns you with lovingkindness and tender mercies, Who satisfies your mouth with good things, so that your youth is renewed like the eagle's. (Psalm 103:1–5 NKJV)

Wow! How awesome is that? When a believer reads this through the eyes of the Holy Spirit, he or she realizes their welfare is secure. These benefits of the kingdom of heaven are the promises of God to which he's already said yes. The kingdoms of this world do not come close to measuring up to the level and expanse of benefits and standard of life available to kingdom citizens nor can they. Kingdom benefits are both spiritual and physical—heaven on earth and the best of both realms.

To believe, receive, and act on these benefits require a kingdom mindset as opposed to a religious mindset. What country or kingdom of this world can promise that our sins are forgiven? Just the opposite—the systems of the world are designed through legislation to condemn and sentence us for our iniquities. "Who Himself bore our sins in His own body on the tree, that we, having died to sins, might live for righteousness – by whose stripes you were healed" (1 Peter 2:24 NKJV).

What country or kingdom of this world can promise that we're healed from all our diseases? Just the opposite—the systems of the world are designed through legislation to provide health care at exorbitant costs, rendering no health care to millions of people who cannot afford it. As a result many suffer for most of their lives, and some die from lack of medical treatment. "He Himself took our infirmities and bore our sicknesses" (Matthew 8:17 NKJV).

What country or kingdom of this world promises to redeem our lives from destruction? Just the opposite—the systems of the world are designed to plow us into more and more debt, which at the very least ends up destroying us and relegating us to a subpar life of being stuck in a rut. Through faith in Jesus Christ, citizens of the kingdom of heaven are redeemed from the curse of sin, sickness, disease, poverty, lack, and debt! Jesus has been made a curse for us (Galatians 3:13–14 NKJV).

What country or kingdom of this world promises to crown us with loving kindness and tender mercies? Just the opposite—the systems of the world are designed to enslave, promote, project, and enact hate-related treatment toward our fellow humans. Jesus's commandment is that we love one another (John 15:12 NKJV) and esteem others higher or better than ourselves (Romans 12:3, 15 NKJV).

> *Yes, I have loved you with an everlasting love; therefore with lovingkindness I have drawn you.*
>
> **—Jeremiah 31:3 NKJV**

> *Let Your tender mercies come to me, that I may live; for Your law is my delight.*
>
> **—Psalm 119:77 NKJV**

What country or kingdom of this world promises to satisfy us with good things? Just the opposite—the systems of the world are designed to give us just enough to get by, and those who never learn how to play the game of life from a physical, intellectual perspective end up losing.

In the kingdom, it is our mouth that makes us thrive. As we study the Word of God consistently, it becomes a seed planted and rooted in our heart that grows and matures, then sprouts out of our mouth as new growth that produces good things—abundant harvests. Whatever good thing we desire, we speak by faith in alignment with the specific promise God made for that thing.

The Word of God works by that same principle. There's miraculous power within it. It is a seed that, once planted by faith in a human heart, will produce more blessings than we can imagine. The Word of God is a seed. That's the kingdom way (Mark 4:26–32 NKJV).

> *A man will be satisfied with good by the fruit of his mouth.*
>
> **—Proverbs 12:14 NKJV**

> *Death and life are in the power of the tongue, and those who love it will eat its fruit.*
>
> **—Proverbs 18:21 NKJV**

> *And He said to me, "Son of man, feed your belly, and fill your stomach with this scroll that I give you." So I ate, and it was in my mouth like honey in sweetness.*
>
> **—Ezekiel 3:3 NKJV**

> *I am the Lord your God, Who brought you out of the land of Egypt; Open your mouth wide, and I will fill it.*
>
> **—Psalm 81:10 NKJV**

What country or kingdom of this world promises to renew our youth like the eagle's? Just the opposite—the systems of the world are designed to wear out the saints (Daniel 7:25 NKJV) because Satan is the ruler of this world (John 12:32; John 14:30 NKJV). "But those who wait on the Lord Shall renew their strength; They shall mount up with wings like eagles, They shall run and not be weary, They shall walk and not faint" (Isaiah 40:31 NKJV).

> *He causes the grass to grow for the cattle, and vegetation for the service of man, That he may bring forth food from the earth, And wine that makes glad the heart of man, Oil to make his face shine, And bread which strengthens man's heart.*
>
> **—Psalm 104:14–15 NKJV**

Whose benefits would we rather have? The benefits of the kingdom of heaven, that are promised and backed by a covenant signed by God himself, or the lack of benefits which are sure to pressure us into submission to the evil systems of this world? "No man can serve two masters; for either he will hate the one and love the other, or else he will be loyal to the one and despise the other. You cannot serve God and mammon" (Matthew 6:24 NKJV).

Mammon's economy—the trust in money over trust in God—holds people hostage to what they want and desire but cannot have, while the economy of the kingdom frees believers from fear and worry about money. It looks at life as one of abundance because we are fixated on the king and his wealth. And in him, through the benefits—the promises of God—we have everything we will ever need, in addition to so much more. We are blessed to be a blessing! That, too, is one of the benefits believers can rely on as we stand firm in our faith in God's Word, giving it first place and final authority.

Enjoyment of the benefits of the kingdom is a Holy Spirit wavelength that transmits the frequency of heaven to earth. Stay tuned-in!

CHAPTER 10

The Frequency of Heaven

If then you were raised with Christ, seek those things which are above, where Christ is, sitting at the right hand of God. Set your mind on things above, not on things on the earth.

—Colossians 3:1–2 NKJV

I begin this chapter by saying that I am not a quantum physicist. There are many people who, when they hear the word *frequency*, automatically think physics. But the physics side of frequency is not what this chapter is about. It is about how conscious we are of who God is and who we are in him. It is about being eternally minded so as to be in constant communication with God by our faith in his word, through our oneness, our relationship with Jesus, our faith in his name, and our relationship with the Holy Spirit—my most treasured friend—as a person.

This frequency is about being God conscious, Christ centered, and Holy Spirit focused as our point of reference in all things. It is about how often you and I are conscious of our oneness with God and the regularity in which we meditate on those things which are above where

Christ is. It's about the repetition, constancy, and persistence in which we seek heaven's operation manual as opposed to how often we set our minds on things on the earth.

If we are to pray, as Jesus taught his disciples, "Thy will be done in earth, as it is in heaven" (Matthew 6:10, KJV), then it stands to reason that we should know what God's will in heaven is before we can replicate it on earth. But we have an age-old problem to deal with before we can truly align ourselves with the will of God in heaven: we must understand how to transport heaven to earth and earth to heaven. After all, God has blessed us with every kind of spiritual blessing in the heavenly places in Christ (Ephesians 1:3 NKJV).

The Father has chosen us in him before the foundation of the world to have access to every kind of spiritual blessing—all things that pertain to life and godliness in the unseen realm of spiritual realities in which believers have life abundantly and receive grace from our Apostle and High Priest, Christ Jesus.

In other words, when believers worship God and praise him for who he is, and for his blessings to us, we have access to every kind of spiritual blessing—the promises of God. Some things that believers ask for are not necessarily spiritual; some are actually carnal. Many times we ask amiss or out of wrong motives that are not in alignment with his promises. Remember, our heavenly Father knows what we have need of before we ask. "You ask and do not receive, because you ask amiss, that you may spend it on your pleasures" (James 4:3 NKJV).

When believers ask God for things of this world with the intent of spending or using them for the expression of their lustful pleasures, they become adulterers and adulteresses. Lack of devotion to God is called adultery, and those believers who do so are unfaithful to God and a friend of the world, which makes them enemies of God (James 4:4 NKJV).

But when believers ask something of our heavenly Father by faith, out of a right motive, and in alignment with his promises, we know we have what we asked of him, and we praise God for another spiritual blessing manifested in our physical hands (1 John 5:14–15 NKJV).

What is a spiritual blessing?

The Greek words used for *spiritual* are *pneumatikos* taken from *pneuma* and comparative to *psuchikos* from *psuche*, which taken together means noncarnal—that is, (humanly) ethereal; (divinely) supernatural; (the human spirit) the rational immortal soul; the higher renovated, regenerated nature; (superhuman) an angel; (divine) God, Christ's spirit, the Holy Spirit, as opposed to the lower, natural, sensual bestial nature.[50]

Blessing is the Greek word *eulogia*, taken from *eulogeo*, which mean benefit or largess; something freely given; a gift: a matter of bounty; to speak well of, to bless; prosper; bless, praise.[51]

Pneumatikos eulogia (spiritual blessing), then, refers to the supernatural, noncarnal gifts and benefits that are ethereal—heavenly, celestial—bountiful blessings specifically for those whose inner spirit has been regenerated by Holy Spirit, whose human spirit—spirit and soul—has merged in a rhythm that prospers and speaks well of them to the praise of God, which blessings are manifested to us by angels because we are heirs of salvation.

This is the complete opposite of our lower, natural, and sensual nature, which is what we unleash when we strive and pray to acquire things through the lust of our flesh, to spend and consume on our pleasures, and then ask God to bless them.

> *Beloved, I pray that you may prosper in all things and be in health, just as your soul prospers.*
>
> **—3 John 2 NKJV**

> *Are they not all ministering spirits sent forth to minister for those who will inherit salvation?*
>
> **—Hebrews 1:14 NKJV**

> *Bless the Lord, you His angels, Who excel in strength, who do His word, Heeding the voice of His word. Bless the Lord, all you His hosts, You ministers of His, who do His pleasure.*
>
> **—Psalm 103:20–21 NKJV**

Spirit and soul work together through regeneration. That's why believers, especially new believers, should feed their newly regenerated spirit a consistent diet of the Word of God. Feeding on the Word of God is nutrition to our spirit like food is to our natural man. If we don't eat

---

[50] *Strong's Exhaustive Concordance of the Bible, NT,* 4152, 4151, 5591, 5590.

[51] *Strong's Exhaustive Concordance of the Bible, NT,* 2129, 2127.

consistently in the natural, our physical body will get weak. The same process takes place when our spirit is not fed with the Word of God.

> *Whoever drinks of the water that I shall give him will never thirst. But the water that I shall give him will become in him a fountain of water springing up into everlasting life.*
>
> **—John 4:14 NKJV**

> *He who believes in Me, as the Scripture has said, out of his heart will flow rivers of living water.*
>
> **—John 7:38 NKJV**

Too many Christians are deceived by their soul—mind, will, emotions, and intellect—when they allow religion and legalism to yoke them in the bondage of self-righteousness and pride, not knowing that their soul is their partner in success when properly joined with their spirit. Spirit and soul are very closely related, yet each has its own agenda. Only the Word of God can distinguish the two (Hebrews 4:12 NKJV).

Let's compare spirit and soul in the context of kingdom and religion, respectively. Our spirit represents God and his kingdom of righteousness, while our soul represents our carnal mind bent on the evil systems of the world. But whenever our minds are renewed by the Word of God, our soul is regenerated and can "move in" with our spirit. Together, spirit and soul engage heaven and earth at the same time, confirming that believers live in both the spiritual realm and the natural realm at the same time. Sadly, many Christians have never gotten a revelation of that fact.

Scripture proves that Jesus was on earth and in heaven at the same time. Scripture also proves that those who are born again live on earth and in heaven at the same time:

> If I have told you earthly things and you do not believe, how will you believe if I tell you heavenly things? No one has ascended to heaven but He who came down from heaven, that is, the Son of Man who is in heaven. (John 3:12–13 NKJV)

> But God, who is rich in mercy, because of His great love with which He loved us, even when we were dead in trespasses, made us alive together with Christ (by grace you have been saved), and raised us up together, and made us sit together in the heavenly places in Christ Jesus. (Ephesians 2:4–6 NKJV)

In Jesus, believers have access to all of heaven here on earth because we are one spirit with him (1 Corinthians 6:17 NKJV). All authority has been given to Jesus in heaven and on earth (Matthew 28:18 NKJV). Therefore, in Jesus, believers are immersed, concealed, and smeared with his anointing—the Spirit of Christ. This is our spiritual position in right standing with God.

Frequency is the number of occurrences of a repeating event per unit of time. For example, if a newborn baby's heart beats at a frequency of 120 times per minute, its period—the time interval between beats—is half a second—sixty seconds divided by 120 beats.

Frequency is the state or fact of being frequent—frequent occurrence or rate of occurrence. For example, the doctor has increased the frequency of his visits.

Let's define frequency again from the perspective of how it is to be used in accordance with the theme of this book. I like to think of frequency as being God conscious, Christ centered, and Holy Spirit focused—the ability to access a sustainable, regular, or consistent mind filled with God's Word, God thoughts, and meditation on the word and the goodness of God; a mind at peace knowing that we have "access on demand" to the wisdom and power of God in "supernatural high definition."

> *You will keep him in perfect peace, Whose mind is stayed on You, Because he trusts in You.*
>
> **—Isaiah 26:3 NKJV**

I could easily frame the above verse to read: Abba Daddy keeps me in perfect peace because my mind stays tuned-in to his frequency.

When I was a boy in church, I remember the old saints singing a song that said, "I woke up this morning with my mind stayed on Jesus." Well, that is exactly the point I'm trying to convey here. How often are we conscious of God, Jesus, the Holy Spirit, and the Word of God? How often is our mind fixed on Jesus? Do we wake up every morning with our mind focused on Jesus? When we wake up each morning, are we conscious of God, prayer, worship, thanksgiving?

Let's take notice of how King David stayed God conscious—how he thirsted for God. In spite of all his faults, David knew how to stay tuned-in to heaven's frequency:

> O God, You are my God; Early will I seek You; My soul thirsts for You; My flesh longs for You In a dry and thirsty land Where there is no water. [2]So I have looked for You in the sanctuary, To see Your power and Your glory. (Psalm 63:1–2 NKJV)
>
> As the deer pants for the water brooks, So pants my soul for You, O God. My soul thirsts for God, for the living God. When shall I come and appear before God? (Psalm 42:1–2 NKJV)

Notice that David says, "You are my God" (Psalm 63:1 NKJV). How personal is that? Staying tuned-in to the frequency of heaven begins with relationship. God is found by those who seek him. He satisfies those who are spiritually thirsty. Those who worship him in spirit and in truth discover and experience his power and his glory. David exemplified a man whose mind was focused on God—his God!

For believers, frequenting heaven should be common or customary. Believers who are astute frequent heaven all the time, since we are already there and have the mind of Christ (1Corinthians 2:16 NKJV) on the earth. Again, we live in two realms simultaneously: heaven and earth.

Our problem as believers is that we are not consistent to keep our minds fixed on Jesus. The things of this world—the lust of the flesh, the lust of the eyes, and the pride of life (1 John 2:16 NKJV) seem to slip in more often than we would like to admit. The writer of The Epistle to the Hebrews warns us of the danger of neglect: "Therefore we must give the more earnest heed [all the more careful attention] to the things we have heard, lest we drift away" (Hebrews 2:1 NKJV).

> *But each one is tempted when he is drawn away by his own desires and enticed. [15]Then, when desire has conceived, it gives birth to sin; and sin, when it is full-grown, brings forth death. [16]Do not be deceived, my beloved brethren.*
>
> **—James 1:14–16**

This is why believers must be God conscious, Christ centered, and Holy Spirit focused at all times. And this is not difficult when the Word of God has been sown or planted in our heart. It has taken root and grown down—fully saturating our spirit—before it grows up and, as a spring, produces living water—revelatory knowledge of the Word of God via the Holy Spirit.

The Holy Spirit is the teacher of the Word of God, and he searches all things, even the deep things of God (1 Corinthians 2:10 NKJV). My desire for and my invitation to the Holy Spirit to release the deep things of God into my spirit makes my spirit vibrate as if it were sending out wavelengths and sound waves that attract the deep things of God—a rhythmic repetition of Holy Spirit revelation that expands my spiritual bandwidth, what things are on God's heart and mind.

I consistently ask the Holy Spirit to fill my spirit with those deep things of God. As believers, we can go as deep into God as our faith will take us. But some believers are afraid of the deep—the realm of their true identity—spirit! The thirsty soul does not sit around waiting for someone to provide answers when he can know all things in God by inviting the Holy Spirit to "take him there" and release into his spirit the mind of God. It is our spirit who knows everything relative to who we are in and through God. Our spirit understands our true identity in Christ. Likewise, no one knows the things of God except the Spirit of God (1 Corinthians 2:11 NKJV).

WHAT BELIEVERS TEND TO MISS CONCERNING HOLY SPIRIT

In the previous nine chapters, I've used the Holy Spirit rather than Holy Spirit, as such is the case in the scriptures; however, for me, Holy Spirit personalizes my relationship with him as my most treasured best friend.

Holy Spirit is not a thing or an "it." His presence is evidence that he is a person who will teach us all things (John 14:26 NKJV), which means he is a mentor. Whether or not we refer to God's Spirit as the Holy Spirit or Holy Spirit is our choice. What matters is that he is or becomes our best friend on earth.

I like to think of Holy Spirit as the satellite of heaven in the earth. Holy Spirit is the power of God, his word initiated on earth. He is the supercharge of God in the earth who searches the deep things of God and beams them from heaven into man's regenerated spirit here on earth. It is the faith of the believer who is Holy Spirit conscious that locates and tunes in to his frequency consistently. Faith plugs in to the Holy Spirit and releases his power.

Staying tuned-in to the frequency of heaven via Holy Spirit is the key to receiving from heaven and living our best life here on earth. The more we nourish and develop our relationship with Holy Spirit, the easier it becomes to tune-in to the clarity of his still, small voice. And when we hear the voice of God clearly, it becomes easier to heed the wisdom or instruction of God by faith. It becomes easier to say no to the devil and yes to God's Word, which separates us from the world and locks us in to His truth.

> *I still have many things to say to you but you cannot bear them now. However, when He, the Spirit of truth, has come, He will guide you into all truth; for He will not speak on His own authority, but whatever He hears He will speak; and He will tell you things to come. He will glorify Me, for He will take of what is Mine and declare it to you.*
>
> **—John 16:12–14 NKJV**

Many believers fall into the category of not being able to hear or bear the many things Jesus still has to say to them. It seems that their spiritual antennas are down and not functioning; therefore, instead of being tuned-in to the frequency of heaven via Holy Spirit, they do not receive the things to come—all truth—that Jesus sends Holy Spirit to guide them into.

What I'm saying is that they are not very mature, spiritually. Believers who are spiritually mature walk by the Spirit and his fruit is manifested in and through their lifestyle as godly character. A believer's love walk and faith walk will generally speak volumes as to whether or not he or she is spiritually mature, since faith works by love. This is a major distinction between spiritually mature saints and the lack of spiritual maturity often seen in the lives of baby Christians. Spiritual maturity is a process, and Holy Spirit plays a major role in its development.

What is the role of Holy Spirit in the life of the believer to assist with the maturation process?

It is Holy Spirit who leads us into sonship and who makes us Christlike. He glorifies Christ by bringing to our remembrance what he taught; this gives believers a deeper appreciation for Holy Spirit and his work, his divine attributes; his distinct personality in the Godhead; his operation in connection with the Lord Jesus and his birth, his life, baptism, and his death; his operations in the world; in the church; his having been sent at Pentecost by the Father and by Christ; his operations in the individual believer; in local churches; his operations in the production of Holy Scripture; his work in the world.[52]

In the scripture above, Jesus said, "I still have many things to say to you but you cannot bear them now" (John 16:12 NKJV). I believe Jesus wanted to release much more revelation to his disciples, but they couldn't handle it. Likewise, the Spirit of Truth, who resides in our spirit, provides the believer a consistent flow of rhema, revelatory knowledge from heaven that he wants to channel into our inner being, but many are not tuned-in to his frequency.

Why does it seem to be difficult for believers to hear what Jesus, via Holy Spirit, has to say to us? I believe the apostle Paul can answer that question for us:

> And I, brethren, could not speak to you as to spiritual people but as to carnal, as to babes in Christ. I fed you

[52] *Expository Dictionary of New Testament Words: A Comprehensive Dictionary of the Original Greek Words with Their Precise Meanings for English Readers.*

> with milk and not with solid food; for until now you were not able to receive it, and even now you are still not able; for you are still carnal. For where there are envy, strife, and divisions among you, are you not carnal and behaving like mere men? For when one says, "I am of Paul," and another, "I am of Apollos," are you not carnal? (1 Corinthians 3:1–4 NKJV)

Notice that the apostle Paul basically says to the believers at Corinth the same thing that Jesus said to his disciples prior to his crucifixion. Paul implies that the saints at Corinth were not fully spiritual, because they were not living in obedience to the Holy Spirit. Therefore, it was impossible for them to receive the things of God. Even though they knew Christ, they still lived in envy, strife, and divisions because their minds were carnal.

"According to the Scriptures, the 'spiritual' state of soul is normal for the believer, but to this state all believers do not attain, nor when it is attained is it always maintained. Thus, the apostle Paul suggests a contrast between the spiritual state and that of the babe in Christ among the believers at Corinth, i.e., of the man who because of immaturity and inexperience has not yet reached spirituality, and that of the man who by permitting jealousy, and the strife to which jealousy always leads, has lost it. The spiritual state is reached by diligence in the Word of God and in prayer; it is maintained by obedience and self-judgment. Such as are led by the Spirit are spiritual, but, of course, spirituality is not a fixed or absolute condition, it admits of growth; indeed growth in 'the grace and knowledge of our Lord and Savior Jesus Christ,' (2 Peter 3:18), is evidence of true spirituality."[53]

> *For those who live according to the flesh set their minds on the things of the flesh, but those who live according to the Spirit, the things of the Spirit. For to be carnally minded is death, but to be spiritually minded is life and peace. Because the carnal mind is enmity against God; for it is not subject to the law of God, nor indeed can be. So then, those who are in the flesh cannot please God.*
>
> **—Romans 8:5–8 NKJV**

[53] The NIV Study Bible, footnotes on Romans 8:5–8.

Let's take a closer look at the word *carnal* from its Greek rendition, *sarkikos*, from *sarx*. It means pertaining to flesh, bodily, temporal, unregenerate; the body as opposed to the soul or spirit, or as the symbol of what is external, or as the means of kindred, or human nature with its frailties and passions, or a human being as such" carnally minded, fleshly.[54]

The believers at Corinth were not growing spiritually, but Paul does not suggest they were antispiritual, which would imply a hardness of their hearts of flesh, as in "fleshy tables of the heart" (2 Corinthians 3:3 KJV), but they were charged by Paul with being fleshy or fleshly, which is carnally minded.

Let's take a look at another context of scripture pertaining to why believers are not consistently tuned-in to the frequency of heaven:

> Of whom we have much to say, and hard to explain, since you have become dull of hearing. For though by this time you ought to be teachers, you need someone to teach you again the first principles of the oracles of God; and you have come to need milk and not solid food. For everyone who partakes only of milk is unskilled in the word of righteousness, for he is a babe. But solid food belongs to those who are of full age, that is, those who by reason of use have their senses exercised to discern both good and evil. (Hebrews 5:11–14 NKJV)

The writer of The Epistle to the Hebrews makes yet another point as to why believers remain babes in Christ and cannot consistently set their spiritual dial to the frequency, the sound waves and wavelengths of heaven via Holy Spirit.

Prior to Hebrews 5:11–14, the Hebrew writer was teaching the difference between the priesthood of Aaron and the priesthood of Melchizedek—that the priesthood of Melchizedek is superior to that of Aaron. He attempts to explain this difference to the Hebrews, but their minds were slow to grasp this highly spiritual revelation. They were slow

---

[54] *Expository Dictionary of New Testament Words: A Comprehensive Dictionary of the Original Greek Words with Their Precise Meanings for English Readers*, 1088.

of heart; their inborn sluggishness was too entwined with their immoral lifestyle. In other words, the Hebrew believers were lazy.

Does this strike a chord within one's mental capacity to make the effort toward spiritual maturity?

The priesthood of Aaron is representative of the flesh—a high priest taken from among men and appointed for men in things pertaining to God, that he may offer every year both gifts and sacrifices for sins because he himself was also subject to weakness of the flesh, and it was required, as it was for the people, so also for himself, to offer sacrifices for sin (Hebrews 5:1–3 NKJV).

The priesthood of Melchizedek is spiritual—king of Salem, priest of the Most High God, without father or mother, without genealogy, having neither beginning of days nor end of life, but made like the Son of God and remains a priest continually (Hebrews 7:1–3 NKJV).

It is important that we delve into what it means to be dull of hearing spiritual things via Holy Spirit. And yes, laziness in seeking God and failure to continue in his word are at the forefront as to why so many saints are dull of hearing spiritual things.

The Greek word for *dull* as used in the text above is *nothros*, which means to be slow, sluggish, indolent, dull in connection with hearing; slow of heart as in *kardia*, the mind; moral blame. There is a deeper, more inborn sluggishness (laziness) implied here, and bound up in the very life of the believer.[55]

There is yet a deeper level of dullness that I want to explore because it is the teaching of Jesus, who draws upon Old Testament scripture to make his point:

> And the disciples came and said to Him, "Why do You speak to them in parables?" He answered and said to them, "Because it has been given to you to know the mysteries of the kingdom of heaven, but to them it has not been given. For whoever has, to him more will be given, and he will have abundance; but whoever does not have, even what he has will be taken away from

[55] *Expository Dictionary of New Testament Words: A Comprehensive Dictionary of the Original Greek Words with Their Precise Meanings for English Readers.*

> him. Therefore I speak to them in parables, because seeing they do not see, and hearing they do not hear, nor do they understand. And in them the prophecy of Isaiah is fulfilled, which says: "Hearing you will hear and shall not understand, and seeing you will see and not perceive; for the hearts of this people have grown dull. Their ears are hard of hearing, and their eyes they have closed, lest they should see with their eyes and hear with their ears, lest they should understand with their hearts and turn, so that I should heal them. But blessed are your eyes for they see, and your ears for they hear; for assuredly, I say to you that many prophets and righteous men desired to see what you see, and did not see it, and to hear what you hear, and did not hear it. (Matthew 13:10–17 NKJV)

The Greek word rendered *dull* as used in the above text is *bareos*, which means heavily, with difficulty; to be heavily dull of hearing.[56] Jesus taught in parables to avoid giving clear truth and understanding to those who rejected him or those who did not believe on him and his words.

So there is a difference between believers today, who are dull of hearing because they are mentally lazy and choose not to seek the revelation of Jesus through continuing in his word and allowing Holy Spirit to feed their spirit with the deep things of God, and those who Jesus deliberately hid his words from, rendering them dull of hearing.

The above passage of scripture should never apply to spiritually mature believers. Our spiritual ears should always be opened to hear the rhema of God and revelatory knowledge of the logos. Jesus said to his disciples, whom spiritually mature saints are today, "It has been given to you to know the mysteries of the kingdom of heaven, but to them it has not been given" (Matthew 13:11 NKJV). Those who did not believe in Jesus were not given the ability to hear his words because their ears

[56] *Expository Dictionary of New Testament Words: A Comprehensive Dictionary of the Original Greek Words with Their Precise Meanings for English Readers.*

were made to be dull of hearing; Jesus taught in parables so that their ears would be heavily dull of hearing.

Believers today, who do not hear the Word of God, have not attained and maintained a consistent relationship with the Father because of their own sluggish behavior; therefore they have not grown spiritually, and they still cannot hear or bear what Father wants to release into their spirit via Holy Spirit, because they are babes. And babes are not skilled in the use of the word, knowing how to discern both good and evil.

The result is they have a difficult time maintaining their spiritual focus—that is, their consistency in reading, studying, speaking the Word of God by faith, and applying it to their situation because they have not prioritized the Word of God as first place and final authority; and, it shows through the dullness of their spiritual minds. In other words, the eyes of their minds are blind.

> *Whose minds the god of this age has blinded, who do not believe, lest the light of the gospel of the glory of Christ, who is the image of God, should shine on them.*
>
> **—2 Corinthians 4:4 NKJV**

> *This I say, therefore, and testify in the Lord, that you should no longer walk as the rest of the Gentiles walk, in the futility of their mind, having their understanding darkened, being alienated from the life of God, because of the ignorance that is in them, because of the blindness of their heart … that you put off, concerning your former conduct, the old man which grows corrupt according to the deceitful lusts, and be renewed in the spirit of your mind, and that you put on the new man which was created according to God, in true righteousness and holiness.*
>
> **—Ephesians 4:17–18, 22–24 NKJV**

Jesus said, "It is the Spirit who gives life; the flesh profits nothing" (John 6:63b NKJV). But I'm more concerned as to why he said it, and to whom. Jesus had been teaching "I am the bread of life" (John 6:48 NKJV) to his disciples. "Whoever eats My flesh and drinks My blood has eternal life, and I will raise him up at the last day. For My flesh is food indeed, and My blood is drink indeed" (John 6:54, 55 NKJV).

> Therefore many of His disciples, when they heard this, said, "This is a hard saying; who can understand it?" When Jesus knew in Himself that His disciples complained about this, He said to them, "Does this offend you?" ... The words that I speak to you are spirit and they are life. But there are some of you who do not believe ... From that time many of His disciples went back and walked with Him no more. Then Jesus said to the twelve, "Do you also want to go away?" But Simon Peter answered Him, "Lord, to whom shall we go? You have the words of eternal life. Also we have come to believe and know that You are the Christ, the Son of the living God. (John 6:60–61, 63b–64, 66–69 NKJV)

It is Holy Spirit who enlivens us, who renews our minds with revelatory knowledge of the Word of God. Believers today have a choice: they can continue to be offended by the Word of God and not believe and turn their backs and walk with him no more, or they can get a revelation here and now, like Simon Peter did, and say, "Lord, You have the words of eternal life; and from this day forward, I believe and know that You are the Christ, the Son of the living God."

Holy Spirit is at the forefront of providing wisdom and power to those whose faith is secure in the Word of God. He spearheads our victories in and through us as a witness of Jesus Christ and to the glory of God, our heavenly Father.

Tune in to the satellite of heaven, Holy Spirit. He will fine-tune our spiritual dial to the frequency of heaven. It's up to us whether or not we stay tuned-in. Holy Spirit knows the exact plan of God for our lives; he knows what tomorrow holds. He wants us to trust Him. He uses the Word of God to change us more and more as we consistently spend time in his presence.

We will know Him as our most treasured best friend as we bask in his presence and meditate on his Word. Our consistent fellowship and communion with him will become our normal custom, and our spirit will hunger and thirst for more of Him. He will respond to us as the deep calling at the noise of our uproar—our hunger, our agitation, our willingness to root out and destroy those sad experiences of life. If we seek him with our whole heart, we will be found of him.

This is the beginning of fine-tuning our renewed mind to the frequency, where the Word of God is broadcast 24-7 so that we never miss what heaven requires us to do on earth—things that bring glory to our heavenly Father.

In the 1980s, my favorite radio disc jockey coined a phrase for the station he worked for, which was quite popular for years. He'd state the call letters of the station and say, "Lock it in and rip the knob off." I invite everyone to do the same by seeking and worshiping God with our whole heart and inviting Holy Spirit to lead and guide us into all truth. In other words, "Lock in his eternal truth and leave the evil systems of the world out!"

This is what we should do mentally so that we stay tuned-in to the frequency of heaven. Lock it, etch it—the Word of God—in your regenerated spirit, and renew our minds by frequenting the word, making it first place and final authority. Remember: "In consistency lies the power!" Lock it in and renew our minds consistently, and we will stay tuned-in to the frequency of heaven.

CHAPTER 11

Ensuring Kingdom-Compliant Generations

For though you might have ten thousand instructors in Christ, yet you do not have many fathers; for in Christ Jesus I have begotten you through the gospel. Therefore I urge you, imitate me. For this reason I have sent Timothy to you, who is my beloved and faithful son in the Lord, who will remind you of my ways in Christ, as I teach everywhere in every church.

—1 Corinthians 4:15–17 NKJV

As an apostle, bishop, pastor, and spiritual father, I can confidently say nothing makes a spiritual father happier than to experience spiritual fatherhood as the apostle Paul did with his spiritual son Timothy.

Paul refers to Timothy as his beloved and faithful son in the Lord. What a powerful bestowal of honor toward Timothy from Paul, who had many spiritual sons. Why did Timothy stand out as beloved and faithful? He stood out among Paul's other sons not because he was the only son that was beloved and faithful to Paul but because he reminded the people of Paul's ways in Christ, which he displayed over the years and through his many missionary journeys.

Paul makes it clear that believers may have ten thousand instructors in Christ, yet not many fathers in Christ. The distinctive difference between instructors in Christ and fathers in Christ is found in the phrase "imitate me." Paul said, "Imitate me, just as I also imitate Christ" (1 Corinthians 11:1 NKJV).

Paul could urge his spiritual sons to imitate him because he was *in Christ.* Paul was in union with Christ through his faith in Jesus. Paul was committed to the ministry of the Lord, Jesus Christ. The apostle Peter said Christ has left us an example that we should follow in His steps (1 Peter 2:21 NKJV), which makes Christ the supreme example. Paul consistently speaks of his commitment to Christ. His opening statement in his epistle to the Corinthians says, "Paul, called to be an apostle of Jesus Christ through the will of God" (1 Corinthians 1:1 NKJV).

Paul was called by God to be an apostle of Jesus Christ, and as Christ's apostle he became an ambassador for Christ (2 Corinthians 5:20 NKJV), following his example. Paul said, "As I imitate or follow Christ" (1 Corinthians 11:1 NKJV). Believers are to follow or imitate the apostle's example: "Now I praise you, brethren, that you remember me in all things and keep the traditions just as I delivered them to you" (1 Corinthians 11:2 NKJV).

This is what the father-son relationship is all about. It's a relationship rooted in the relationship Jesus had with his Father, to say what he heard his Father say and to do what he saw his Father do (John 5:19 NKJV).

To imitate means to follow as a model or a pattern; to make a copy, counterpart, or semblance of. Obviously, Timothy was a most trusted spiritual son to Paul. As an apostle of Jesus Christ and spiritual father, I know from personal experience that there is so much comfort in knowing one has a spiritual son or daughter in whom they trust completely because they remind them so much of themselves—commitment to Christ Jesus and the ministry he has entrusted to our care.

> *Paul, an apostle of Jesus Christ, by the commandment of God our Savior and the Lord Jesus Christ, our hope, to Timothy, a true son in the faith.*
>
> **—1 Timothy 1:1–2 NKJV**

> *Paul, an apostle of Jesus Christ by the will of God, according to the promise of life which is in Christ Jesus, to Timothy, a beloved son.*
>
> **—2 Timothy 1:1–2 NKJV**

> *You therefore, my son, be strong in the grace that is in Christ Jesus. And the things that you have heard from me among many witnesses, commit these to faithful men who will be able to teach others also.*
>
> **—2 Timothy 2:1–2 NKJV**

All three of the above scriptures are opening statements from Paul concerning Timothy, his spiritual son. Paul refers to Timothy as a true son in the faith, a beloved son, and a son who could commit to other faithful men and women the things he heard and learned from Paul in the presence of many witnesses. Timothy was with Paul on all three missionary journeys and had heard him preach and teach on many occasions. Paul trusted Timothy like the Father trusted Jesus. And Paul bestowed upon Timothy the ultimate commendation prior to sending him to Philippi to minister and report on the state of the church there.

> But I trust in the Lord Jesus to send Timothy to you shortly, that I also may be encouraged when I know your state. For I have no one like-minded, who will sincerely care for your state. For all seek their own, not the things which are of Christ Jesus. But you know his proven character, that as a son with his father he served with me in the gospel. (Philippians 2:19–22 NKJV)

Timothy's attributes as a spiritual son to Apostle Paul included qualities that can only be developed in spiritual maturity, being led and guided by the Holy Spirit and exhibiting his fruit. Paul could send Timothy on missions to represent him; Timothy was sincere in his care for the people; his character was proven; he served faithfully with Paul; and Paul could think of no other spiritual son who was more like-minded of him than Timothy. Wow! Oh, for spiritual sons of this spiritual magnitude—those like Timothy, possessors of a servant's heart and attitude.

> But you have carefully followed my doctrine, manner of life, purpose, faith, longsuffering, love, perseverance, persecutions, afflictions, which happened to me at Antioch, at Iconium, at Lystra – what persecutions I endured. And out of them all the Lord delivered me … But you must continue in the things which you have learned and been assured of, knowing from whom you have learned them. (2 Timothy 3:10–11, 14 NKJV)

> If you instruct the brethren in these things, you will be a good minister of Jesus Christ, nourished in the words of faith and of the good doctrine which you have carefully followed. (1 Timothy 4:6 NKJV)

In the above scriptures, Paul continues to heap accolade after accolade after spiritual accolade upon Timothy as a true and faithful spiritual son. No one throws around words and describes people the way Paul speaks and describes Timothy. When I read about the life of Paul as an apostle, it doesn't take long to conclude that his life as an apostle was not necessarily an easy one, according to the flesh.

His doctrine at times was too difficult for many to understand. Even Peter commented on this in his second epistle: "As also our beloved brother Paul, according to the wisdom given to him, has written to you, as also in all his epistles, speaking in them of these things, in which are some things hard to understand, which untaught and unstable people twist to their own destruction, as they do also the rest of the Scriptures" (2 Peter 3:15b–16 NKJV).

Paul's manner of life was at times harsh; his purpose extensive; his faith insurmountable; his long-suffering endured a lifetime; his love was unsurpassed; his perseverance uncanny; his persecutions and his many afflictions too often; he was treated as the scourge of the earth, as the filth of the world. This is the man Timothy imitated. And this is what made Timothy a true, beloved, and faithful spiritual son to Paul (2 Corinthians 11:22–31 NKJV; 1 Corinthians 4:9–13 NKJV).

Timothy continued in the things that he had learned and was assured of, knowing from whom he had learned them—his spiritual father, the apostle Paul. Timothy was considered a good minister of Jesus Christ and could instruct and nourish others in the words of faith and of the good doctrine, which he himself carefully followed.

INSTRUCTORS IN CHRIST VERSUS FATHERS

Paul makes a pretty major distinction between instructors and fathers: "Ten thousand instructors in Christ, yet you do not have many fathers" (1 Corinthians 4:15a NKJV). Paul places greater emphasis on fathers, from the perspective that they play a greater role in the spiritual development of sons and daughters in Christ. He implies that in Christ fathers actually birth their sons and daughters spiritually through the steadfast teaching of the gospel: "For in Christ Jesus I have begotten you through the gospel" (1 Corinthians 4:15b NKJV).

"In Christ" would suggest being united with him through faith in him and commitment to him. So, then, during the course of our spiritual lives, we may have thousands of instructors in Christ but few fathers who instruct their sons and daughters concerning the gospel of the kingdom. True spiritual fathers birth and nurture their sons and daughters in the gospel.

According to Paul, there is a great divide between the instructor in Christ and the father who, in Christ, begets sons and daughters through the gospel.

The Greek word *paidagogos* is used to denote *instructor*, which means a boy-leader—that is, a servant whose office it was to take the children to school; schoolmaster.[57] *Paidagogos* further denotes a guide, or guardian or trainer of boys; a child-leader, a tutor; here the thought is that of pastors rather than teachers; the idea is of training and discipline, not of impartation of knowledge. The *paidagogos* was not the instructor of the child; he exercised a general supervision over him and was responsible for his moral and physical well-being. Thus, understood, *paidagogos* is appropriately used with "kept in ward" and "shut up," whereas to understand it as equivalent to "teacher" introduces

---

[57] *Expository Dictionary of New Testament Words: A Comprehensive Dictionary of the Original Greek Words with Their Precise Meanings for English Readers.*

an idea entirely foreign to the passage and throws the apostle's argument into confusion.[58]

According to the above definitions and descriptions, the major distinction between an instructor and a father, from Paul's perspective, is training, discipline and supervision as opposed to teaching and imparting knowledge. The instructor in Christ was not a teacher, but rather a supervisor responsible for the moral and physical well-being of young boys. It was these instructors who kept young boys "in ward" or "shut up" as in keeping them out of trouble or protected against predators.

The Greek word *pater* is used in Paul's context for *father*, signifying one who nourishes, a protector, upholder; of one who, as a preacher of the Gospel and a teacher, stands in a father's place, caring for his spiritual children.[59]

Spiritual fathers nourish, protect, and uphold their spiritual sons and daughters by teaching and imparting to them knowledge of the gospel. A spiritual father stands in the place of a father, as in a daddy who takes responsibility for his children's welfare and safety. In other words, Daddy is at home. An instructor may be among those he or she supervises for a period of time, but at the end of the day the instructor and those supervised part ways. In the spiritual sense, the father stays with his sons and daughters; they are spiritually connected or like-minded.

The Greek word *pater—father*—has a specific reference to the ministry of the Apostle. First of all, we are built upon the foundation of the "apostles and prophets" (Ephesians 2:20 NKJV). The New Testament was written by the fathers of the universal church. They laid the foundation upon which we build. There is also a contemporary usage of this word, *pater*, to speak of those five-fold ministers—specifically the ministry of the apostle—who birth and then nurture younger ministers in this walk. *Pater*, as it is used in the context of 1 Corinthians 4:15, is valid though sometimes abused in a one-to-one relationship that is imbalanced.

---

[58] *Strong's Exhaustive Concordance of the Bible, NT.*

[59] *Strong's Exhaustive Concordance of the Bible, NT.*

> *And you, fathers, do not provoke your children to wrath, but bring them up in the training and admonition of the Lord.*
>
> **—Ephesians 6:4 NKJV**

> *I have written to you, fathers, Because you have known Him who is from the beginning. I have written to you, young men, Because you are strong, and the word of God abides in you, And you have overcome the wicked one.*
>
> **—1 John 2:14 NKJV**

I find it interesting that the Greek word *pater* used for *father* has a specific reference to the ministry of the apostle, which means that the father-son paradigm is one of divine order. apostolic fathers guide, govern and guard the welfare and proper spiritual growth of their spiritual sons and daughters. And that spiritual growth is based on discipline, divine order, and direction.

The heart of an apostolic father should be to see Christ formed in his spiritual sons and daughters, as was the heart of the apostle Paul who said, "My little children, for whom I labor in birth again until Christ is formed in you" (Galatians 4:19 NKJV). Apostolic fathers impart themselves, a compilation of what they are, spiritual gifts, anointing, mantles, etc., into their sons and daughters building them to the position of emerging apostles who will also set their sights on raising spiritual sons and daughters to become kingdom-compliant servant-leaders. Spiritual fathers impart their gifts to their sons and daughters so that in the process of being established as kingdom-compliant servant-leaders they, too, will become apostles and spiritual parents.

> *For I long to see you, that I may impart to you some spiritual gift, so that you may be established – that is, that I may be encouraged together with you by the mutual faith both of you and me.*
>
> **—Romans 1:11–12 NKJV**

The mandate of a spiritual father is to thoroughly equip and train his sons and daughters for generation succession. But first they must be established in the faith of their spiritual father so that both father and son are encouraged together by their mutual faith. When spiritual sons and daughters are not thoroughly equipped for generation succession through the mutual faith of both father and son, they generally break rank or divine order of God by ministering independently of their father. Establishment in the mutual faith of the father and son is crucial to the father-son relationship.

What exactly was the apostle Paul alluding to when he said, "So that you may be established" (Romans 1:11 NKJV)?

Sterizo and *stereos* are the Greek words used in this context to describe *established*. They are a derivative of *histemi*. Their collective meaning is to stand, abide, continue, covenant; solid, stable; steadfast, strong, sure. To turn resolutely in a certain direction, to confirm; fix, establish, set, and strengthen.[60]

Establish means to make stable or firm; to confirm; to form; to found; to institute; to set up in business. To appoint or adopt, as officers, laws, regulations, guidelines, etc.; to enact; to ordain. To prove and cause to be accepted as true; to establish a fact; to demonstrate.

The apostle Paul was called by the Lord to establish his sons and daughters—to confirm them as steadfast, strong, and solid in abiding resolutely in covenant. Paul's mandate as a spiritual father was to make sure his sons and daughters were proven, ordained, and caused to be accepted as true, stable, and firm.

Paul knew ultimately that the confirmation of his true sons and daughters was a work of God by his spirit. Whenever Paul could not be in a certain place himself to strengthen, confirm, and establish the saints, he sent his spiritual sons.

> *Now to Him who is able to establish you according to my gospel and the preaching of Jesus Christ, according to the revelation of the mystery kept secret since the world began.*
>
> **—Romans 16:25 NKJV**

> *And sent Timothy, our brother and minister of God, and our fellow laborer in the gospel of Christ, to establish you and encourage you concerning your faith.*
>
> **—1 Thessalonians 3:2 NKJV**

[60] *Strong's Exhaustive Concordance of the Bible, NT*, 4741, 4731, 2476.

> *Strengthening the souls of the disciples, exhorting them to continue in the faith, and saying, "We must through many tribulations enter the kingdom of God."*
>
> **—Acts 14:22 NKJV**

Spiritual sons and daughters are successors of their spiritual father. Spiritual sons and daughters receive the blueprint on how to build generationally from their spiritual father. Although we don't see this recorded in biblical canon, I believe that Timothy was Paul's successor in ministry. Paul poured himself into Timothy, and at the time of his death he counseled Timothy to "be watchful in all things, endure afflictions, do the work of an evangelist, fulfill your ministry. For I am already being poured out as a drink offering, and the time of my departure is at hand" (2 Timothy 4:5–6 NKJV).

The pattern of the spiritual father-spiritual son relationship finds its roots in the same relationship that our Heavenly Father had with his Son, Jesus. And Father Yahweh said of his Son, "*This is My beloved Son, in whom I am well pleased*" (Matthew 3:17 NKJV). True spiritual sons and daughters are birthed out of their spiritual father's bosom. Like Jesus, sons and daughters come in the volume of their spiritual father's book. In other words, spiritual sons and daughters complete their spiritual father's life mission, expanding the family name through generation succession.

Spiritual sons and daughters are birthed by their spiritual father. This is a birth of spiritual origin, which means it is about relationship. Spiritual fathering doesn't take place just because someone who is well respected and has been a leader in a church for thirty years says to someone, "You are my spiritual son or daughter."

Paul said, "For in Christ Jesus I have begotten you through the gospel" (1 Corinthians 4:15b NKJV).

Instructors in Christ may guide and govern, but they cannot beget or give birth to sons and daughters; only spiritual fathers have this God-ordained ability. Building sons is the responsibility of fathers. And in the process, the son's spirit becomes joined to the spirit of his father.

The problems that the church faces today are largely due to the fact there is a lack of spiritual fathering taking place. Many would-be fathers have fallen into their own personality-driven desires for fame and fortune. Instead of building the next generation of sons and daughters who can expand the kingdom of God on earth, they are building and promoting themselves and their platform and projects.

Today our heavenly Father is appealing to spiritually mature men and women of God to become spiritual parents, to birth from their spirit those sons and daughters that are like-minded. As Paul said of Timothy:

> When I call to remembrance the genuine faith that is in you, which dwelt first in your grandmother Lois and your mother Eunice, and I am persuaded is in you also. Therefore I remind you to stir up the gift of God which is in you through the laying on of my hands … Hold fast the pattern of sound words which you have heard from me, in faith and love which are in Christ Jesus. That good thing which was committed to you, keep by the Holy Spirit who dwells in us. (2 Timothy 1:5–6, 13–14 NKJV).

Spiritual fathers deposit the righteousness of the kingdom into the spirit of their sons and daughters, building them over time to become kingdom-compliant commissioned servant-leaders who will build other generations of sons and daughters that will occupy the earth, advancing the kingdom of God in it, until Jesus's return.

BUILDING KINGDOM-COMPLIANT GENERATIONS: SONS AND DAUGHTERS WHO REFLECT THE SPIRITUAL DNA OF THEIR SPIRITUAL FATHER

Kingdom-compliant saints are those who are willing to be submissive; to yield, bend, become pliable, and comply with the government, rule, and authority of God on the earth. They hold firm to the Word of God being first place and final authority in their lives. These are the saints who consistently pray, "Your kingdom come. Your will be done on earth as it is in heaven" (Matthew 6:10 NKJV).

True spiritual fathers build kingdom-compliant sons and daughters who reflect them through their lifestyle and activities. Since the kingdom of God is ever evolving in the earth, each generation of kingdom-compliant sons and daughters must, of necessity, become more efficient in their responsibility to produce their own spiritual sons and daughters who can also generate generations. Each generation of spiritual sons and daughters must evolve to be changed into the image of Christ and model the Father-Son relationship. We are transformed more and more fully into this image by the Holy Spirit.

> *But we all, with unveiled face, beholding as in a mirror the glory of the Lord, are being transformed into the same image from glory to glory, just as by the Spirit of the Lord.*
>
> **—2 Corinthians 3:18 NKJV**

True spiritual sons and daughters reflect their father's image, his spiritual patterns, and kingdom behaviors. When a spiritual father sees himself in his sons and daughters, he knows that his offspring is legitimate and has his spiritual DNA to maintain and advance the heritage. These legitimate sons and daughters are now able to reproduce themselves in the future. In order to make the kingdom more visible on earth, there must be a consistent upgrade of spiritual sons and daughters who reflect generational increase, taking up and putting on the mantle of their spiritual father.

Furthermore, spiritual sons and daughters reflect, as does Jesus's Father-Son paradigm, equality with their spiritual father in power. Spiritual fathers who raised faithful spiritual sons and daughters make spiritual impartations into their inner being, which allows them to carry out their own ministry with a greater anointing and power than their spiritual father. Spiritual sons and daughters who maintain an intimate relationship with their father should qualify for a double portion of his anointing.

> *Most assuredly, I say to you, the Son can do nothing of Himself, but what He sees the Father do; for whatever He does, the Son also does in like manner. For the father loves the Son, and shows Him all things that He Himself does; and He will show Him greater works than these, that you may marvel.*
>
> **—John 5:19–20 NKJV**

> *Believe Me that I am in the Father and the Father in Me, or else believe Me for the sake of the works themselves. Most assuredly, I say to you, he who believes in Me, the works that I do he will do also; and greater works than these he will do, because I go to My Father.*
>
> **—John 14:11–12 NKJV**

While on earth, Jesus was a reflection, the very image of his Father. Jesus is the Father's revelation of himself to the world. This unique Father-Son relationship is expressed through their oneness. The Father and Jesus are in one another, and the words of the Son, Jesus, come with the authority of the Father.

Let's take a look at the transfer of a double-portion anointing from spiritual father to spiritual son through the father-son relationship of the prophets Elijah and Elisha. This is the pattern of a spiritual son reflecting the anointing, power, and spiritual behavior of a spiritual father.

I'm always fascinated by this story taken from 2 Kings. A chariot of fire is about to take Elijah into heaven by a whirlwind. And Elisha, his spiritual son, was in line to become his successor. Elijah understood the necessity of a successor. His spiritual DNA would be lost without a successor. And there would never be another reproduction or reflection of himself and his anointing and power. Today's apostles, prophets, bishops, and elders would do well to study this father-son pattern.

Elisha served Elijah for years, developing the intimacy that can only be produced from a father-son relationship. At God's instruction, Elijah was told to anoint Elisha as prophet in his place. When Elijah found Elisha, he was plowing with twelve yoke of oxen. "Then Elijah passed by him and threw his mantle on him … then he arose and followed Elijah, and became his servant" (1 Kings 19:19–21b NKJV).

I love that Elijah threw his mantle—his glory, his splendor, his shawl of nobility, greatness, and power, magnificence and honor—on Elisha prior to the father-son relationship. It tells us that Elijah trusted God to choose his successor; this is yet another lesson that today's spiritual fathers should learn.

Elijah treated his successor the way a spiritual father would treat his spiritual son. And when it was his time to be taken into heaven, Elijah and his spiritual son, Elisha, left from Gilgal and traveled to Bethel. From Bethel they traveled to Jericho, and from Jericho they traveled to Jordan. Each of these villages hosted a prophetic school for the training and preparation of young future prophets.

I like the fact that each of these villages has prophetic significance, each of which play a significant role in assuring the proper transfer of the father's DNA to the son, and the establishment of the son, Elisha, to repeat the process with his spiritual son which never happened, because Elisha's protégé Gehazi did not have the spiritual perception or character to receive Elisha's mantle. This spiritual misalignment happens too often today as well.

Gilgal represents a place to roll away reproach; a whirlwind: heaven, rolling thing; to commit, remove, roll away, seek occasion, trust, wallow—place of *mediocrity.* Bethel means house of God, a house of family, obtain children—place of *sacrifice.* Jericho represents the fragrant smell or wind, breath of the ruwach; to perceive, anticipate, enjoy: to make of quick understanding; a lunation, a month: moon—place of *warfare.* Jordan means to descend, to go downwards; to subdue, take down—a place of *descent exchanged for an eternal ascent.*

Elijah made the great exchange—the spiritual father's anointing, mantle and power to his spiritual son, for his life in eternity with the Father. But in order to receive the double-portion anointing of his spiritual father, Elisha first had to "wrap his face in his mantle." In other words, Elisha had to endure the doubts, envies, and jealousies of other would-be prophets who wanted to be Elijah's successor but did not have the intimate relationship and seal of true sonship as Elisha did.

Elisha followed Elijah from the place of mediocrity to the place of sacrifice; from there, he followed him to the place of spiritual warfare, anticipation, expectation, and action. Finally, Elisha stilled the sons of the prophets and stood with Elijah at the Jordan, the place of descent; to take down or relieve himself of his earthly duties and sojourn in exchange for his glorious eternal state with the Father.

Just as Jesus did what he saw his Father do, Elisha is about to do what his spiritual father, Elijah, did.

> Now Elijah took his mantle, rolled it up, and struck the water; and it was divided this way and that, so that the two of them crossed over on dry ground. And so it was, when they had crossed over, that Elijah said to Elisha, "Ask! What may I do for you, before I am taken away from you?" Elisha said, "Please let a double portion of your spirit be upon me." So he said, "You have asked a hard thing. Nevertheless, if you see me when I am taken from you, it shall be so for you; but if not, it shall not be so. Then it happened, as they continued on and talked, that suddenly a chariot of fire appeared with horses of fire, and separated the two of them; and Elijah went up by a whirlwind into heaven. And Elisha saw it, and he cried out, "My father, my father, the chariot of Israel and its horsemen!" So he saw him no more. And he took hold of his own clothes and tore them into pieces. He also took up the mantle of Elijah that had fallen from him, and went back and stood by the bank of the Jordan. Then he took the mantle of Elijah that had fallen from him, and struck the water, and said, "Where is the Lord God of Elijah?" And when he also had struck the water, it was divided this way and that; and Elisha crossed over. (2 Kings 2:8–14 NKJV)

What a fitting climax to a spiritual father-son relationship. Elisha managed to ward off all opposition to receive what was rightfully his. He crossed over the Jordon with Elijah on dry ground. The cross over from one state or dimension into another was the deciding factor. Now Elijah knew that Elisha was ready to receive his anointing. Still, Elisha had to step into a higher spiritual dimension in order to supernaturally wear the mantle of his spiritual father and use it to fulfill his divine assignment.

Elijah did not ask Elisha what he could do for him before his departure until the two had crossed over the Jordan. Now Elijah could "take down" and the "ascent" could take place. Elisha asked for a double portion of Elijah's anointing, a request based on inheritance laws of the Old Testament in which the firstborn son received a double portion of his father's estate.

Sonship is the central theme here. But I love Elijah's response. "If you see me when I am taken from you, it shall be so for you" (2 Kings 2:10 NKJV). Elijah was a true spiritual father. He knew that in order for Elisha to walk in a double portion of his anointing, he would have to reflect his anointing.

The supernatural separation took place suddenly and Elisha saw it. He honored his spiritual father as the spiritual defender of Israel; and he saw him no more. Elisha embraced his new identity by tearing his old clothes into pieces; then he took Elijah's mantle that had fallen from him and went back to the bank of the Jordon.

Elisha was about to become a reflector —an image, a likeness of his spiritual father. He was about to exhibit or give back what his spiritual father had given to him. His first miracle was identical to his spiritual father, Elijah. He took the mantle that had fallen from Elijah and struck the water saying, "Where is the Lord God of Elijah" (2 Kings 2:14 NKJV)? And the waters parted for him to cross back over on dry land. Today, because we live under the New Testament, we would say, "In the Name of Jesus, I command this river to be parted to provide a dry path!"

The transfer was complete. The double-portion anointing rested on Elisha not only because he saw Elijah when he was taken up to heaven by a whirlwind but also because Elisha could see Elijah through himself. What Elijah told Elisha was actually a spiritual revelation. The revelation that I received from the Holy Spirit is, Elijah told Elisha, "If you see me in you after I've been taken from you, the double portion anointing is yours." In all of Elisha's subsequent miracles, he could see Elijah, his spiritual father. He was always reminded of his spiritual father; he carried Elijah's spiritual DNA after he was taken to heaven. And Elisha doubled the miracles performed by his spiritual father, Elijah. That's what sonship looks like; that's what "generating generations" looks like.

The Body of Christ is in dire need of spiritual fathers who will teach, train, develop and produce kingdom-compliant sons and daughters who will occupy the earth, utilizing their gifts, anointing, and talents for kingdom expansion until Jesus's return.

Too many leaders, who should have become spiritual parents leading their sons and daughters into becoming kingdom-compliant commissioned servant-leaders, have viewed the urgent mandate to father spiritual sons and daughters as overbearing—too difficult or beyond what they were willing to do. Spiritual fathering that leads to spiritually mature kingdom-compliant sons and daughters requires spiritually mature parents who are willing to give themselves wholeheartedly to the process of transforming the mind of their sons and daughters for kingdom use—to advance the kingdom of God in the earth one generation after another, until, "The kingdoms of this world have become the kingdoms of our Lord and of His Christ, and He shall reign forever and ever" (Revelation 11:15 NKJV)!

DO BUSINESS (OCCUPY) TILL I COME

"Occupy til I come" (Luke 19:13 KJV) is a kingdom mandate given to the body by its head, our commanding officer—Jesus Christ. I like the dual-mandate approach to this commandment. It is both a military command and a business-investment command.

> There was once a man descended from a royal house who needed to make a long trip back to headquarters to get authorization for his rule and then return. But first he called ten servants together, gave them each a sum of money, and instructed them, "Operate with this until I return." But the citizens there hated him. So they sent a commission with a signed petition to oppose his rule: "We don't want this man to rule us." When he came back bringing the authorization of his rule, he called those ten servants to whom he had given the money to find out how they had done. The first said, "Master, I doubled your money." He said, Good servant! Great work! Because you've been trustworthy in this small job, I'm making you governor of ten towns." The second said, "Master, I made a fifty percent profit on your money." He said, "I'm putting you in charge of five towns." The next servant said, "Master, here's your money safe and sound. I kept it hidden in the cellar. To

> tell you the truth, I was a little afraid. I know you have high standards and hate sloppiness, and don't suffer fools gladly." He said, "You're right that I don't suffer fools gladly - and you've acted the fool! Why didn't you at least invest the money in securities so I would have gotten a little interest on it?" Then he said to those standing there, "Take the money from him and give it to the servant who doubled my stake." They said, "But Master, he already has double ..." He said, "That's what I mean: Risk your life and get more than you ever dreamed of. Play it safe and end up holding the bag. As for these enemies of mine who petitioned against my rule, clear them out of here. I don't want to see their faces around here again." (Luke 19:12–27 Message)

In the parable above, Jesus is clearly teaching about himself—his first earthly sojourn and his subsequent return. When Jesus returns to reign as King over all the kingdoms of the world, he will require his servants to give an account of their stewardship of the assignments that he left with them. Every person will have to answer the Lord.

Abba Daddy has given every one of us at least one significant talent, gift, or skill. Some people may have more than one, but no one is more important than the other. Through divine purpose, the Father has matched our talent to our ability—his assignment for our lives on earth.

According to the parable, a certain nobleman, Jesus, distributed his talents to his servants, believers, and took a long journey to receive a kingdom for himself and return home. This nobleman instructed his servants to use their talent(s), the equivalent of money, to occupy, operate, do business until he returned.

Occupy, as used in the King James Version of the Bible, is the Greek word *pragmateuomai*. It means to busy oneself with or to trade. It is related to another Greek word, *prasso*, which means to practice, perform repeatedly or habitually. It also means to do business, execute, and accomplish.[61]

---

[61] *Strong's Exhaustive Concordance of the Bible, NT*, 4231, 4229, 4238.

From a military standpoint, *occupy* means to have, or to have taken, possession or control of a territory.

Basically, the nobleman entrusted his money to his servants as an investment into their lives and future. The accompanying instruction from the nobleman focused on management of the money by trading, investing, or exchanging the money in the marketplace for profit. In other words, the nobleman told his servants to do business in the marketplace and use the money to possess or control the territory Jesus had marked out for himself.

Jesus himself did the same by going to all the cities and villages, teaching in their synagogues, and preaching the gospel of the kingdom, healing every sickness and every disease, and making people whole. We are to use our talents in the marketplace as well as in our local assembly. With his talents, the Holy Spirit's gifts, Jesus occupied each city and village he entered.

We, too, as saints of God, are to use the gifts, talents, and anointing received from the Lord to occupy not only the ministry but also the marketplace and municipality, repeatedly and habitually teaching and preaching the Gospel of the kingdom. This doesn't mean that believers who are not assigned to the pulpit to teach and preach the gospel of the kingdom should go into the marketplace or municipalities preaching. "The Kingdom of God is within you" (Luke 17:21 NKJV).

Believers simply have to live the kingdom of God from the inside out. This happens when we are kind to others; when we love others, trade fairly with others, and smile and respect one another. We say and do things that compliment godly character. The anointing is wrapped in our demeanor, our behavior. It's who we are.

As we do so, we will have the same accomplishments Jesus had when He ministered in all the cities and villages. The kingdom of God lived through our daily lifestyle will execute and perform, change worldly atmospheres, environments, and worldly mindsets by divine influence—the prevailing grace and power of Jesus's governmental authority for kingdom increase and peace: "Because as He is, so are we in this world" (1 John 4:17 NKJV).

Obviously, trading our talents in ministry, the marketplace and in municipalities for money to be used to occupy and operate the kingdom of God in worldly kingdoms is a risk that requires our faith, which is why I believe the servant who received only one talent hid it rather than use it to gain more money.

Taking faith risks can be very fearful. And one of the pitfalls of believers has been their unwillingness to trust God and take faith risks. A faith risk is simply appropriating the promises of God and acting—worshipping and praising God—as if we already possess whatever we are believing God for, even though we don't have a tangible or physical manifestation of it. It is complete trust in God.

Believers must take faith risks as we exchange our talents in the marketplace for money. We must understand that the marketplace is a place of commerce. It is where we acquire the financial, technological, and material resources that will advance God's kingdom in the earth.

Faith risks increase our faith, even if it seems that we've failed in previous efforts to achieve a thing. We've not failed because faith never gives up; keep trusting and keep praising God, who sees the end from the beginning, and the things that are not yet done. His counsel will stand, and he will do all his pleasure, for he has spoken it (Isaiah 46:10 NKJV).

People who buy and sell stocks in the stock exchange take risks every day, not necessarily faith risks but risks taken by faith—their belief in the market's trends. They know that good things will happen eventually if they stay the course and not yield to panic, and it usually does. When they are successful, they call it luck; however, there is no such thing as luck in the realm of spiritual faith.

"The wealth of the sinner is stored up for the righteous" (Proverbs 13:22 NKJV). But where is the wealth of the sinner? It is in the marketplace. Therefore, if believers never establish trade or do business or operate in the marketplace with the talents given us by the Lord Jesus, it is unlikely we will acquire the sinner's wealth that awaits us there.

Once believers acquire substantial billions from the marketplace, we will have a massive influence spiritually and physically within municipalities worldwide. We will set the stage for Jesus's return as the governmental ruler of the earth, where "the government will be upon His shoulder" (Isaiah 9:6 NKJV).

People who live according to this world's system of covetousness take risks daily, speculating that the good things of life will come to them. This is a type of faith, not godly faith, but faith as a law or principle. Faith is faith no matter who uses it because faith is a law. For the believer, faith is spiritual law. It is our Father in heaven who does the work. "The blessing of the LORD makes one rich, And He adds no sorrow with it" (Proverbs 10:22 NKJV).

Therefore, the person of faith who believes in God as the Source of all things need not speculate at all. Abba Daddy has already promised to supply all our needs "according to His riches in glory by Christ Jesus" (Philippians 4:19 NKJV). The person of spiritual faith lives in full assurance of an abundant life filled with success, knowing that, as an heir of God, he or she has an inheritance in him.

In other words, the person of spiritual faith is blessed to be a blessing to others. As he or she serves and obeys God, he or she shall spend their days in prosperity and their years in pleasures (Job 36:11 NKJV).

We don't want to be like the slothful servant who said to the nobleman upon his return, "Master, here's your money safe and sound. I kept it hidden in the cellar. I was a little afraid. I know you have high standards and hate sloppiness, and don't suffer fools gladly" (Luke 19:20–21 Message).

This man did not exchange his talent in the marketplace for money, because it required taking a faith risk. This servant did not mix the instruction of the nobleman with faith; therefore the instruction given did not profit him. Whenever the person of faith places his trust in God, he becomes a faith risk-taker who will eventually become a faith success-maker.

Verses 23–26 seal the fate of the unbelieving believer:

> Why didn't you at least invest the money in securities so I would have gotten a little interest on it?" Then he said to those standing there, "Take the money from him and give it to the servant who doubled my stake." They said, "But Master, he already has double …" He said, "That's what I mean: Risk your life and get more than you ever dreamed of. Play it safe and end up holding the bag. (Luke 19:23–26 Message)

Our Holy Father will take money from those slothful believers who do not mix faith with his words, his instructions, and give it to those servants who through their faith double his money by doing business in the marketplace and occupying the earth with his kingdom presence until Jesus returns in glory and in power.

God's consuming fire is being released upon the saints, purifying, and releasing us suddenly into this new season of awakening, where we're being reformed and refreshed through supernatural manifestations. What held us back in past seasons is being burnt away and Father is manifesting Himself as an all-consuming fire, initiating a deep level of refinement that will prepare and release the body of Christ into this kingdom age glory. We will advance the kingdom of God in the earth beyond what we've ever imagined. We will experience furtherance in the five-fold ministry ascension gifts of the Lord Jesus and the gifts of the Holy Spirit, and we will soar to heights and dimensions above what we've dreamed.

There is an urgent need in the body of Christ today for spiritual fathers to teach, train, and develop spiritual sons and daughters to become kingdom-compliant commissioned servant-leaders who occupy, operate, and do business until Jesus returns.

This is a fullness of time season—a season of no restraints to God to do what he has already ordained from before the foundation of the world. The saints must embrace the fact that God is with us. We cannot fail! Our faith in Jesus's finished work at Calvary has sealed our victory. "It may be that the Lord will work for us. For nothing restrains the Lord from saving by many or by few" (1 Samuel 14:6b NKJV). All kingdom—all the time! Stay tuned-in to the frequency of heaven.

CHAPTER 12

Advance the Kingdom of Heaven on Earth

But I want you to know, brethren, that the things which happened to me have actually turned out for the furtherance of the gospel, so that it has become evident to the whole palace guard, and to all the rest, that my chains are in Christ; and most of the brethren in the Lord, having become confident by my chains, are much more bold to speak the word without fear.

—Philippians 1:12–14 NKJV

You therefore must endure hardship as a good soldier of Jesus Christ.

—2 Timothy 2:3

The apostle Paul was the quintessential, prototypical advancer of the kingdom of heaven on the earth. Paul's amazing journey of teaching and preaching the Gospel of the kingdom did not begin without controversy and downright skepticism, especially among believers.

Prior to his transformation from sinner to saint, from Pharisee to God fearing, from the law and religion to New Testament grace and freedom, and prior to God changing his name from Saul to Paul, Saul watched in approval as Stephen the first Christian martyr was being stoned to death because of his faith. Saul's mission was to persecute and scatter the saints and destroy the church.

What a stark contrast between the person that Saul was, a Jew who was born a Roman citizen and educated in Greek culture, and the person Paul became—the apostle who did more to advance the kingdom of God on the earth, showing Christians how to face persecution and endure hardness as a good soldier of Jesus Christ with faith and courage.

Paul was indeed a witness to the end of the earth. In the natural realm, it is quite obvious that his ministry portfolio is very impressive. In our physical world, men honor and highly esteem the kinds of ministry accomplishments that Paul attained, including three missionary journeys, the Jerusalem Council, and the trip to Rome. Add to that amazing list of accomplishments his writing two-thirds of the New Testament, which includes at least thirteen of the twenty-one epistles to the churches.

Today the person of faith who rises to such a pinnacle as Paul's ministry lifework would be considered an icon, idol or deity, a portrait of success having a mega church, his name in lights and his ministry broadcast on every available social media platform—not that this is a bad thing, except many have risen to ministry heights where their character couldn't sustain them. And unlike Paul, they did not keep the faith and they did not endure hardness as a good soldier of Jesus Christ.

Instead, they allowed the enemy to slip in subtly—a testament to their lack of consistency in prioritizing the kingdom of God and making his word first place and final authority in their lives. Fame and fortune destroyed the noble seed of the word that had been planted in their hearts, and they turned before God "into the degenerate plant of an alien vine" (Jeremiah 2:21 NKJV).

In other words, "the cares of this world, the deceitfulness of riches, and the desires for other things entering in choke the word, and it becomes unfruitful" (Mark 4:19 NKJV).

The body of Christ needs kingdom-compliant commissioned

servant-leaders who, like the apostle Paul, will put their confidence in the Lord Jesus Christ rather than their flesh. Even with his extensive and eloquent resume, Paul's desire to know Jesus intimately superseded his desire to be known and honored in the world by people. Paul loved the praise of God more than the praises of man (John 12:43 NKJV). After his conversion he did not allow his ministry, his office as an apostle or the Holy Spirit's gifts operating in and through him to sway him from his first love. He was willing to give up all his earthly accolades and count them as loss to gain Christ and be found in him:

> For we are the circumcision, who worship God in the Spirit, rejoice in Christ Jesus, and have no confidence in the flesh … But what things were gain to me, these I have counted loss for Christ. Yet indeed I also count all things loss for the excellence of the knowledge of Christ Jesus my Lord, for whom I have suffered the loss of all things, and count them as rubbish, that I may gain Christ and be found in Him, not having my own righteousness, which is from the law, but that which is through faith in Christ, the righteousness which is from God by faith. (Philippians 3:3, 7–9 NKJV)

Paul exemplifies the transformation that takes place through the washing of regeneration and the renewing of the mind with the Word of God. The natural mind has to be transformed for kingdom use, if we are to advance the kingdom of heaven on earth.

> So here's what I want you to do, God helping you: Take your everyday, ordinary life – your sleeping, eating, going-to-work, and walking around life – and place it before God as an offering. Embracing what God does for you is the best thing you can do for him. Don't become so well-adjusted to your culture that you fit into it without even thinking. Instead, fix your attention on God. You'll be changed from the inside out, Readily recognize what he wants from you, and quickly respond

> to it. Unlike the culture around you, always dragging you down to its level of immaturity, God brings the best out of you, develops well-formed maturity in you. (Romans 12:1–2 Message)

Like the apostle Paul, today's believers must embrace what God does for us as the best thing we can do for him—that's covenant. And I believe that true covenant with God, Creator and Sustainer of the universe, begins with discipleship, and discipleship has its beginning in discipline. "Therefore I run thus: not with uncertainty. Thus I fight: not as one who beats the air. But I discipline my body and bring it into subjection, lest, when I have preached to others, I myself should become disqualified" (1 Corinthians 9:26–27 NKJV).

Notice that Paul says, "I discipline my body" (1 Corinthians 9:27 NKJV). Discipline begins with the person, and it is not a one-time event. It is an ongoing process that requires diligence, steady effort, and obedience.

> Endure hardship as discipline; God is treating you as his children. For what children are not disciplined by their father? If you are not disciplined - and everyone undergoes discipline - then you are not legitimate, not true sons and daughters at all. Moreover, we have all had human fathers who disciplined us and we respected them for it. How much more should we submit to the Father of spirits and live! Our fathers disciplined us for a little while as they thought best; but God disciplines us for our good, in order that we may share in his holiness. No discipline seems pleasant at the time, but painful. Later on, however, it produces a harvest of righteousness and peace for those who have been trained by it. (Hebrews12:7–11 NIV)

The Greek word for *discipline* as used in the above text is *paideia*, which means tutorage—that is, education or training; disciplinary correction; chastening, chastisement, instruction, nurture. Discipline is a controlled behavior; enforced compliance; self-control.[62]

---

[62] *Strong's Exhaustive Concordance of the Bible, NT*, 3809.

The Greek word for *disciple* is *mathetes*, which means a learner—that is, pupil. But the process toward becoming a disciple comes from the Greek word *matheteuo*, meaning to become a pupil; to disciple—that is, enroll as scholar; be a disciple, instruct, teach. This indicates thought accompanied by endeavor to imitate the teacher.[63]

Jesus told those Jews who believed on Him that if they would continue in His word, then they would be His disciples indeed (John 8:31 NKJV).

There is a sad dilemma being played out in our churches today to our shame, because the Church has not generationally trained disciples who can imitate and reflect a spiritual parent who took the time and patience required to teach, train and develop them to become spiritually mature sons and daughters—disciplined disciples—kingdom-compliant commissioned servant-leaders who discover their kingdom assignment to advance the kingdom of heaven on the earth, who teach, train, and develop other faithful men and women to do the same, generating like-minded generations.

Since the last spiritual awakening, the church has become complacent. It has barricaded itself within its four-walled structures and allowed social media outlets to be the basis of teaching and training without the intimate relationship that is required of a spiritual parent to raise sons and daughters who also know their parent intimately, who not only imitate and reflect their anointing but also their godly character and lifestyle.

With the advent of global social media platforms, many would-be spiritual fathers and mothers abandoned the physical, hands-on relationship and embraced the easier, less stringent mode of raising spiritual sons and daughters. For the most part, many leaders have done what some parents do when they are tired or don't want to be bothered with little Taquana and little Bakari: they turn on the television or give them a tablet or gaming device to keep them busy.

While this may work for a period of time, and even though learning on some level is taking place, it neither supplies the proper learning style nor the tools required to establish the discipline the children need to become studious pupils. In similar likeness, many church leaders

---

[63] *Strong's Exhaustive Concordance of the Bible, NT,* 3809, 3101, 3100.

stopped training and developing their members and allowed them to learn on their own from their electronic devices without any revelatory knowledge of scripture.

Any Facebook page will reveal that one out of every ten people is a Facebook minister releasing word from scripture of which they have little to no intimate, spiritual relationship. In many cases, church leaders have traded the process that develops and transforms ordinary humans into disciples—spiritually mature stewards of the faith who disciple others—for fame, fortune, and the easy, less-hassled life. We no longer give of ourselves and our time to plant wholly righteous seeds of the Word of God into the hearts of those to whom we are called to shepherd. What matters to many leaders, would-be spiritual parents, is the number of followers they can amass on social media outlets.

As the apostle James says, "My brethren, these things ought not to be so" (James 3:10 NKJV).

The church has lacked spiritual fathers who teach, train, and develop the discipline required for their sons and daughters to become disciples indeed who aggressively advance the kingdom of heaven on earth. "And from the days of John the Baptist until the present time, the kingdom of heaven has endured violent assault, and violent men seize it by force [as a precious prize – a share in the heavenly kingdom is sought with most ardent zeal and intense exertion]" (Matthew 11:12 The Amplified Bible).

There must be a return of apostolic parenting if the church is to maintain a generational succession of disciples commissioned for kingdom-compliant servant-leadership. Saints must be spiritually *transformed* into disciples—transfigured, changed, to fashion, shape, form, a share. The Greek word that denotes these things is *metamorphoo*.[64] Saints have to be morphed into disciples.

To *transform* means to change in composition or structure; to change the outward form or appearance of; to change in character or condition.

Transformation is the act of transforming or the state of being transformed. It is a marked change in appearance or character, especially one for the better.

Spiritual conversion takes place from the inside out. So, then,

[64] *Strong's Exhaustive Concordance of the Bible, NT*, 3339, 3445, 3313.

discipleship transformation is the process of changing the nature and character of a believer through a sequence of advancements in which the believer is converted by the instruction, teaching, training, development and mentoring of a spiritual parent into a pupil, a learner who endeavors to imitate his spiritual parent. The proof of his discipleship can be seen and affirmed through his commitment to give up his life to follow Christ, continue in the Word of God, and advance the kingdom on earth by teaching and training other faithful men and women for generational succession as kingdom-builders.

"True disciples are not manufactured wholesale. They are produced one by one because someone has taken the pains to discipline; to instruct and enlighten; to nurture and train one that is younger." I believe this is the job of the apostolic parent.

What if Jesus had not humbled himself and become a disciple, a learner, a true spiritual Son to his Father? We forget that Jesus was also son of man, and he had to submit himself to the spiritual mentorship of his Father in order to fulfill his earthly assignment. Jesus was led and guided by the Holy Spirit just as believers, who are true sons and daughters, must do. Jesus is our example. If Jesus had refused to become a disciple, a spiritual Son of God, he never would have humbled himself. He never would have learned obedience, and He never would have become the author of our eternal salvation.

> *Though He was a Son, yet He learned obedience by the things which He suffered. And having been perfected, He became the author of eternal salvation to all who obey Him.*
>
> **—Hebrews 5:8–9 NKJV**

> *Who being in the form of God, did not consider it robbery to be equal with God, but made Himself of no reputation, taking the form of a bondservant, and coming in the likeness of men. And being found in appearance as a man, He humbled Himself and became obedient to the point of death, even the death of the cross.*
>
> **—Philippians 2:6–8 NKJV**

Jesus did not take any shortcuts as a man. He emptied himself of his deity, although equality with God was his right and heritage. Jesus continuously allowed His Father to teach, train and develop him for kingdom expansion on earth. As a pupil of his Father, Jesus learned through many experiences, the things which he suffered—things that were excruciatingly painful, yet they completed him to carry out his earthly mandate.

Because Jesus willingly became a disciple, a true spiritual Son to his Father, he became the author of our eternal salvation. Jesus remained steadfast in the will of his Father. He showed genuine commitment as he endured the process that led him to be crucified. His mind was transformed for kingdom expansion, and that transformation took place at Calvary, where Jesus was made sin for us, so that we might be made the righteousness of God through him (2 Corinthians 5:21 NKJV).

That was Jesus's kingdom assignment, and he fulfilled it. But fulfillment didn't come without challenges. Jesus teaches us that there can be no fulfillment of purpose where there is no commitment. And where there is no commitment, there will be no transformation.

Jesus endured the process that led him to the cross, even as he discipled twelve men. He endured Gethsemane, the betrayal of Judas Iscariot, his arrest and arraignment, Peter's denial, judgment before Pontius Pilate, being stripped naked, a crown of thorns thrust onto his head, spat on by Roman soldiers, slapped, mocked, beaten with a whip of thorns that literally tore and pulled his flesh apart, nails that weighed two pounds each driven into his hands and feet, and being nailed on a cross between two criminals.

During the process of discipleship and becoming a spiritual son, there will be many opportunities to give up before full transformation of the mind is complete. Yet Jesus had the presence of mind while dying on the cross to save one of the criminals who repented, to forgive those who crucified him, and to commit the care of his mother, Mary, to the care of the apostle John. What a transformation!

Jesus's passion empowered him to endure the shame—to look beyond it—and see the glory of a Father who was well pleased. That is what true commitment to advancing the kingdom on earth looks like. Jesus's life on earth is the permanent model of discipleship and spiritual maturity. His life on earth was an example of what transformation of the mind for kingdom use looks like and the commitment that powers it.

Spiritual maturity does not form in a vacuum. It grows over time through personal relationship with God, and by allowing the Holy Spirit to empower us. This kind of commitment is formed out of a foundation of love, humility, faithfulness, obedience, and patience. It forms as we willfully confront and overcome every challenge, difficulty, struggle, hardship, and pain.

Jesus's life on earth exemplifies this process, and we are encouraged to follow his model of discipleship and spiritual maturity, which will lead us also to the place where our minds are transformed for kingdom use and advancement.

Our attitude as believers must be one of complete and continual submission to God so that we, too, will be completed to become true disciples of Jesus Christ to the fulfillment of our divine assignment, which include advancing God's kingdom on earth.

ADVANCEMENT IS A STANDARD OF THE KINGDOM OF GOD

Advancement is about promotion; it is about a unique advantage one has. In our case, as believers, it is a supernatural advantage we have that unbelievers do not. To advance means to further or to help the progress of something. It means to move forward in space or time; to move or push something forward, especially forcefully; to make something happen at an earlier time or date; and, to bring forward, to hasten.

A standard is an established method of accomplishing a task; a principle, example or measure used for comparison. Standard is also defined as something set up and established by authority as a rule for the measure of quantity, weight, extent, value, or quality; the personal flag of the head of a state or of a member of a royal family; an organization flag carried by a mounted or motorized military unit. Standard applies to any definite rule, principle, or measure established by authority.

The Hebrew word for *standard, nec* taken from *nacac*, denotes a flag; also a sail; a flagstaff; generally a signal; banner, a conspicuous signal; to raise a beacon; lift up as an ensign.[65]

[65] *Strong's Exhaustive Concordance of the Bible, OT*, 5251, 5264.

For our purpose, we will approach advancement and standard as military terms. In other words, our mandate as believers is to subdue the earth, making it ready for Jesus's return. Jesus's commission to the saints says so and is a military command from our commanding officer, Jesus Christ.

> *Go therefore and make disciples of all the nations, baptizing them in the name of the Father and of the Son and of the Holy Spirit, teaching them to observe all things that I have commanded you; and lo, I am with you always, even to the end of the age. Amen.*
>
> **—Matthew 28:19–20 NKJV**

> *You have given a banner to those who fear You, that it may be displayed because of the truth. Selah.*
>
> **—Psalm 60:4 NKJV**

This is the twenty-first-century. God has reestablished the ministry offices of the apostle and prophet as foundations of the church (Ephesians 2:20 NKJV). And God now requires the full measure of the stature of Christ to arise within his body. This is the season of manifestation of the sons of God, the army of the Lord full of love, spiritually mature, doing exploits and subduing earthly kingdoms. The standard has been raised for citizens of the kingdom of heaven. The requirement is that we are standard-bearers, kingdom soldiers, who carry the flag, ensign, or banner that display the territories that God has decreed are his. This is the season of supernatural manifestations—demonstration of Holy Spirit and of power (1 Corinthians 2:4 NKJV)—which can only take place through accelerated advancement of the church for supernatural lift and dominion.

> Lift up a banner on the high mountain, Raise your voice to them; Wave your hand, that they may enter the gates of the nobles. I have commanded My sanctified ones; I have also called My mighty ones for My anger - those who rejoice in My exaltation. The noise of a multitude in the mountains, like that of many people! A tumultuous noise of the kingdoms of nations gathered together! The

> Lord of hosts musters the army for battle. They come from a far country, from the end of heaven - the Lord and His weapons of indignation, to destroy the whole land. Wail, for the day of the Lord is at hand! It will come as destruction from the Almighty. Therefore all hands will be limp, every man's heart will melt, And they will be afraid. Pangs and sorrows will take hold of them; they will be in pain as a woman in childbirth; they will be amazed at one another; their faces will be like flames. Behold, the day of the Lord comes, cruel, with both wrath and fierce anger, to lay the land desolate; and He will destroy its sinners from it. (Isaiah 13:2–9 NKJV)

The spearheads—apostles and prophets—of this remnant army of the Lord are challenging believers to live above the systems of the world through the grace of the Lord Jesus Christ and God's faithfulness to his word. As members of the universal body of Christ, we must now put into practice the governmental principles of the kingdom of heaven that produce spiritual, physical, and materialistic prosperity and wealth for advancing God's kingdom on earth.

This standard of the kingdom requires that saints be purified by the fire of the Holy Spirit, refined and tested in the furnace of affliction, so that everything that isn't of God can be shaken, and that which cannot be shaken may remain (Hebrews 12:27 NKJV).

> *The LORD gives voice before His army, For His camp is very great; For strong is the One who executes His word. For the day of the Lord is great and very terrible; Who can endure it?*
>
> **—Joel 2:11 NKJV**

> *Who is she who looks forth as the morning, fair as the moon, clear as the sun, awesome as an army with banners?*
>
> **—Song of Solomon 6:10 NKJV**

Yes, the standard for kingdom advancement has been raised. Now believers must ascend into the culture of the kingdom through righteousness and peace and joy driven by the Holy Spirit (Romans

14:17 NKJV). If a person knows God has called and ordained them to be a kingdom-compliant commissioned servant-leader, he or she must rise to that level. Here is the kingdom command: "Go through, go through the gates! Prepare the way for the people. Build up, build up the highway! Take out the stones, lift up a banner for the peoples!" (Isaiah 62:10 NKJV).

Kingdom-compliant commissioned servant-leaders have arisen to the standard of the kingdom. These kingdom leaders prioritize the pattern and government of the kingdom of heaven as taught by Jesus and the apostles of the first-century church.

Our earlier study of Paul's ministry plainly shows that the apostle stands out as the standard of the kingdom, and he held himself accountable to it, fathering other sons and daughters who could also adhere to that standard.

This standard separates those leaders who have endured the God process to spiritual maturity and whose priority it is to advance the government of the kingdom of heaven on earth as opposed to simply "having church" or some other inspirational meetings that make people feel good but do not hold them accountable for spiritual growth.

I sense that the days of church leaders who are not kingdom compliant, who do things and make things happen by their own might and power—the abundance of their resources, along with their ability to influence others, which leads to personal fame and fortune—are over!

The church, the end-time remnant army of God, representing his kingdom, must be led by those who prioritize his plans and purposes—commissioned servant-leaders, not commissioned "served leaders."

The Father is commissioning those who are his as kingdom-compliant servant-leaders. Commissions are not given; they are earned. Our earnest commitment to endure God's process of development toward spiritual maturity—being equipped and deployed for success into our kingdom assignments—all play a role in our rise to the place of a commission.

A commission is an authorization or command to act in a prescribed manner or to perform prescribed acts; a Charge; authority to act for, in behalf of, or in place of another.

The Hebrew word translated to *commission* is *dath*, meaning a royal edict or stature; commandment, commission, decree, law, and manner.[66] Its Greek companion is *epitrope*, which means to give permission—that is, by implication full power; allow; give leave, liberty, license, let, and permit.[67]

Commissioned servant-leaders are standard-bearers. They have been called and ordained by God to be commanders. God has given them a charge and authorization to act on behalf of his Son, Jesus. God has given them full authority and power as ambassadors for Christ. As such, they are those who bear or carry the standard, the banner, ones who lead an organization, movement, party, or corporation on behalf of the kingdom of heaven.

In the United States, our form of government is a representative democracy—government by the people, for the people; rule of the majority driven by capitalism, free enterprise or money. God is the Sovereign King of the kingdom of heaven, and the constitution that governs his kingdom—the Word of God—is his government of his people, for his people, driven by obedience and willful servitude, and the benefits of the kingdom are given to all citizens without partiality—a theocracy.

Commissioned servant-leaders are also commanders. A commander is one in an official position of command or control; commanding officer. The presiding officer of a society or organization; a commissioned officer.

The Hebrew word translated *commander* is *tsavah*, which means to constitute, enjoin; appoint, give a charge, send with a charge; commander, send a messenger, put in order.[68]

Commissioned servant-leaders are kingdom-compliant commanders sent forth by the authority of the King of kings and given a charge to put or set things in kingdom order. They are Commanders of the Lord's army who protect and defend and advance the Kingdom of Heaven on the earth. Their assignment is to carry out the plans and purposes of God, their Commander in Chief and to please their Commanding Officer, Jesus Christ.

---

66 *Strong's Exhaustive Concordance of the Bible, OT,* 1881.

67 *Strong's Exhaustive Concordance of the Bible, NT,* 2011.

68 *Strong's Exhaustive Concordance of the Bible, OT,* 6680.

> *You therefore must endure hardship as a good soldier of Jesus Christ. [4]No one engaged in warfare entangles himself with the affairs of this life, that he may please him who enlisted him as a soldier.*
>
> **—2 Timothy 2:3–4 NKJV**

This is a dangerous time to be spiritually lazy! One of the end-time schemes of Satan is to keep the saints of God busy doing good things, but not necessarily God-things. He wants to keep us busy doing what seems right to man, but not pleasing to God. The devil can't do very much about our salvation, but he consistently attacks our purpose. His goal is to keep Christians stagnant, sitting idly, waiting for the Lord to return. This is called religion.

The devil knows that our purpose is anointed and leads us into sonship, where we learn to hear the voice of our heavenly Father and obey him, and he'll use our minds as a battlefield where he releases fiery darts in the form of evil thoughts that, if we're not tuned-in to heaven's frequency, can become strongholds. But for the spiritually alert, who are always God conscious, Christ centered and Holy Spirit focused, obedience and service to God leads to fulfillment of our kingdom assignments.

The fulfilling of divine assignment requires spiritual maturity, commitment, loyalty and faithful devotion to God, which will always lead to advancement of His kingdom on earth. And, advancing the kingdom of heaven on earth begins with advancing people.

Let's take a slightly different slant on the scripture text above. This time from the Good News Bible: "Take your part in suffering, as a loyal soldier of Christ Jesus. A soldier on active duty wants to please his commanding officer and so does not get mixed up in the affairs of civilian life … Think about what I am saying, because the Lord will enable you to understand it all" (2 Timothy 2:3–4, 7 GNB).

The Father has prepared a remnant of the body of Christ for the end-time harvest of souls. The church can no longer be a collection of saved folk with no power. The church cannot afford to simply be slumbering saints, sleeping with vessels that contain no oil.

The five foolish virgins were just as much saints as were the five wise virgins. What was the difference? Spiritual maturity! The five wise virgins had been processed and prepared by God with a readiness to will and to do God's good pleasure. The five foolish virgins had enough oil to live in the kingdom, but not enough to operate within next level assignments where advancement takes place. This requires mantles of spiritual anointing along with the superior heavenly mindset of a victor's mentality.

This is where the church finds herself today. Father has ushered his preserved kingdom-compliant remnant of spiritually mature faith warriors into next level advancement and new realms and assignments for supernatural manifestation and exponential increase and multiplication of resources for the advancement of his kingdom on earth and for the fulfillment of our kingdom assignments.

Our heavenly Father knows that the saints must be fully committed and possess an abundance of his word (oil) for distribution to the unprepared world-oriented multitude—unbelievers and faithless believers alike. Supernatural manifestations are being released through the saints, convincing proof of the power of the Holy Spirit.

For those who are mature saints and servant-leaders, this reformation of the church and advancement of the kingdom of heaven on earth signifies the beginning of our time of fulfillment. All our preparation to become commissioned servant-leaders, kingdom-compliant commanders, has been leading us to and positioning us for such a time as this.

You are no longer a foot soldier, getting beat up by the demonic schemes of the systems of the world. You are a Kingdom horseman, who will ride with Jesus as a Commander in the Armies of Heaven clothed in clean, white, fine linen.

We have been pruned, shaped, and molded, shifted and sifted over the years. And it has all been leading us to this God season, this kairos time in which things that God has ordained should and must be done. The invitation of God's heart to us is for a deeper level of seeking him—a deeper level of consecration; a deeper level of abiding in his presence; and a deeper level of yielding, worship, and praise. This is to keep us pure. We've entered a season of radical shifts, sudden transformation, and instant alignment with the heart of God's plans and purposes.

Yes, we are one body. We need not look for another because there is no other. God does not have an alternate plan. His counsel will stand. We are the spiritually mature remnant church of which God has patiently waited. And I say to readers, commissioned kingdom-compliant servant-leaders, "You are commanders. Arise! Advance the kingdom of heaven on earth." We are about to be married! We are the bride of Christ. Let's occupy, do business, operate with the talents the Lord has given us, and advance the kingdom of heaven on earth. All kingdom, all the time!

CHAPTER 13

Learn to Walk with Jesus

Enoch lived sixty-five years, and begot Methuselah. After he begot Methuselah, Enoch walked with God three hundred years, and had sons and daughters. So all the days of Enoch were three hundred and sixty-five years. And Enoch walked with God; and he was not, for God took him.

—Genesis 5:21–24 NKJV

The above context of scripture is of profound magnitude. It is deep! It is weighty with the splendor of God, and it expresses an unfathomable amount of revelatory knowledge that many believers miss. I like to relate the verse of scripture that says, "Deep calls unto deep at the noise of Your waterfalls; all Your waves and billows have gone over me" (Psalm 42:7 NKJV), to scriptures like the one above because they contain secrets and mysteries of which the Holy Spirit is willing to reveal to any believer who sincerely desire Holy Spirit revelation of the Word of God and makes himself available to receive it.

As a child and young adult growing up in the holiness church my family attended, the old saints would sing a song called "We've Come This Far by Faith, Leaning on the Lord." Today many saints not only sing that song but they also pray it to the Lord. They say, "Lord, just let me lean on You 'cause I can't walk this out by myself."

Two other versions of this song, "Let Me Lean on You" and "Jesus said, 'I Won't Let You Fall if You Lean On Me'" have had great success. Over the years, these songs have had many variations. Songs like these have survived because they have constantly been upgraded to meet the cultural, technological, and innovative times and lifestyles in which we live. The question is, how many saints are still leaning on Jesus with the same religious mindset they had twenty-five years ago?

There is nothing wrong with leaning on Jesus. I have very real memories of times I had to do just that; but those times were also seasons of consistent spiritual growth as well. As a novice, a new believer, I did not yet possess the faith to do anything other than lean on Jesus. I had to lean on Him for just about everything, especially when the devil would bombard my mine with all the "pleasures of the world" I was missing. So it really is okay for a new believer to lean on Jesus; and because spiritual maturity involves the planting of the word in ones heart, it begins as a seed and requires proper spiritual cultivation before the word planted is activated to produce fruit. God really does want to bring forth those deep seated anointings and powers that are within you.

Here's the problem. Many saints have been saved for decades and have not grown up in Christ as spiritually mature saints. God will sometimes manifest supernatural feats for a new believer as a beginning to building their faith and trust in him. But he is too wise to leave them in that place because faith grows. Faith comes by hearing, and hearing the Word of God —being sensitive to what is heard with an attentive ear to receive and obey or act on it (Romans 10:17 NKJV).

God does not want his children to be babes in Christ all their Christian lives. So he allows situations that will present an opportunity to trust him. As the author of the Epistle to the Hebrews said, and I believe it to be Paul: "But, beloved, we are confident of better things concerning you, yes, things that accompany salvation, though we speak in this manner" (Hebrews 6:9 NKJV).

Paul's exhortation to spiritual maturity was not lost in any of his epistles. He was a constant advocate of spiritual growth for the saints, and he chastised the Hebrews for not being spiritually mature when they should have been, because many were weary and wanted to give up on their Christian way of life.

> For though by this time you ought to be teachers, you need someone to teach you again the first principles of the oracles of God; and you have come to need milk and not solid food. For everyone who partakes only of milk is unskilled in the word of righteousness, for he is a babe. But solid food belongs to those who are of full age, that is, those who by reason of use have their [spiritual] senses exercised to discern both good and evil. (Hebrews 5:12–14 NKJV)

The saints that apostle Paul is speaking to were not recent converts; they'd been believers for quite some time. Yet they needed to be taught again. This implies these believers had taken positive steps toward becoming spiritually mature Christians, and for lack of spiritual exercise—a consistent regimen of trusting God and mixing his word by faith—they either stopped growing or slipped back to the place where they were when they first accepted Christ.

The word *again* as used in verse 12 carries significant weight, as it suggests a reverse direction, or to an original starting point; back to a former place or state.

The Greek word for *again* is *palin*, which means oscillatory repetition; anew—that is, of place; back; of time; once more.

The above context of scripture paints for us a picture of adult saints who look and carry on like babies who have yet to be weaned from milk. And because they are babes in Christ, they also are unskilled in the word of righteousness. They have not developed the spiritual skill of how to wield the sword of righteousness. Baby Christians can never become wise master builders. They have to mature, be weaned from the first principles of the oracles of God, and consume solid food—advanced teaching of the Word of God of which they hear and obey by faith.

Advanced teaching belongs to spiritually mature saints; those who show steady growth because they consistently exercise their spirit with the Word of God. Remember, in consistency lies the power. Spiritually mature saints consistently use—hear, study, and act in faith—the Word of God.

Paul lets us know that we cannot properly discern between good and evil unless our spiritual senses are consistently exercised by our continuous use of the Word of God. The spiritually mature have progressed in their spiritual life and have become believers who exercise sound judgment and discernment.

As stated above, there is a time to lean on Jesus. Most assuredly as a novice in the Christian faith but also in times when it seems we are overwhelmed with an extended barrage of misfortune, sorrow, or calamity. That is a time when even spiritually mature believers tend to lean on Jesus, but they tend to recover quickly. It's like laying in the bosom or on the breast of Jesus for immediate strength, energy, and recovery of their faith. They remember who they are in and through Him, and they pick themselves up, recover their faith, and resume their walk with Him. "I can do all things through Christ who strengthens me" (Philippians 4:13 NKJV).

The apostle John was very close to Jesus, and at times he would lean on Jesus's breast. John was somewhat discouraged at times, and one of those times took place at the Last Supper prior to Judas's betrayal of Jesus. This was a time when John leaned on Jesus not from a position of fear and unbelief but from a relational position born out of intimacy.

> When Jesus had said these things, He was troubled in spirit, and testified and said, "Most assuredly, I say to you, one of you will betray Me." Then the disciples looked at one another, perplexed about whom He spoke. Now there was leaning on Jesus' bosom one of His disciples, whom Jesus loved. Simon Peter therefore motioned to him to ask who it was of whom He spoke. Then leaning back on Jesus' breast, he said to Him, "Lord, who is it?" [26]Jesus answered, "It is he to whom I shall give a piece of bread when I have dipped it." And

> having dipped the bread, He gave it to Judas Iscariot, the son of Simon. (John 13:21–26 NKJV)
>
> Then Peter, turning around, saw the disciple whom Jesus loved following, who also had leaned on His breast at the supper and said, "Lord, who is the one who betrays You?" (John 21:20 NKJV).

The Greek word translated for *lean* is *anapipto*, which means to fall back, lean back.[69] John was actually lying back, leaning back on Jesus's breast.

I know what today's saints mean when they say, "I'm leaning on Jesus." They're simply saying, "I can't get through this situation, trouble, calamity without you, Jesus." They're saying, "Lord, I trust you to bring me out of this or do it for me." But that's not biblical faith. Again, the problem here is that these are requests void of faith or complete trust in God. They are likened to wishing or hoping God rescues them without the required ingredients added to the request or supplication—the promises of God and their faith in the promises of God. "We then, as workers together with Him, also plead with you not to receive the grace of God in vain" (2 Corinthians 6:1 NKJV).

The prophet Jeremiah is known as the "weeping prophet" who mourned over Jerusalem's sorrowful plight. He lamented, crying in despair over the destruction of Jerusalem and its desolation due to the grievous sins of the people. Jeremiah prayed for mercy. And his prayer is one of which I suppose some would say, "Jeremiah leaned on the Lord." Even so, Jeremiah did not allow this terrible tragedy to put him in a faithless quagmire. He cried to God in despair, but he recovered himself by remembering who and what he was in God.

> I am the man who has seen affliction by the rod of His wrath. He has led me and made me walk In darkness and not in light. Surely He has turned His hand against me Time and time again throughout the day. He has aged my flesh and my skin, And broken my bones. He

---

[69] *Strong's Exhaustive Concordance of the Bible, NT*, 377.

> has besieged me And surrounded me with bitterness and woe. He has set me in dark places Like the dead of long ago … You have moved my soul far from peace; I have forgotten prosperity. And I said, "My strength and my hope have perished from the Lord." (Lamentations 3:1–6, 17–18 NKJV)

Obviously, that is a prayer of one who is grief-stricken. But it is more of a complaint consisting of Jeremiah's plight as a consequence of the destruction of Jerusalem, which the Lord allowed at the hands of Babylon. He starts out praying as if God is the enemy; but what an amazing recovery of Jeremiah's faith.

> Remember my affliction and roaming, The wormwood and the gall. My soul still remembers and sinks within me. This I recall to my mind, therefore I have hope. Through the Lord's mercies we are not consumed, because His compassions fail not. They are new every morning; great is Your faithfulness. "The LORD is my portion," says my soul, "Therefore I hope in Him." The LORD is good to those who wait for Him, To the soul who seeks Him. It is good that one should hope and wait quietly for the salvation of the Lord. (Lamentations 3:19–26 NKJV)

Wow! What a remarkable statement of faith by the prophet Jeremiah: "Through the Lord's mercies we are not consumed, because His compassions fail not. They are new every morning; great is Your faithfulness" (Lamentations 3:22–23 NKJV). Notice that Jeremiah had to recall to his mind those times when he had gone through afflictions and hard times prior to the siege of Jerusalem. Notwithstanding the immediate horror and terror of what Jeremiah was experiencing, along with what seemed to be God's silence in not answering his prayers to save Jerusalem and allowing the destruction, Jeremiah remembered all the proof of God's compassion and faithfulness. He refused to give up hope, and he attached his faith to God's faithfulness. Though Jeremiah's life was steeped in affliction, by faith he maintained the Lord as his inheritance. He had faith in God's faithfulness to his own word.

Jeremiah's ability to wait on God further points out the advantage or leverage saints have through their God-given ability to be patient. God is a good God, and his goodness is found even when we are distressed because of trouble or calamity. During these times, we must earnestly worship or seek God and wait for his deliverance. This isn't something we can do halfheartedly. We must encourage ourselves in the Lord and endure the afflictions and tribulations patiently, without complaint (Hebrews 10:36 NKJV). This is where real faith meets the problem. It is a total submission to God. Real faith doesn't struggle to produce results through selfish or fleshly means; it simply rests and lets our heavenly Father do the work.

There are times also when saints find themselves leaning on their own sense knowledge. King Solomon, the earthly king of all wisdom, points out to us the vain glory associated with doing so. It is impossible for believers to use their human insight or intelligence when standing in faith for the wisdom of God. We must learn the righteous ways of our heavenly Father, our Abba Daddy, and trust him completely, for he sees all and knows all.

> *Trust in the Lord with all your heart, and lean not on your own understanding; In all your ways acknowledge Him, And He shall direct your paths. Do not be wise in your own eyes; Fear the Lord and depart from evil. It will be health to your flesh, And strength to your bones.*
>
> **—Proverbs 3:5–8 NKJV**

Saints are God's spiritual architects, his master builders, whom he has placed on earth to build and advance his kingdom. "According to the grace of God which was given to me, as a wise master builder I have laid the foundation, and another builds on it. But let each one take heed how he builds on it. For no other foundation can anyone lay than that which is laid, which is Jesus Christ" (1Corinthians 3:10–11 NKJV).

The Father has equipped his spiritually mature sons and daughters with his nature, power, and glory to build upon the foundation of his dear Son, to walk with him as his representatives on earth, not to lean on him or our own understanding. The apostle Paul said we should take heed how we build. Jesus was not a weak, immature Son of God. He was strong, mature, and he learned obedience through the things he suffered.

Yet Jesus didn't simply lean on his Father, expecting him to do the work of bringing salvation to all people without Jesus's working together with him. Jesus provided the passion to willingly obey his Father, and his Father supplied the resurrection power that raised Jesus from the dead.

As saints, we, too, must be perfected or fitted for completion of our kingdom assignment through the things that will definitely require us to endure for Christ's sake and the Gospel's by walking with God in faith and not leaning on him, expecting that he's just going to make everything all right.

As we grow spiritually, we will learn how to walk with God as Enoch did; we will learn how to stay tuned-in to the frequency of heaven and walk and talk with God in the "cool of the day" (Genesis 3:8 NKJV). And we will be transformed to become the author of our kingdom purpose.

May our sincere desire be to reflect our loyalty, devotion, and faithful commitment to our wise master builder, Jesus Christ, by walking with him as spiritually mature saints as opposed to leaning on him as baby Christians. Be assured, baby Christians can never become wise master builders!

MATURE SAINTS WALK WITH GOD

The Bible says that Enoch walked with God. "Enoch lived sixty-five years, and begot Methuselah. After he begot Methuselah, Enoch walked with God three hundred years, and had sons and daughters. So all the days of Enoch were three hundred and sixty-five years. And Enoch walked with God; and he was not, for God took him" (Genesis 5:21–24 NKJV).

What exactly does it mean to walk with God?

Halak is the Hebrew word translated for *walk*. It means to walk continually, be conversant, be eased, enter, exercise self, follow, grow, walk abroad, to and fro, up and down to places.[70]

---

[70] *Strong's Exhaustive Concordance of the Bible, OT*, 1980.

Halak is akin to *yalak*, which means to walk; to carry away, follow, grow, lead forth, prosper, pursue, spread, to be weak.

The Greek translation of *walk* is *peripateo*, which means a path under foot; to tread all around—that is, walk at large as proof of ability; to live, deport oneself, follow as a companion or votary; be occupied with, walk about.[71]

I am convinced the New Testament saints of the first century walked with God, signifying the lifestyle and activities of the individual life, their observance of kingdom ordinances as well as moral conduct. Their walk with God was one of walking in the newness of life—after Holy Spirit, in love, by faith, in wisdom, in honesty, in truth, in good works, after the commandment of the Lord, Jesus, and not after their flesh—not after the manner of men in craftiness nor in the vanity of the mind nor disorderly.

> Therefore we were buried with Him through baptism into death, that just as Christ was raised from the dead by the glory of the Father, even so we also should walk in newness of life. For if we have been united together in the likeness of His death, certainly we also shall be in the likeness of His resurrection, knowing this, that our old man was crucified with Him, that the body of sin might be done away with, that we should no longer be slaves of sin. (Romans 6:4–6 NKJV)

> For what the law could not do in that it was weak through the flesh, God did by sending His own Son in the likeness of sinful flesh, on account of sin: He condemned sin in the flesh, that the righteous requirement of the law might be fulfilled in us who do not walk according to the flesh but according to the Spirit. For those who live according to the flesh set their minds on the things of the flesh, but those who live according to the Spirit, the things of the Spirit. For to be carnally minded is death, but to be spiritually minded is life and peace. (Romans 8:3–6 NKJV)

---

[71] *Strong's Exhaustive Concordance of the Bible, NT,* 4043.

> Therefore be imitators of God as dear children. And walk in love, as Christ also has loved us and given Himself for us, an offering and a sacrifice to God for a sweet-smelling aroma. (Ephesians 5:1–2 NKJV)

> For we walk by faith, not by sight. (2 Corinthians 5:7 NKJV)

> Walk in wisdom toward those who are outside, redeeming the time. (Colossians 4:5 NKJV)

> Let us walk honestly, as in the day; not in rioting and drunkenness, not in chambering and wantonness, not in strife and envying. But put ye on the LORD Jesus Christ, and make no provision for the flesh, to fulfill the lusts thereof. (Romans 13:13–14 KJV)

> I rejoiced greatly that I have found some of your children walking in truth, as we received commandment from the Father. (2 John 4 NKJV)

> For we are His workmanship, created in Christ Jesus for good works, which God prepared beforehand that we should walk in them. (Ephesians 2:10)

> This is love, that we walk according to His commandments. This is the commandment, that as you have heard from the beginning, you should walk in it. (2 John 6 NKJV)

Let's go back to the life of Enoch. There is a difference between walking with God and leaning on Him. Leaning on God implies merely living, survival mode. But walking with God signifies thriving in life, living the best life on earth as God does in heaven. The things that accompany our salvation are ours in abundance as we obey and serve him. "If they obey and serve Him, they shall spend their days in prosperity, And their years in pleasures" (Job 36:11 NKJV).

Salvation is both a spiritual and physical reality. It is the object of our confident hope. We have eternal life with God, but we live on the physical earth now; therefore the things that accompany our eternal life are enjoyed physically on earth. The Greek word for *salvation* is *soteria*, which denotes deliverance, preservation, health, rescue, safety, maintenance of peace and harmony, do well and make whole.[72] These are things we need here on earth, not in heaven.

Enoch's walk with God, the distinguishing factor in his life, entailed both the spiritual and the physical realms. Something transpired or shifted in Enoch after he turned sixty-five years old and after he begot Methuselah. As we know, Methuselah is believed to have lived 969 years, longer than any recorded human beings physical life. But Enoch, Methuselah's father, was taken to eternity with God after only 365 years. So, then, Methuselah symbolizes longevity of physical life on earth and Enoch symbolizes our eternal existence with God, which is far greater, even if our life on earth is short.

After the birth of Methuselah, Enoch walked with God for three hundred years. For three hundred years, Enoch's lifestyle and activities signified his observance of God's Kingdom ordinances, as well as his personal moral conduct. His walk with God was one of walking in the newness of life—after the Spirit of God, in love, by faith, in wisdom, in honesty, in truth, in good works, after the commandment of the Lord, and not after his flesh—not after the manner of men in craftiness nor in the vanity of the mind nor disorderly. And he did so among a generation of ungodly people who sinned continually, and whom God would destroy by the Flood.

> Then the Lord saw that the wickedness of man was great in the earth, and that every intent of the thoughts of his heart was only evil continually. And the Lord was sorry that He had made man on the earth, and He was grieved in His heart. So the Lord said, "I will destroy man whom I have created from the face of the earth, both man and beast, creeping thing and birds of the air, for I am sorry that I have made them. (Genesis 6:5–7 NKJV)

---

[72] *Strong's Exhaustive Concordance of the Bible, NT*, 4991.

Enoch's walk with God over a period of three hundred years, living a lifestyle that signified his reverence for God in observing and obeying God's ordinances, reveals to us God's secret blueprint detailing how we will be taken away by God, not that we won't see death or die physically, like Enoch and like Elijah, both of whom God took so that they didn't experience death, but in the sense that as we get older and abide in our walk with God the devil can't kill us prior to the fulfillment of our kingdom assignment. After our divine assignment is fulfilled, like the apostle Paul, to die is gain (Philippians 1:21 NKJV).

Enoch walked with God for three hundred years! I am assured he maintained that walk, not by his might nor by his power but by the power of God's spirit (Zechariah 4:6 NKJV), since Holy Spirit had not been personally manifested in the earth to abide in the heart of man.

The key to how we experience death rests in our sustained walk with God.

> *But God will redeem my soul from the power of the grave, For He shall receive me. Selah.*
>
> **—Psalm 49:15 NKJV**

> *You will guide me with Your counsel, and afterward receive me to glory.*
>
> **—Psalm 73:24 NKJV**

I believe that there is a difference between experiencing physical death and being received in death by God, the latter of which signifies our supernatural leverage as saints. As his sons and daughters, heirs of salvation, saints are valuable to God—we're priceless! "Precious in the sight of the Lord Is the death of His saints" (Psalm 116:15 NKJV). God receives the death of those who walk with him and brings us into his glory—his heavenly bliss.

Receive is the Hebrew word *laqach*, which means to take; accept, bring, buy, carry away, drawn, reserve, send for, and take away, take up. Win.[73]

For all nonbelievers and those faithless believers, death has a sting to it, which is sin. If sin is the lifestyle of nonbelievers, and also those

[73] *Strong's Exhaustive Concordance of the Bible, OT*, 4991, 3947.

saints who initially used their faith to enter into eternal salvation but afterward lived a lifestyle of unbelief, death has a sting which is God's judgment equal to the accumulated sin committed.

Sting is the Greek word *kentron*, which means to prick; a point—that is, a sting (poison) or goad for poking and pricking, a divine impulse; prick, sting.[74]

> *For we must all appear before the judgment seat of Christ, that each one may receive the things done in the body, according to what he has done, whether good or bad.*
>
> **—2 Corinthians 5:10 NKJV**

This is the judgment reserved for saints only. The following text of scripture describes the judgment of those who have an unrepentant heart. And the judgment of God is according to truth:

> But in accordance with your hardness and your impenitent heart you are treasuring up for yourself wrath in the day of wrath and revelation of the righteous judgment of God, who "will render to each one according to his deeds": eternal life to those who by patient continuance in doing good seek for glory, honor, and immortality; but to those who are self-seeking and do not obey the truth, but obey unrighteousness – indignation and wrath, tribulation and anguish, on every soul of man who does evil, of the Jew first and also of the Greek; but glory, honor, and peace to everyone who works what is good, to the Jew first and also to the Greek. For there is no partiality with God. (Romans 2:5–11 NKJV)

If we go back to the life of Enoch and look closely at the wording of scripture relative to family genealogy, we will observe that every person from Adam to Noah lived and died, with the exception of Enoch. They lived, begat sons and daughters and they died. Enoch lived sixty-five years, and his life shifted. Enoch did not live the normal custom of the genealogy of those from Adam to Noah. Enoch not only lived but he

---

[74] *Strong's Exhaustive Concordance of the Bible, NT*, 2759.

walked with God for three hundred years. I'd say that was a major shift. Where the others lived and died, Enoch walked with God and was taken away by God.

My questions would be, "Why did God take Enoch? Why didn't God allow Enoch to live eight hundred, nine hundred or so years as he had allowed others?"

The answer to each of the two questions is not only pertinent to our walk with God today but also significant to our life purpose and divine assignment. Why did God take Enoch that he didn't experience the sting of death? I believe it is because Enoch was not a sinner. He lived among the vilest of sinners, yet he maintained his walk with God for three hundred years without sin. God did not allow Enoch to live for eight hundred or nine hundred years, because Enoch had fulfilled his divine purpose in three hundred years.

I believe that longevity of life is directly related to divine purpose and assignment. Satan's plan was to kill Enoch because he could not persuade him to sin, as he had persuaded all the generation of Enoch's time. Satan knew that Enoch's life was a testimony of his trust and faith in God and he wanted Enoch dead. So death was looking for Enoch but couldn't find him because his life testimony pleased God and was his life shield against experiencing the sting of physical death.

> *By faith Enoch was taken away so that he did not see death, "and was not found [by death], because God had taken him," for before he was taken he had this testimony, that he pleased God.*
>
> **—Hebrews 11:5 NKJV**

It is our walk, our lifestyle, with God as a testimony of our faith, not our leaning on Him for survival, that distinguishes us from being received by God through death or experiencing the sting of death when we die. Enoch's life testimony of faith, walking with God, saved him from a premature death and experiencing its sting. Saints today have the same opportunity as Enoch. We can choose to walk with God or live in this world according to its evil systems. We should always remember that we live in the world, but we are not of the world. We walk with the Lord both spiritually and physically while we live on the earth by being God conscience, Christ centered, and Holy Spirit-focused.

Enoch was the seventh generation from Adam. The number seven symbolizes completion. Enoch's final testimony regarding God's future judgment of false teachers and those who opposed Christ (anti-Christ) was a prophetic rhema from God, and it completed him:

> Now Enoch, the seventh from Adam, prophesied about these men also, saying "Behold, the Lord comes with ten thousands of His saints, to execute judgment on all, to convict all who are ungodly among them of all their ungodly deeds which they have committed in an ungodly way, and of all the harsh things which ungodly sinners have spoken against Him." These are grumblers, complainers, walking according to their own lusts; and they mouth great swelling words, flattering people to gain advantage … These are sensual persons, who cause divisions, not having the Spirit. But you, beloved, building yourselves up on your most holy faith, praying in the Holy Spirit, keep yourselves in the love of God, looking for the mercy of our Lord Jesus Christ unto eternal life. (Jude 14–16, 19–21 NKJV)

As we walk with God, we keep ourselves in his love, where we have access to his perpetual grace and mercy unto eternal life. As we do so, we grow spiritually, and we learn to walk in the newness of life, walking by faith, not by sight. We grow into our walk with God. Enoch didn't begin his life walking with God; that shift of the spirit took place after he was sixty-five years old and had begotten Methuselah.

I believe our holy Father has shifted or changed times and seasons, making them compatible with our walk with him, no longer leaning on Jesus as a crutch or leaning post or portraying ourselves, our physical bodies, as an old house with so many leaks that we need to find us a better home. That is not a mentality of victory but of defeat—religion and escapism—hoping the Lord hurries to rapture the church out of the earth.

Saints, we are anointed to change the world and bring it under the authority of the kingdom of heaven and its King, who also is King and Lord of all earthly kings and kingdoms. Our walk with God, our oneness with him through faith to represent his holiness on the earth, will determine our life testimony. The power of God and our security in him is in our walk with God. But when we walk with God, the world sees us as weak. Ungodly people don't necessarily recognize our humility before God, but therein lies our strength.

Jesus said to the apostle Paul, "My grace is sufficient for you, for My strength is made perfect in weakness."

Paul's reply: "Therefore most gladly I will rather boast in my infirmities, that the power of Christ may rest upon me. Therefore I take pleasure in infirmities, in reproaches, in needs, in persecutions, in distresses, for Christ's sake. For when I am weak, then I am strong" (2 Corinthians 12:9–10 NKJV).

I encourage readers to ask the Father to shift their mentality from religion to kingdom, from surviving to thriving, and from leaning on the Lord to walking with him. He may not let us fall if we lean on him, but we're assured there is no earthly way we can fall as we walk with him.

Stay tuned-in to the frequency of heaven—walk with God!

CHAPTER 14

Leave a Legacy of Faith to Future Generations

Therefore you are no longer a slave but a son, and if a son, then an heir of God through Christ.

—Galatians 4:7 NKJV

A good man leaves an inheritance to his children's children.

—Proverbs 13:22a NKJV

God's idea surrounding generating families focuses on giving or leaving an inheritance to future generations, the family heirloom—for instance, a valued possession passed down from one generation to the next. Jesus is God's Son, which makes him an heir. God is a "Good Man" who has left an inheritance to his children's children through his Son, Jesus. As saints, we are heirs of God and joint heirs with Christ (Romans 8:17 NKJV).

A legacy is something inherited from a predecessor—a heritage. The blessing of a father is an inheritance, an acquisition of a possession, condition, or trait from past generations; a valuable possession that is a common heritage from nature; a birthright. A legacy and an inheritance are closely related because both involve something left or given from a predecessor. Successive heirs must steward well the legacy, the inheritance, as the improper care of any legacy or inheritance could signify the end of the family name.

I sincerely believe faith is a family heirloom in the form of a legacy that can be handed down to future generations of believers not only from biological parents, but also from spiritual parents. Faith is a spiritual legacy, inheritance, which manifests its visibility through people.

I often thank God for the legacy of faith that my father and mother left me. They did not have a large estate or a family heirloom, those material things that family members generally fight over. What they left me and my siblings is worth so much more. It is supernatural, and it is backed by the power of the Holy Spirit. No one generally fights for a spiritual or invisible legacy or inheritance. Therefore, I consider the legacy of faith left to me by my parents, a blessing. As I said earlier, a blessing is an inheritance.

Let's take a look at the life of Jacob, son of Isaac, grandson of Abraham. God left a legacy of faith to Abraham, who believed God and it was accounted to him as righteousness. To that end, Abraham has become the "father of faith." So, then, faith is an inheritance, a legacy.

> For this is the word of promise: "At this time I will come and Sarah shall have a son." And not only this, but when Rebecca also had conceived by one man, even by our father Isaac (for the children not yet being born, nor having done any good or evil, that the purpose of God according to election might stand, not of works but of Him who calls), it was said to her, "The older shall serve the younger." As it is written, "Jacob I have loved, but Esau I have hated." What shall we say then? Is there unrighteousness with God? Certainly not! For He says to Moses, "I will have mercy on whomever I will have mercy, and I will have compassion on whomever I will have compassion." So then it is not of him who wills,

> nor of him who runs, but of God who shows mercy. (Romans 9:9–16 NKJV)

Without having mentioned the words legacy or inheritance in the above context of scripture, God had already predestinated or predetermined Jacob's inheritance and his legacy. It was God's sovereignty at work. God said, "The older shall serve the younger. Jacob I have loved, but Esau I have hated" (Romans 9:12–13 NKJV).

The promise God made to Abraham did not fail. Isaac was indeed the seed of promise. And his son Jacob's seed, Judah, was used by God, through many generations, to bring salvation to the world by Jesus Christ. God is true to his word. "My counsel shall stand, And I will do all My pleasure" (Isaiah 46:10 NKJV).

This should make saints very happy. As the apostle Paul testifies, "In Him also we have obtained an inheritance, being predestined according to the purpose of Him who works all things according to the counsel of His will" (Ephesians 1:11 NKJV).

The legacy, the inheritance of the saints where faith is concerned, is based also on God's sovereign freedom, and not on the fulfillment of any prior conditions.

> For whom He foreknew, He also predestined to be conformed to the image of His Son, that He might be the firstborn among many brethren. Moreover whom He predestined, these He also called; whom He called, these he also justified; and whom He justified, these He also glorified. (Romans 8:29–30 NKJV)

> Just as He chose us in Him before the foundation of the world, that we should be holy and without blame before Him in love, having predestined us to adoption as sons by Jesus Christ to Himself, according to the good pleasure of His will. (Ephesians 1:4–5 NKJV)

The Greek word for predestined is *proorizo*, which comes from *horidzo*. It means to determine before, ordain and predetermine; it also means to mark out by boundary, to appoint, decree, specify—declare, determine, limit, ordain.[75]

> *And He has made from one blood every nation of men to dwell on all the face of the earth, and has determined their preappointed times and the boundaries of their dwellings.*
>
> **—Acts 17:26 NKJV**

The Father has given us a legacy, a heritage—a divine destiny inclusive of leaving an inheritance to our children's children and a legacy of faith to future generations.

As heirs of God and joint heirs with Christ, we have been chosen by the Father, redeemed by the Son, and sealed by the Spirit. The Father has decreed both the inheritance and the legacy that will be entrusted to our care, bearing our names for a season. As we steward our spiritual inheritance well, it will increase in value; and at our death reception to the Father, our legacy of faith will be passed down to our children and their children as a spiritual heirloom, a spiritual inheritance. What a way to live! And what a way to be received by God at our death!

Yes, faith can be passed down as a legacy. Abraham passed his faith to Isaac; Isaac passed down his faith to Jacob; Jacob to Joseph, to David, and to Jesus. Through Jesus, we, too, can claim faith as an inherited legacy. Faith speaks (Romans 10:6a NKJV) and so do legacies.

The sovereignty of God is reflected even in our inheritance, spiritually and physically. Let's take a look at the life of Jacob and how inheritance played a key role in determining the outcome of his life and the legacy of faith that he left to his children's children. God prophesied over Jacob's life and his future legacy.

> Now Isaac pleaded with the Lord for his wife, because she was barren; and the Lord granted his plea, and Rebekah his wife conceived. But the children struggled together within her; and she said, "If all is well, why am I like this?" So she went to inquire of the Lord. And the Lord said to her: "Two nations are in your womb, two

[75] *Strong's Exhaustive Concordance of the Bible, NT,* 4309.

> peoples shall be separated from your body; One people shall be stronger than the other, And the older shall serve the younger." (Genesis 25:21–23 NKJV)

This is a prophetic word from God to Rebekah. By his sovereignty, God had predetermined that the two boys that Rebekah carried in her womb were two nations, and one would be stronger than the other, and the older would serve the younger.

Of course, this would be totally contrary to what most mothers would want to hear. Through his sovereignty, God intervened and flipped the script on what would have been culturally expected—that is, the older son gets the inheritance. It seems here that God is true to his sovereign nature; he takes the weaker or lesser people and things and uses them to confound our human intelligence (1 Corinthians 1:25–29 NKJV).

Esau came out first, but Jacob took hold of Esau's heel. Hostility between the two boys began at their birth. As they grew, Esau became a skilled hunter, but Jacob was a mild-mannered man. Isaac loved Esau because he loved to eat his game, and Rebekah loved Jacob because he dwelled in tents.

God is the Master Orchestrator of events! Let's revisit the scripture from Romans chapter nine: "For the children not yet being born, nor having done any good or evil, that the purpose of God according to election might stand, not of works but of Him who calls, it was said to her, 'The older shall serve the younger.' As it is written, 'Jacob I have loved, but Esau I have hated'" (Romans 9:11–13 NKJV).

God masterfully orchestrated the challenge of the birthright in order that his purpose—the older shall serve the younger—should stand. It was according to divine election, not through works of the flesh. Somehow the birthright had to be reversed so that Esau, the firstborn son, would not inherit it, but Jacob would. According to their law and custom, a birthright could be sold. So, while it is true that Esau's action was legal, it is also true that it was morally wrong, as it was done out of a selfish motive.

> Now Jacob cooked a stew; and Esau came in from the field, and he was weary. And Esau said to Jacob, "Please

> feed me with that same red stew, for I am weary." … But Jacob said, "Sell me your birthright as of this day." And Esau said, "Look, I am about to die; so what is this birthright to me?" Then Jacob said, "Swear to me as of this day." So he swore to him, and sold his birthright to Jacob. And Jacob gave Esau bread and stew of lentils; then he ate and drank, arose, and went his way. Thus Esau despised his birthright. (Genesis 25:29–34 NKJV)

In Old Testament times, the term *birthright* referred to the inheritance rights of the firstborn son in a Hebrew family. The father's property was normally divided among his sons at his death. But the larger part, sometimes double, was given to the oldest son to exercise authority over the household and assume care of his mother and unmarried sisters, thus honoring his father's name.

Esau acted foolishly by trading his birthright to his brother Jacob for a mere bowl of stew; he squandered it. "Thus Esau despised his birthright" (Genesis 25:34 NKJV).

Bazah is the Hebrew word translated *despised*. It means to disesteem; despise, disdain, contemptible, to scorn, vile person.[76]

Esau treated his birthright as if it had no value and literally bartered it away for bread and stew. Notice, however, that Jacob is quite the schemer in all this. He lives up to his name—trickster or supplanter. He did not discourage his brother from making a generational decision in the immediacy of his weakened state of hunger. I believe he'd made up his mind to take advantage of his brother by any means necessary.

I say that knowing that Jacob acted upon God's sovereign will and appointed time to scheme his brother out of his birthright, not because Jacob was so bright or intelligent that he could finagle the birthright from his brother. Jacob sealed the deal by demanding a verbal oath from his brother, which made the transaction legal and binding.

Jacob knew the covenant promises that his father, Isaac, had received from his father, Abraham, was at stake. This proves Jacob knew the gravity of the inheritance, but it also proves Jacob did not yet know the God of his fathers.

[76] *Strong's Exhaustive Concordance of the Bible, OT*, 959.

It was the custom of the father to bless the elder son prior to his death. This was Jacob's opportunity to fully receive the blessing and birthright—the inheritance he "divinely swindled" from his brother Esau. The verbal blessing would legally transfer the property and authority to him.

As the story goes, Isaac was old, and his eyes were so dim he couldn't see when he called Esau to him to inform him of his impending death:

> Now therefore, please take your weapons, your quiver and your bow, and go out to the field and hunt game for me. And Make me savory food, such as I love, and bring it to me that I may eat, that my soul may bless you before I die. Now Rebekah was listening when Isaac spoke to Esau his son … So Rebekah spoke to Jacob her son, saying, "Indeed I heard your father speak to Esau your brother, saying, "Bring me game and make savory food for me, that I may eat it and bless you in the presence of the Lord before my death. Now therefore, my son, obey my voice according to what I command you … And Jacob said to Rebekah his mother, "Look, Esau my brother is a hairy man, and I am a smooth-skinned man. Perhaps my father will feel me, and I shall seem to be a deceiver to him; and I shall bring a curse on myself and not a blessing." But his mother said to him, "Let your curse be on me, my son; only obey my voice … Then Rebekah took the choice clothes of her elder son Esau, which were with her in the house, and put them on Jacob her younger son. And she put the skins of the kids of the goats on his hands and on the smooth part of his neck. Then she gave the savory food and the bread, which she had prepared, into the hand of her son Jacob. So he went to his father and said, "My father." And he said, "Here I am. Who are you, my son?" (Genesis 27:3–8, 11–13, 15–18 NKJV)

Throughout this story, *birthright* and *blessing* are used interchangeably, both of which Jacob deceitfully sought to obtain. The

Hebrew word translated for *birthright* is *bekorah*, meaning the firstling of man or beast; primogeniture: firstborn.[77] The Hebrew word translated as *blessing* is *berakah*, which means benediction; prosperity; blessing.[78]

We know *Jacob* means supplanter, deceiver, or schemer, but what does Rebekah's name mean? The Hebrew name translated for *Rebekah* is *Ribqah*, which means to clog by tying up the fetlock; fettering by beauty.[79]

Both their names play a role in their deceptive act against Isaac and Esau. Jacob and Rebekah become coconspirators: Jacob, through his deception to take the birthright of Esau; and Rebekah, through her beauty to restrain Isaac and her ability to put a plot to Jacob's scheme. Rebekah shows favoritism to her son, Jacob, and together they pull off the "divine exchange."

Rebekah successfully disguised Jacob to resemble and smell like Esau. And she used this cunning scheme to bind or restrict her near-blind husband, Isaac. She went so far as to tell Jacob to let the curse fall on her. This was her way of making sure that Jacob, instead of Esau, got the birthright due to inheritance, which includes the blessing. Before Isaac could give the blessing, the inheritance, to his son, he asked a legal question of sorts, "Who are you, my son?" (Genesis 27:18 NKJV).

> Jacob said to his father, "I am Esau your firstborn; I have done just as you told me; please arise, sit and eat of my game, that your soul may bless me." But Isaac said to his son, "How is it that you have found it so quickly, my son?" And he said, "Because the Lord your God brought it to me." Then Isaac said to Jacob, "Please come near, that I may feel you, my son, whether you are really my son Esau or not." So Jacob went near to Isaac his father, and he felt him and said, "The voice is Jacob's voice, but the hands are the hands of Esau." And he did not recognize him, because his hands were hairy like his brother Esau's hands; so he blessed him. (Genesis 27:19–23 NKJV)

---

[77] *Strong's Exhaustive Concordance of the Bible, OT*, 1062.

[78] *Strong's Exhaustive Concordance of the Bible, OT, 1293.*

[79] *Strong's Exhaustive Concordance of the Bible, OT*, 7259.

Jacob seeks to hasten the blessing and birthright, the inheritance of the firstborn. But Isaac was suspicious enough to question him. When Jacob answers his father concerning how he found, killed, dressed, and cooked the venison stew so quickly, Jacob said, "The Lord your God brought it to me" (Genesis 27:20 NKJV), meaning that Jacob did not yet recognize the Lord as his God. Still suspicious, Isaac called Jacob to come near so he could feel him and determine whether or not he was indeed Esau. Isaac went so far as to distinguish the voice as Jacob's, but the hands were of Esau, yet he did not recognize that it truly was Jacob. So he blessed him:

> Then his father Isaac said to him, "Come near now and kiss me, my son." And he came near and kissed him; and he smelled the smell of his clothing, and blessed him and said: "Surely the smell of my son is like the smell of a field which the Lord has blessed. Therefore may God give you of the dew of heaven, of the fatness of the earth, and plenty of grain and wine. Let peoples serve you, and nations bow down to you. Be master over your brethren, and let your mother's sons bow down to you. Cursed be everyone who curses you, and blessed be those who bless you!" Now it happened, as soon as Isaac had finished blessing Jacob, and Jacob had scarcely gone out from the presence of Isaac his father, that Esau his brother came in from his hunting. (Genesis 27:26–30 NKJV)

Jacob betrayed his father with a kiss, the same as Judas Iscariot betrayed Jesus. This act of betrayal shows the depth of control the spirit of deception wielded over Jacob. But I can imagine Jacob on pins and needles wanting to quickly receive the blessing from Isaac before his scheme fell apart. It was a huge blessing, for it not only included physical prosperity, but also authority over the immediate family and brethren within the extended family. His older brother serving him was the fulfillment of the prophetic word given to Rebekah by God while she was pregnant with the twins. Also, peoples of other nations would serve and bow down to Jacob. Wow. What an inheritance!

What transpired next is what I believe happens today when siblings squabble and fight over the inheritance left by their parents. Esau revealed himself to his father, and the deception was known, but too late:

> "Let my father arise and eat of his son's game, that your soul may bless me." And his father Isaac said to him, "Who are you?" So he said, "I am your son, your firstborn, Esau." Then Isaac trembled exceedingly, and said, "Who? Where is the one who hunted game and brought it to me? I ate all of it before you came, and I have blessed him - and indeed he shall be blessed." When Esau heard the words of his father, he cried with an exceedingly great and bitter cry, and said to his father, "Bless me - me also, O my father!" But he said, "Your brother came with deceit and has taken away your blessing." And Esau said, "Is he not rightly named Jacob? For he has supplanted me these two times. He took away my birthright, and now look, he has taken away my blessing!" And he said, "Have you not reserved a blessing for me?" Then Isaac answered and said to Esau, "Indeed I have made him your master, and all his brethren I have given to him as servants; with grain and wine I have sustained him. What shall I do now for you, my son?" And Esau said to his father, "Have you only one blessing, my father? Bless me - me also, O my father!" And Esau lifted up his voice and wept. (Genesis 27:31–38 NKJV)

Ouch! That really hurt. Isaac had already blessed Jacob, and it could not be reversed. Isaac solemnly transferred the inheritance to Jacob by an oral statement made as his deathbed bequest, which was legally binding.

Esau cried with an exceedingly great and bitter cry. I sense it was the type of "dry cry"—no more power to weep—that David and his men cried after their wives and children were taken from their camp in Ziglak by the Amalekites. Esau cried bitterly, yet to no avail. All his wailing could not change the legality of the transfer of the covenant blessing, birthright—the inheritance—from Isaac to Jacob.

After he could not retrieve the blessing, Esau acknowledged that Jacob's character lived up to his name. "Isn't he rightly named Jacob? For he has supplanted me these two times. He took away my birthright, and now look, he has taken away my blessing!" (Genesis 27:36 NKJV). "These two times" imply a separation of the birthright and the blessing; however, according to the scripture, the birthright led to the blessing because both are inclusive of the inheritance.

"Have you only one blessing, my father? Bless me – me also, O my father!" (Genesis 27:38 NKJV). Esau is in a stuck position of servitude to his younger brother, Jacob, according to divine election and the purpose of God. Paul, in his epistle to the Hebrews, while exhorting the Jewish Christians to endure God's chastening, mentions Esau's despising of his birthright as a godless, profane act:

> Pursue peace with all people, and holiness, without which no one will see the Lord: looking carefully lest anyone fall short of the grace of God; lest any root of bitterness springing up cause trouble, and by this many become defiled; lest there be any fornicator or profane person like Esau, who for one morsel of food sold his birthright. For you know that afterward, when he wanted to inherit the blessing, he was rejected, for he found no place for repentance, though he sought it diligently with tears. (Hebrews 12:14–17 NKJV)

Despising one's birthright is a profane or godless act. Paul used Esau's example to encourage the Jewish believers not to give up their Christian walk and return to Judaism. He was telling them not to compromise their faith, even though they were being persecuted. He warned them not to exchange their spiritual inheritance or birthright for temporary relief from persecution; this would deprive them of Christ's blessing.

Esau never understood the gravity of the inheritance. He devalued his birthright to a single meal. He was deceived twice by Jacob, for his birthright and for his blessing. And when he finally understood the strong force of the blessing and inheritance, it was too late. His bitter tears could not bring it back and he was rejected, turned away from his inheritance, because he did not have a repentant heart; he simply regretted the loss. "So Esau hated Jacob because of the blessing with which his father blessed him, and Esau said in his heart, 'The days of mourning for my father are at hand; then I will kill my brother Jacob" (Genesis 27:41 NKJV).

According to the story, Jacob ran from Esau to his uncle Laban's house. On the way, he met the God of his fathers, Abraham and Isaac, at Bethel, where he dreamed of a ladder that reached from earth to heaven. There he made a vow to God, saying, "If God will be with me, and keep me in this way that I am going, and give me bread to eat and clothing to put on, so that I come back to my father's house in peace, then the Lord shall be my God … and of all that You give me I will surely give a tenth to You" (Genesis 28:20–22 NKJV).

Knowing God intimately is a process, and Jacob was about to take a twenty-year tour in the progression toward spiritual maturity. He made it to Haran, his uncle Laban's homeland, where he learned a long, difficult, and valuable lesson from Laban about deception. In the twenty years that he worked for Laban, fourteen for his wives, Leah and Rachel, and six for his cattle, Laban changed his wages ten times and stole his cattle.

After God gave Jacob a rhema concerning how to boost the strength and enlarge his herd more than all of Laban's cattle, Laban and his sons were jealous. And when Jacob knew that Laban and his sons were out to get him, he took his wives and children and fled. "Thus the man became exceedingly prosperous, and had large flocks, female and male servants, and camel and donkeys … Now Jacob heard the words of Laban's sons, saying, 'Jacob has taken away all that was our father's, and from what was our father's he has acquired all this wealth'" (Genesis 30:43, 31:1 NKJV).

It became a matter of inheritance for Jacob, who wanted to leave his own inheritance to his own children. Laban's plan was to keep tricking Jacob to stay with him. That way, he not only could control Jacob but he also could keep his daughters and grandchildren with him. God informed Jacob of Laban's plan and told him to "get out of this land, and return to the land of your family" (Genesis 31:13 NKJV). Before

Jacob left, he went to his wives to get their approval: "Then Rachel and Leah answered and said to him, 'Is there still any portion or inheritance for us in our father's house? Are we not considered strangers by him? For he has sold us, and also completely consumed our money. For all these riches which God has taken from our father are really ours and our children's; now then, whatever God has said to you, do it'" (Genesis 31:14–16 NKJV).

Birthright, blessing, inheritance—legacy—was Jacob's portion, for he would go on to leave an inheritance to his children's children, as his son Joseph's legacy and inheritance to his sons Ephraim and Manasseh will attest (Genesis 49 NKJV).

I believe it is important that today's saints understand that, even as heirs of God, we, too, can devalue our inheritance. Like it was with Esau, we can despise our inheritance. But we don't have to, since we live under New Testament grace, where all saints are God's firstborn. Jesus is the Firstborn of firstborns, which means God sees all his children as his firstborn. We are joined to the Lord, which means we are one spirit with Him (1 Corinthians 6:17 NKJV). And as he is in heaven, so are we on the earth (1 John 4:17b NKJV). We have confidence as heirs of God, his firstborn, and we simply receive our inheritance—birthright, blessing. We let the blessing work!

If saints were still under Old Testament law, the principle that the eldest child had an exclusive right of inheritance certainly would not bode well for us today, because there would still be only one blessing—from father to the firstborn or elder son—and the blessing of the elder son would trump all other blessings the father might give.

New Testament believers receive their inheritance, the blessing of the covenant, from God by faith. It is through unbelief that we forfeit our birthright by allowing the enemy to steal it from us. As we receive our inheritance from God, the blessing of the covenant sworn by God to Abraham and to his seed, Jesus, we also build our faith legacy—our godly lifestyle lived by faith. And we can leave that legacy of faith to future generations, including our children's children.

> *Train up a child in the way he should go, And when he is old he will not depart from it.*
>
> **—Proverbs 22:6 NKJV**

Leave a legacy of faith to future generations. I believe that parents who are born again and live consistent and persistent godly lifestyles produces children who will eventually walk by faith in God's Word and whose faith and commitment to the Gospel of the kingdom are unwavering.

I should know: I'm one of those children produced by godly parents who rebelled as a young man. "When I was a child, I spoke as a child, I understood as a child, I thought as a child; but when I became a man, I put away childish things" (1 Corinthians 13:11 NKJV). In Proverbs 22:6, the emphasis is on the phrase *when he is old*, which is parallel to being a child.

When I became independent of my parents and times got hard, and when there was no money and I was sinking in sin, I remembered how my parents raised me and realized all that my parents had taught me about Jesus, the Word of God, and the power of the Holy Spirit to wash and cleanse me through regeneration, I received a revelation. "I'm not a child any longer. Only you, Father, can make me a man. I yield my life to You."

Like the apostle Paul, "I have been crucified with Christ; it is no longer I who live, but Christ lives in me; and the life which I now live in the flesh I live by faith in the Son of God, who loved me and gave Himself for me" (Galatians 2:20 NKJV). That's the legacy of faith that I desire to leave to future generations, inclusive of my children's children, for I am a good man.

We must prepare ourselves consistently to leave a legacy of faith in Christ Jesus to future generations, inclusive of our children's children. It's one of the ways we stay tuned-in to the frequency of heaven.

CHAPTER 15

It Is the Father's Good Pleasure to Give Us the Kingdom

Do not fear, little flock, for it is your Father's good pleasure to give you the kingdom.

—Luke 12:32 NKJV

It is the Father's good pleasure to give his sons and daughters a share of his royal realm called earth. The purpose of which is to rule and to reign in life through the One, Jesus Christ, as in reigning with him, on earth as it is in heaven.

The above verse is powered by the word give. Yet it is a word that we tend to look past, focusing instead on the kingdom and the Father's good pleasure. And while those two components of the verse certainly add the major thrust to this power verse, it is the word give that provides the fuel.

The Hebrew word translated *give* in this context is *didomi*, which means to be greatly modified by the connection; adventure, bestow, bring forth, deliver, give, grant, minister, have power, receive, take, set, suffer, yield.[80]

What an amazing word. It is our heavenly Father's good pleasure to greatly modify or transform us through our connection to him, the King of kings, who daily loads us with benefits and "who gives us richly all things to enjoy" (1 Timothy 6:17b NKJV). He holds us near to him, furnishes the occasion, and presents richly all things for us to enjoy.

It is our father's good pleasure to bestow upon us good things, to bring forth good things in our lives, to deliver us from evil and grant us clemency, forbearance, through our faith in Jesus. He ministers to our needs, and through his spirit we have power to prevail and live life abundantly and to the full. Therefore, we believe, we receive, and we take the blessing of the kingdom by faith.

It is the Father's good pleasure to give every believer the kingdom, and it should be every believer's good pleasure to take or receive it by faith. We yield to the Holy Spirit, and we obey and willingly serve our King. We are fools for Christ, addicted to the ministry of the Gospel of the kingdom, and willing to suffer for the sake of Christ and for the Gospel.

What we need to understand now is the phrase *good pleasure* and how the Father's good pleasure is released to us through relationship. The more intimate the relationship the more good pleasure we can expect from our heavenly Father.

The Greek phrase *kalos eudokeo* is translated to "good pleasure" and signifies that which is beautiful, valuable, or virtuous for appearance or use.[81] It denotes that which is intrinsically good; of that which is ethically good, right, noble, and honorable. It implies how well God thinks of us—as in, "well done good and faithful servant." It means to approve of, to approbate a person or thing: think good, be well pleased, be the good pleasure, be willing. It is not merely an understanding of what is right and good, but stressing the willingness and freedom of *an intention or resolve regarding what is good*, "It is your Father's good pleasure."

---

[80] *Strong's Exhaustive Concordance of the Bible, OT,* 1325.

[81] *Strong's Exhaustive Concordance of the Bible, NT,* 3930.

Did you get that? There is no pressure on our heavenly Father concerning His good pleasure to give Kingdom benefits to his sons and daughters. The good pleasure is a part of the Father's nature, for He is intrinsically good, ethically good, virtuous, noble, honorable and righteous. Our heavenly Father releases all of who He is to us willingly or intentionally. It is His resolve to do or give what is good. Right here is where we say, "Thank you, Lord. I believe I receive!

In the world in which we live, people are in constant disputes over money. We tend to prioritize money over everything else, including God, who created money as a means of exchange for greater expansion of life, which includes blessing others. Sadly, most of the world sees money only as a means of influence, control, submission, and fulfillment of lustful desires of the flesh, which stems from a spirit of greed or covetousness. In other words, money has become their god. They don't simply possess money; money possesses them.

> *For what profit is it to a man if he gains the whole world, and loses his own soul? Or what will a man give in exchange for his soul?*
>
> **—Matthew 16:26 NKJV**

> *No one can serve two masters; for either he will hate the one and love the other, or else he will be loyal to the one and despise the other. You cannot serve God and mammon.*
>
> **—Matthew 6:24 NKJV**

And for the love of money, people will do just about anything. Their insatiable appetite for money and their unethical plans and systems to acquire and amass as much as they can, even to the extent that they take away the welfare and life of others, is a testimony to the depth of their greed and superior mindset. It is as if God didn't create enough resources for all people to prosper, which really boils down to a poverty mentality. Yes, we can be rich and yet possess a poverty mentality based on fear of lack or never having enough. That's why we see so many money hoarders in these last days, but they are never satisfied.

> *For the love of money is a root of all kinds of evil, for which some have strayed from the faith in their greediness, and pierced themselves through with many sorrows. But you, O man of God, flee these things and pursue righteousness, godliness, faith, love, patience, gentleness.*
>
> *—1 Timothy 6:10–11 NKJV*

What God requires us to seek and pursue is in stark contrast to the pursuit of money as our first priority. Paul warns believers that the unrighteous love of money—prioritizing money over relationship and trust in God—is a root of all kinds of evil acts, and those who wrongfully pursue it actually end up thrusting themselves with many sorrows, as in being pierced in the heart with a very sharp object.

Both saints and nonbelievers can quote this part of Ecclesiastes 10:19b NKJV: "But money answers everything." People tend to quote that verse putting their twisted or contorted spin on human values, noting the versatility of money not only to provide a great living but also to fulfill the first part of that verse: "A feast is made for laughter, and wine makes merry" (Ecclesiastes 10:19a NKJV). The truth is, yes, money is the answer to all mundane things—worldly, earthly, profane, vulgar, as opposed to heavenly.

> Come now, you rich, weep and howl for your miseries that are coming upon you! Your riches are corrupted, and your garments are moth-eaten. Your gold and silver are corroded, and their corrosion will be a witness against you and will eat your flesh like fire. You have heaped up treasure in the last days. Indeed the wages of the laborers who mowed your fields, which you kept back by fraud, cry out; and the cries of the reapers have reached the ears of the Lord of Sabaoth. You have lived on the earth in pleasure and luxury; you have fattened your hearts as in a day of slaughter. You have condemned, you have murdered the just; he does not resist you. (James 5:1–6 NKJV)

As a believer, I'd like to think that this context of scripture only refers to nonbelievers. But more and more believers are being sucked into the cesspool of the evils of the world. Many believers have become hoarders of money, weapons, and foodstuff. They've built bunkers for their personal survival. Personally, I don't see any faith or trust in God as their Protector, Provider, Sustainer, and Refuge: "For whoever desires to save his life will lose it, but whoever loses his life for My sake and the gospel's will save it" (Mark 8:35 NKJV).

> *He who loves his life will lose it, and he who hates his life in this world will keep it for eternal life. If anyone serves Me, let him follow Me; and where I am, there My servant will be also. If anyone serves Me, him My Father will honor.*
>
> **—John 12:25–26 NKJV**

Brother and sister Christians, serving Christ Jesus must become more important to us than valuing life. As his servants, his representatives on the earth, we must die to every purpose that is contrary to the will of God. Jesus promises two things to those who follow him. They will be where he is, and they will be honored by his Father, our heavenly Father. What a glorious promise! Jesus doesn't tell us to depend on, hang on to, or hoard anything in this life that doesn't please God. "But without faith it is impossible to please Him" (Hebrews 11:6 NKJV).

What pleases the Father is our willingness to lose our life for Jesus's sake and the Gospel's, which is a display of complete, absolute, uncompromising trust in God—loyalty to the King! "For the eyes of the Lord run to and fro throughout the whole earth, to show Himself strong on behalf of those whose heart is loyal to Him" (2 Chronicles 16:9 NKJV).

As I've already said, too many believers are running away. They are hiding in bunkers and stockpiling foodstuffs and weapons, when they should be on the front line ministering salvation, praying for peoples' deliverance, decreeing their healing, and performing miracles as good soldiers of Jesus Christ.

Yes, we will face opposition through compromise, opposition through slander and persecution, opposition through threats, opposition through ridicule, and opposition through treachery, but like Joshua and Caleb, we are well able to take the land and advance God's kingdom on earth.

The body of Christ needs more Nehemiahs, who will stand firm in compliance with the righteousness of the kingdom and do the will of God, not our own will. We will not love our lives to the death.

> For they all were trying to make us afraid, saying, "Their hands will be weakened in the work, and it will not be done." Now therefore, O God, strengthen my hands. Afterward I came to the house of Shemaiah the son of Delaiah, the son of Mehetabel, who was a secret informer, and he said, "Let us meet together in the house of God, within the temple, and let us close the doors of the temple, for they are coming to kill you; indeed, at night they will come to kill you." And I said, "Should such a man as I flee? And who is there such as I who would go into the temple to save his life? I will not go in!" Then I perceived that God had not sent him at all, but that he pronounced this prophecy against me because Tobiah and Sanballat had hired him. For this reason he was hired, that I should be afraid and act that way and sin, so that they might have cause for an evil report, that they might reproach me. My God, remember Tobiah and Sanballat, according to these their works, and the prophetess Noadiah and the rest of the prophets who would have made me afraid. (Nehemiah 6:9–14 NKJV)

Even now, our biggest enemy may not be the unsaved but the saved. Prophets are prophesying against one another. The body of Christ has a decision to make: Are we going to love this world and the material things thereof, like the Pharisees, who were pleasers and lovers of money (Luke 16:14 NKJV)? Or will we confess that we are not of this world and fix our hearts on things that are above and not beneath? Are we going to say, like Jesus, "Nevertheless not My will, but Yours, be done" (Luke 22:42b NKJV)? Or will we love this world and lose our own soul?

Jesus said, "For whoever wants to save their life will lose it, but whoever loses their life for me and for the gospel will save it" (Mark 8:35 NKJV).

Paul said, "And see, now I go bound in the spirit to Jerusalem, not knowing the things that will happen to me there, except that the Holy Spirit testifies in every city, saying that chains and tribulations await me. But none of these things move me; nor do I count my life dear to myself, so that I may finish my race with joy, and the ministry which I received from the Lord Jesus, to testify to the gospel of the grace of God" (Acts 20:22–24 NKJV).

John said, "And they overcame him by the blood of the Lamb and by the word of their testimony, and they did not love their lives to the death" (Revelation 12:11 NKJV).

As believers, we must appropriate Psalm 23 over our lives, for it is a description of Jesus as our Shepherd in times of crisis: "Yea, though I walk through the valley of the shadow of death, I will fear no evil; For You are with me; Your rod and Your staff they comfort me" (Psalm 23:4 NKJV).

> *Stand therefore, having girded your waist with truth, having put on the breastplate of righteousness.*
>
> **—Ephesians 6:14 NKJV**

"Girding your loins" is what a soldier would do when he was preparing to fight. During biblical times, men wore long tunics. Around the tunic they would wear a belt. When it came time to fight, they had to tuck the hem of the tunic into their belt/girdle so they wouldn't trip, and so they wouldn't be hindered while fighting.

As believers, we will face spiritual battles on a regular basis. The enemy is treacherous and will always look for an opportune time he thinks will derail us from the track of faith; but we know our heavenly Father is with us, and his perfect will for us unfolds even in the midst of these battles. And we can be sure He will provide a way for us to stand, through the power of the Holy Spirit.

As we continue to face pandemics, political unrest, censorship, corruption, and times of testing, let us be like Jesus, Paul, and John. I decree, in the name of Jesus, that when it's time to act, we will do so with love, faith, and courage. Now is certainly the time to teach and preach the gospel of the kingdom and encircle our nations with the truth that God is in control and his perfect will shall be done on earth, as it is in heaven.

THE KINGDOM IS OUR FATHER'S GIFT TO US

One of God's gifts to Queen Esther was to allow her to become queen of a heathen nation for the salvation of the Jews. This was a kairos time in which God had ordained to deliver His chosen people. He used Mordecai to prepare Esther, and He used Esther to soften the hardened heart of the king, "for such a time as this" (Esther 4:14 NKJV).

Esther means *star.* Stars shine and sparkle brightly. Scientists say that maybe the sun is the nearest star to earth. Esther's Hebrew name, Hadassah, is apparently the feminine form of the word for *myrtle*, a plant associated with hope. *Hope*, as used in the Bible, refers to an earnest expectation of something longed for. Believers should earnestly expect not only a royal position in the kingdom at Jesus's return but also a royal position on earth representing the kingdom of heaven for such a time as this.

Satan has a plan to destroy God's people. Just like in the story of Esther, to ascertain the most favorable moment for destroying the Jews, Haman piously consulted his gods by casting lots (or pur). A date eleven months into the future was revealed—Adar, our February-March. Haman immediately persuaded King Ahasuerus (Xerxes) to issue a decree that all the Jews in his realm were to be slaughtered on that day. By way of incentive, the decree proclaimed that anyone who killed a Jew could plunder his possessions. Mordecai reacted immediately by contacting his cousin Esther, whom he raised as his daughter, and commanded her to plead mercy before the king for her people.

But Esther was afraid and replied, "All the king's servants and the people of the king's provinces know that any man or woman who goes into the inner court to the king, who has not been called, he has but one law: put all to death, except the one to whom the king holds out the golden scepter, that he may live. Yet I myself have not been called to go in to the king these thirty days" (Esther 4:11 NKJV).

Mordecai replied, "Do not think in your heart that you will escape in the king's palace any more than all the other Jews. For if you remain completely silent at this time, relief and deliverance will arise for the Jews from another place, but you and your father's house will perish.

Yet who knows whether you have come to the kingdom for such a time as this?" (Esther 4:14 NKJV).

So Esther instructed Mordecai, "Go, gather together all the Jews who are present in Shushan, and fast for me; neither eat nor drink for three days, night or day. My maids and I will fast likewise. And so I will go to the king, which is against the law; and if I perish, I perish" (Esther 4:16 NKJV).

> *Now it happened on the third day that Esther put on her royal robes and stood across from the king's house ... [2]So it was, when the king saw Queen Esther standing in the court, that she found favor in his sight, and the king held out the golden scepter that was in his hand. Then Esther went near and touched the top of the scepter. [3]And the king said to her, "What do you wish, Queen Esther? What is your request? It shall be given to you – up to half the kingdom."*
>
> **—Esther 5:1–3 NKJV**

Every believer has been given a royal position on earth for such a time as this to advance the kingdom. But we must come together in the unity of our faith in order to step into our royal destiny: Let us throw off everything that hinders and the sin that so easily entangles, and let us run with perseverance the race marked out for us. Let us fix our eyes on Jesus (Hebrews 12:1–2 NKJV).

We are anointed for such a time as this. I decree that every saint who is a commissioned kingdom-compliant servant-leader will not remain silent at this time but will provide relief and deliverance for believers and unbelievers alike. Praise God that he turns the wisdom and the power of the world on its head, often using the most surprising tactics to accomplish his plan.

There are so many things happening in the world right now that people need to be delivered from. Even many saints have become easy prey for the devil. God, we ask that Christians in our nation would understand that government is appointed by you and for your purposes—that our lives as believers depend on what we have in our heart. Instead of filling our heart with hate and division, I pray that the body of Christ would arise and walk in the one thing that never fails—love! And God is love. I pray that we will fill our hearts to overflowing all the time with the love of God and the Word of God. Then, when trouble hits, we'll be ready to do our part to save the world. We'll be in the habit of talking like God does, and we will no longer be easy prey for the devil.

When Jesus died on the cross, Satan thought he had won. What Satan didn't know is that Jesus's death would blow his plans to smithereens. His death would save all who receive him as Savior. Keep in mind, when Jesus prayed in the garden before his crucifixion, he said, "Father, if you are willing, take this cup from me; yet not my will, but yours be done" (Luke 22:42 NIV). Notice he says, "Not my will, but yours."

I pray that we call upon Jesus during our times of need and accept his will, whatever it may be.

Whatever we are going through right now, we must remember God knew it was coming before we ever set foot on the earth. He is the Alpha and the Omega. He knows our beginning and end. He also knew exactly what our nation would be facing right here and now.

David reminds us that "my times are in Your hands" (Psalm 31:15 NKJV). This is why our Esther anointing is so critical and will be displayed for such a time as this.

> *For if you remain silent at this time, relief and deliverance for the Jews will arise from another place, but you and your father's family will perish. And who knows that you have come to your royal position for such a time as this.*
>
> **—Esther 4:14 NKJV**

Queen Esther was in a position to save her people, the Jews. But she had to act. She couldn't sit back and let fear rule her life. She had to do something. Realizing her actions were risky, she later said, "And if I perish, I perish" (Esther 4:16 NKJV). She would act, even if it led to her death. She was accepting the will of God and not her own will.

Because Esther obeyed, it was the Father's good pleasure to give her the kingdom. In a physical sense, God literally gave Esther the kingdom of Persia!

RELIGIOUS CHRISTIANS WORK TOO HARD

I love to see believers transformed from religion to kingdom. The shift in mindset is one of a supernatural cleansing, sort of like deleting old information and material no longer used or needed from your computer's hard drive.

When we are transformed, our minds renewed by the Word of God, the Holy Spirit reveals to us the divine nature of the Source of life whom we serve. God is a good God, and his nature is one of giving. It is his good pleasure to give us the kingdom.

Many believers think they somehow have to impress God or do things that add up to what they consider as working for the Lord. These religious types are always "running trying to make a hundred, 'cause ninety-nine and a half won't do." For the most part, they wear themselves out. They become entrenched in "busywork," displaying to anyone who will abide their religious efforts their commitment to work for the Lord. They pride themselves on their godliness, but generally have no life. Religious Christians miss the best that God has to offer:

> Grace and peace be multiplied to you in the knowledge of God and of Jesus our Lord, as His divine power has given to us all things that pertain to life and godliness, through the knowledge of Him who called us by glory and virtue, by which have been given to us exceedingly great and precious promises, that through these [the exceedingly great and precious promises] you might be partakers of the divine nature, having escaped the corruption that is in the world through lust. (2 Peter 1:2–4 NKJV)

Much of the corruption in the world that befalls believers through the lust of their flesh is because they have no revelatory knowledge of God and of Jesus, his Son. The result is usually a forfeiture of divine power which He freely gives to us in the form of all things that pertain to life and godliness.

Remember the word *give*, as used in the context of the Father's good pleasure to give, means to be greatly modified by the connection—our connection as sons and daughters to our loving heavenly Father. His gifts, his bestowals, become our adventure in life as we boldly set forth to fulfill our divine assignment on earth. Our godly adventure is inclusive of the ministry of the Holy Spirit's power working in and through us granting us divine favor as we yield to his will and are willing to suffer for the sake of Christ and for the gospel: "If we suffer, we shall also reign with him" (2 Timothy 2:12 KJV).

This is Father's gift to us which flows from his nature as a good God who cheerfully gives to his sons and daughters. God is a cheerful giver, which is why he urges his sons and daughters to be cheerful givers (2 Corinthians 9:7 NKJV). But we must also learn to be cheerful receivers. If it is our Father's good pleasure to give us the kingdom, it should be our good pleasure to take or receive it cheerfully.

> *Let them shout for joy and be glad, who favor my righteous cause; and let them say continually, "Let the Lord be magnified, who has pleasure in the prosperity of His servant.*
>
> **—Psalm 35:27 NKJV**

Part of what we ask for as we pray the Lord's prayer is that he gives us food to eat daily. "Give us this day our daily bread" (Matthew 6:11 NKJV). How is it that we can ask God to give us food to eat daily and not accept the things he freely gives us besides? As I said earlier, giving is a part of God's nature. Jesus said that as we seek first the kingdom of God and his righteousness, all these things will be added or given besides, inclusive of food, clothing, and shelter (Matthew 6:33 NKJV).

Our heavenly Father gives us gifts. He does not require that we work to receive His gifts. Our good works or good deeds are a product of our faith, our total trust in God, His Word. Why would a good Father "give" good gifts to his children, then turn around and tell them to pay him for the gifts He just gave them? We ask, and our Father gives.

> Ask, and it will be given to you; seek, and you will find; knock, and it will be opened to you. For everyone who asks receives, and he who seeks finds, and to him who knocks

> it will be opened. Or what man is there among you who, if his son asks for bread, will give him a stone? Or if he asks for a fish, will he give him a serpent? If you then, being evil, know how to give good gifts to your children, how much more will your Father who is in heaven give good things to those who ask Him! (Matthew 7:7–11 NKJV)

The body of Christ needs to rid itself of the poverty mentality. God is abundance; and abundance produces more abundance. It is the same for every believer. Jesus is a Seed of abundance planted in our heart that also produces more abundance. He took our poverty, a curse of the law, in His own body on the cross so that we are free from that curse. Poverty is not humility before God; poverty is a curse! Nevertheless, there are many believers who wear this false humility like a badge of honor, thinking that it pleases God. And they display it with zeal - tireless devotion.

But zeal without knowledge is dangerous! There are still many believers who substitute their righteous position before God by their faith in Christ Jesus—knowledge—for their zeal, their intense passion for God. Zeal cannot be substituted for righteousness. But zeal does work well with righteousness through knowledge. There is nothing wrong with having a righteous zeal for God, but it must be according to knowledge of God and his Word.

> *Brethren, my heart's desire and prayer to God for Israel is that they may be saved. For I bear them witness that they have a zeal for God, but not according to knowledge. For they being ignorant of God's righteousness, and seeking to establish their own righteousness, have not submitted to the righteousness of God. For Christ is the end of the law for righteousness to everyone who believes.*
>
> **—Romans 10:1–4 NKJV**

As we pray, like the apostle Paul did, for salvation for the lost among our families, friends, and unbelievers worldwide, we must also pray that they will acquire knowledge of God's righteousness; that they understand righteousness is not something they can put on or do in and of themselves.

In God's sight, our righteousness—what we do to try to impress God without faith in Jesus Christ—is as filthy rags before him (Isaiah 64:6 NKJV). No flesh or human effort can boast or be justified before God. "Therefore by the deeds of the law no flesh will be justified in His sight" (Romans 3:20 NKJV). If righteousness is not by faith in Jesus Christ, whatever we do trying to be righteous is more or less done from our zeal for God, our intense enthusiasm to gain the Lord's approval.

In other words, *zeal* is praiseworthy when God is its object; however, it is faulty when it is not based on knowledge of God's way to salvation. Righteousness, or right standing before God by faith in Jesus Christ, is a gift (Romans 5:17 NKJV); therefore it cannot be earned by human works. If righteousness could be earned by human efforts or works of the flesh, debt or obligation would be involved. But righteous standing before God is based on faith.

Christ is the fulfillment of the law. His perfect obedience to God, his Father, brought completeness of the law. Christ has freed every believer from condemnation of the law. Even though the law still plays a role in our life, we are freed from the fulfillment of its moral demands. Right standing before God is available for everyone who believes.

> What then shall we say that Abraham our father has found according to the flesh? For if Abraham was justified by works, he has something to boast about, but not before God. For what does the Scripture say? "Abraham believed God, and it was accounted to him for righteousness." Now to him who works, the wages are not counted as grace but as debt. But to him who does not work, but believes on Him who justifies the ungodly, his faith is accounted for righteousness, just as David also describes the blessedness of the man to who God imputes righteousness apart from works. (Romans 4:1–6 NKJV)

> Therefore, as through one man's offense judgment came to all men, resulting in condemnation, even so through one Man's righteous act the free gift came to all men, resulting in justification of life. (Romans 5:18 NKJV)

Abraham did no works or performed no rituals of the law. God made promises to Abraham, and he believed God. And God credited or accounted Abraham's belief or faith as righteousness. Therefore, Abraham was justified by faith, not by works. The Pharisees used Abraham as an example of being justified by works, but the apostle Paul teaches us that Abraham is our example of righteousness by faith: "Just as Abraham 'believed God, and it was accounted to him for righteousness,' therefore know that only those who are of faith are sons of Abraham. And the Scripture, foreseeing that God would justify the Gentiles by faith, preached the gospel to Abraham beforehand, saying, 'In you all the nations shall be blessed.' So then those who are of faith are blessed with believing Abraham ... And if you are Christ's, then you are Abraham's seed, and heirs according to the promise" (Galatians 3:6–9, 29 NKJV).

> *Now hope does not disappoint, because the love of God has been poured out in our hearts by the Holy Spirit who was given to us.*
>
> **—Romans 5:5 NKJV**

> *For by grace you have been saved through faith, and that not of yourselves; it is the gift of God.*
>
> **—Ephesians 2:8 NKJV**

> *Of which I became a minister according to the gift of the grace of God given to me by the effective working of His power.*
>
> **—Ephesians 3:7 NKJV**

> *For if by one man's offense death reigned through the one, much more those who receive abundance of grace and of the gift of righteousness will reign in life through the One, Jesus Christ.*
>
> **—Romans 5:17 NKJV**

> *Then Peter said to them, "Repent, and let every one of you be baptized in the name of Jesus Christ for the remission of sins; and you shall receive the gift of the Holy Spirit. [39]For the promise is to you and to your children, and to all who are afar off, as many as the Lord our God will call."*
>
> **—Act 2:38–39 NKJV**

> *If any of you lacks wisdom, let him ask of God, who gives to all liberally and without reproach, and it will be given to him.*
>
> **—James 1:5 NKJV**

> *For the wages of sin is death, but the gift of God is eternal life in Christ Jesus our Lord.*
>
> **—Romans 6:23 NKJV**

I hope I've impressed upon readers that God is a good God, who loves to give gifts. We, through our human efforts, apart from faith, try to earn good gifts from God. That's too much work. It amounts to trying to reinvent the wheel. Believers who possess this mindset are operating under the law, whether they know it or not.

The good gifts of God are already here and waiting for the man or woman of faith to simply receive or take them. God gives good gifts to us because of his amazing love. This means that every gift that God gives is for our good, for his character is unchanging. Through God's great love for all people, he offers salvation as a gift, faith as a gift, grace as a gift, and righteousness as a gift. The Holy Spirit is a gift, and wisdom is a gift. Even eternal life is a gift.

> *Every good gift and every perfect gift is from above, and comes down from the Father of lights, with whom there is no variation or shadow of turning.*
>
> **—James 1:17 NKJV**

Stayed tuned-in to the frequency of heaven, and every good gift and every perfect gift will be spiritually transported from heaven—not because we worked hard through human effort or religious rituals to obtain them but because it is our holy Father's good pleasure to give us the kingdom on earth as it is in heaven, now and in the future. "For it is God who works in you both to will and to do for His good pleasure" (Philippians 2:13 NKJV).

> *But you are those who have continued with Me in My trials. And I bestow upon you a kingdom, just as My Father bestowed one upon Me, that you may eat and drink at My table in My kingdom, and sit on thrones judging the twelve tribes of Israel.*
>
> **—Luke 22:28–30 NKJV**

Taking or receiving cheerfully the kingdom, in alignment with the Father's good pleasure to give it to us, is a Holy Spirit wavelength that transmits the frequency of heaven to earth. Stay tuned-in! "These things I have spoken to you, that My joy may remain in you, and that your joy may be full" (John 15:11 NKJV).

CHAPTER 16

A Job Well Done

> *His lord said to him, "Well done, good and faithful servant; you were faithful over a few things, I will make you ruler over many things. Enter into the joy of your lord."*
>
> **—Matthew 25:21 NKJV**

"Well done, good and faithful servant" (Matthew 25:21 NKJV), is what I believe most believers, including myself, would love our heavenly Father to pronounce over us as we fulfill or complete our divine assignment on earth. But this divine accolade may not be attained as easily as many Christians may think. I sometimes think that people trivialize this most superlative honor, thinking that just because they are a Christian and have performed Christian acts in Jesus's name that have blessed people, and since they have thousands of followers, what they are doing must be right and God must approve it; otherwise, what they're doing in the name of the Lord would not have worked.

> Not everyone who says to Me, "Lord, Lord," shall enter the kingdom of heaven, but he who does the will of My Father in heaven. Many will say to Me in that day, "Lord, Lord, have we not prophesied in Your name, cast out demons in Your name, and done many wonders in Your name?" And then I will declare to them, "I never knew you; depart from Me, you who practice lawlessness!" (Matthew 7:21–23 NKJV).

Sadly, I believe the above context may apply to many believers, especially well-known believers who have never truly humbled and submitted themselves to God. In other words, they never did the will of the Father but chose some other way, mainly through human effort, to accomplish a natural task that should have been a supernatural manifestation of their faith.

Many believers defy the principles of the kingdom of heaven and expect God to oblige them in their defiance of the constitution of heaven—the Word of God. We saw a lot of this happen in 2020 amid the COVID-19 pandemic, the 2020 US presidential election, protests over Black Lives Matter, rioting, and early in 2021, when thousands of people stormed and vandalized the US Capitol on January 6.

And while this may not constitute lawlessness or defiance of the law as a lifestyle, still many Christians were involved in these events and incidents in a manner that would not be considered Godly. As a matter of fact, much of what Christians said and did regarding those events and incidents was downright un-Christian. Their activities did not display godly character.

When believers do things contrary to the will of God, his word, not humbling themselves in complete trust and dependence upon God, they get what they want some other way that is not in alignment with the Word of God. Jesus calls them thieves and robbers. "Most assuredly, I say to you, he who does not enter the sheepfold by the door, but climbs up some other way, the same is a thief and a robber … I am the door. If anyone enters by Me, he will be saved, and will go in and out and find pasture" (John 10:1, 9 NKJV).

Notice Jesus never said those who do not enter the sheepfold by the door couldn't get in. They just didn't enter by the door. They took an alternate route, climbed up, or got elevated to a higher, grander position some other way—a way not prescribed by scripture, contrary to the will of God. They didn't do it God's way. Jesus said, "The same is a thief and a robber" (John 10:1 NKJV), and "The thief does not come except to steal, and to kill, and to destroy" (John 10:10 NKJV). God's way states that Jesus is the Door, and, "No one can come to Me unless the Father who sent Me draws him" (John 6:44 NKJV).

I am often reminded of this quote: "Your gifts can take you to a place where your character can't keep you." I do not know its original author, but I can relate very well to its truth. Over the years I have met many anointed and gifted men and women of God, and I am pleased to have learned from them; however, they had serious character flaws and became "an island to themselves."

They never humbled themselves under the mighty hand of God to be raised up in due season. Instead, they plowed ahead using their gifts—charisma—to advance them until they reached a status, a sphere of influence, where their flawed character could not sustain them: "For the gifts and the calling of God are irrevocable" (Romans 11:29 NKJV).

God does not change his mind concerning his gifts to men. This is why many believers can operate the gifts that Father has bestowed upon them and yet their character is flawed by means of their own selfish actions and lack of accountability to other spiritually mature saints. Some of them preach Christ from selfish ambition driven by covetousness. And yet through their God bestowed gifts they preach Christ and help people. In this, I rejoice. The gifts of God are anointed to bless people even when the bearer of the gift, through his flawed character, doesn't want to.

> Some indeed preach Christ even from envy and strife, and some also from goodwill: The former preach Christ from selfish ambition, not sincerely, supposing to add affliction to my chains; but the latter out of love, knowing that I am appointed for the defense of the gospel. What then? Only that in every way, whether in

> pretense or in truth, Christ is preached; and in this I rejoice, yes, and will rejoice. (Philippians 1:15–18 NKJV)

Nevertheless, God does exhort believers to unity through the gifts—the fivefold ministry offices of the Lord, Jesus Christ, along with the gifts of Holy Spirit—through lowliness and gentleness with long-suffering in love, all of which are components of a godly character, one that shows consideration for others. These attributes make up the character of God, who is love, and brings to us unity and peace, as we endeavor to keep the unity of the Spirit in the bond of peace.

> I, therefore, the prisoner of the Lord, beseech you to walk worthy of the calling with which you were called, with all lowliness and gentleness, with longsuffering, bearing with one another in love, endeavoring to keep the unity of the Spirit in the bond of peace … But to each one of us grace was given according to the measure of Christ's gift. Therefore He says: "When He ascended on high, He led captivity captive, and gave gifts to men." And He himself gave some to be apostles, some prophets, some evangelists, and some pastors and teachers, for the equipping of the saints for the work of ministry, for the edifying of the body of Christ, till we all come to the unity of the faith and of the knowledge of the Son of God, to a perfect man, to the measure of the stature of the fullness of Christ. (Ephesians 4:1–3, 7–8, 11–13 NKJV)

In order to hear our heavenly Father say to us, "Well done, good and faithful servant" (Matthew 35:23 NKJV), believers need to consistently do the things that are pleasing to God. And I do not think a believer can do things pleasing to God without his spirit—the spirit of truth (John 14:17 NKJV). When we do things God's way, when we are trustworthy and reliable as his bond servants, we willfully become subservient to him, allowing him to lead us into sonship (Romans 8:14 NKJV) and guide us into all truth (John 16:13 NKJV). We become Holy Spirit conscious that he is our Helper, our Teacher, our Reminder of truth, and our Keeper because we have turned the reins of our lives over to him. He leads, and we follow.

I take my stand next to the apostle Paul, who consistently made reference to different subjects, including being hindered by Satan to go to Rome, using the phrase, "I do not want you to be ignorant" (Romans 1:13 NKJV). Also, in referencing the mystery concerning God's promise of Israel's restoration (Romans 11:25 NKJV), the mystery of crossing the Red Sea (1 Corinthians 10:1 NKJV), concerning spiritual gifts (1 Corinthians12:1 NKJV), concerning despairing for one's life (2 Corinthians 1:8 NKJV), concerning Satan's evil devices (2 Corinthians 2:11 NKJV), and concerning those who have fallen asleep in Christ (1 Thessalonians 4:13 NKJV).

Ignorant is *agnoeo* in Greek and means not to know through lack of information or intelligence; to ignore through disinclination; not know, not understand, unknown.[82]

The apostle Paul knew a few things about being ignorant of God and his sovereign reign as King eternal. But after his conversion, Paul quickly recovered himself "through the washing of regeneration and renewing of the Holy Spirit" (Titus 3:5 NKJV) by which he received understanding of the mystery of the gospel and was no longer ignorant. He realized he had done many evil things against Jesus Christ and those of that Way because of his unbelief. All believers should learn from Paul's experience.

> And I thank Christ Jesus our Lord, who has enabled me because he counted me faithful, putting me into the ministry although I was formerly a blasphemer, a persecutor, and an insolent man, but I obtained mercy because I did it ignorantly in unbelief. And the grace of our Lord was exceedingly abundant, with faith and love, which are in Christ Jesus. This is a faithful saying and worthy of all acceptance, that Christ Jesus came into the world to save sinners, of whom I am chief. However, for this reason I obtained mercy, that in me first Jesus

[82] *Strong's Exhaustive Concordance of the Bible, NT*, 50.

> Christ might show all longsuffering, as a pattern to those who are going to believe on Him for everlasting life. Now to the King eternal, immortal, invisible, to God who alone is wise, be honor and glory forever and ever. Amen. (1Timothy 1:12–17 NKJV)

FINISH STRONG

The phrase *well done* denotes completion in a superlative way, such as performed well. As saints, we have a duty to fulfill responsibilities related to our kingdom mandate to teach and preach the gospel of the kingdom in all the world as a witness to all nations (Matthew 24:14 NKJV).

Jesus's return is imminent and certain! But while he is away, can we honestly say we are his servant, a bond servant subservient to the will of God? If Jesus were to return today, would he find us faithful—trustworthy, sure, and true; a faith that perseveres in prayer and in loyalty? "Nevertheless, when the Son of Man comes, will He really find faith on the earth?" (Luke 18:8 NKJV).

> And the Lord said, "Who then is that faithful and wise steward, whom his master will make ruler over his household, to give them their portion of food in due season? Blessed is that servant whom his master will find so doing when he comes. Truly, I say to you that he will make him ruler over all that he has. But if that servant says in his heart, "My master is delaying his coming," and begins to beat the male and female servants, and to eat and drink and be drunk, the master of that servant will come on a day when he is not looking for him, and at an hour when he is not aware, and will cut him in two and appoint him his portion with the unbelievers. (Luke 12:42–46 NKJV)

Saints have a duty to fulfill their kingdom responsibilities. But there is a distinction between those who do and those who do not. Those who do are referred to as faithful and wise stewards. These are they whom the Lord will make ruler over his household because he knows they can be trusted to give, bless, and teach the Gospel of the kingdom to others as needed.

I love that the apostle Paul makes clear in several of his epistles that he is first a bond servant of Jesus, called to be an apostle. Paul understood first order—first things first. Paul is saying that his heart is completely knit with Jesus Christ's and God's purposes and plans for his life, inclusive of being chosen and commissioned by Christ to be an apostle, separated or appointed to teach and preach the Gospel of the kingdom.

> *Paul, a bondservant of Jesus Christ, called to be an apostle, separated to the gospel of God.*
>
> **—Romans 1:1 NKJV**

> *Paul, a bondservant of God and an apostle of Jesus Christ, according to the faith of God's elect and the acknowledgment of the truth which accords with godliness.*
>
> **—Titus 1:1 NKJV**

The Greek word for *servant*, *doulos*, means a slave, bondman, bond servant, subservient.[83] In essence, Paul was saying that he is a *slave* who completely belongs to his owner and has no desire to be free, and a *servant* who willingly chooses to serve his master.

Ruler in the above context of Luke 12:42 is the Greek word *kathistemi*, which means to designate, appoint, ordain.[84] God appointed, ordained David to be ruler over his people, Israel.

> *Now therefore, thus shall you say to My servant David, "Thus says the Lord of hosts: I took you from the sheepfold, from following the sheep, to be ruler over My people, over Israel.*
>
> **—2 Samuel 7:8 NKJV**

> *Let every soul be subject to the governing authorities. For there is no authority except from God, and the authorities that exist are*

[83] *Strong's Exhaustive Concordance of the Bible, NT*, 1401.

[84] *Strong's Exhaustive Concordance of the Bible, NT*, 2525.

> *appointed by God. Therefore who ever resist the authority resists the ordinance of God, and those who resist will bring judgment on themselves. For rulers are not a terror to good works, but to evil. Do you want to be unafraid of the authority? Do what is good, and you will have praise from the same.*
>
> **—Romans 13:2–3 NKJV**

It is God who designates or appoints or ordains rulers. The main purpose is for rewarding good and punishing evil. In this case, those saints who are faithful and wise stewards will be appointed or designated as rulers of the Lord's house. The implication is that God's designated rulers, because they are faithful and wise, can be trusted to feed the lambs and the sheep as they have need. "Preach the word! Be ready in season and out of season. Convince, rebuke, exhort, with all longsuffering and teaching" (2 Timothy 4:2 NKJV).

Toward the end of apostle Paul's life, he could say most emphatically, "I have fought the good fight, I have finished the race, I have kept the faith" (2 Timothy 4:7 NKJV). Paul understood how to finish strong in faith. In Lystra, after he had healed a man crippled from birth, he was stoned by Jews from Antioch and Iconium and dragged out of the city, but Paul miraculously got up and went back to Lystra.

During all his missionary journeys, there is ample proof that Paul was an apostle of Jesus Christ who was strong in faith. He was spiritually mature and knew that his human strength and effort was inadequate to fight the spiritual forces of evil that take place in heavenly realms. And he urges us to be strong and put on the armor of God for protection against all kinds of evil—the superhuman craftiness of the devil, capable of drawing careless believers into sin.

But the enemy is not all powerful. As we place our faith in God, he delivers adequate power for us to stand against the evil schemes of the devil.

> Finally, my brethren, be strong in the Lord and in the power of His might. Put on the whole armor of God, that you may be able to stand against the wiles of the devil. For we do not wrestle against flesh and blood, but against principalities, against powers, against the rulers

> of the darkness of this age, against spiritual hosts of wickedness in the heavenly places. Therefore take up the whole armor of God, that you may be able to withstand in the evil day, and having done all, to stand. (Ephesians 6:10–13 NKJV)

Paul talked about finishing strong in the ministry he received from the Lord, Jesus, and he urged his spiritual son, Timothy, to do the same. "But you be watchful in all things, endure afflictions, do the work of an evangelist, fulfill your ministry" (2 Timothy 4:5 NKJV).

Through scripture, we know Paul kept his eyes on the prize to finish strong. Compelled by the Holy Spirit, he went to Jerusalem to continue preaching to Jews and Greeks repentance toward God and faith toward Jesus Christ, not knowing what would happen to him. "But none of these things move me; nor do I count my life dear to myself, so that I may finish my race with joy, and the ministry which I received from the Lord Jesus to testify to the gospel of the grace of God" (Acts 20:24 NKJV).

> *Finally, there is laid up for me the crown of righteousness, which the Lord, the righteous Judge, will give to me on that Day, and not to me only but also to all who have loved His appearing.*
>
> **—2 Timothy 4:8 NKJV**

Our heavenly Father, the Righteous Judge, will give his sons and daughters a crown of righteousness as a reward for our righteous lifestyle—one lived in total submission to his will and purposes for our lives on earth by faith as bondservants who are kingdom-compliant commissioned apostles, prophets, evangelists, pastors, and teachers, along with the spiritually mature remnant body of Christ worldwide who have loved his appearing.

We are on the earth for such a time as this, and we must finish strong for the hastening of Jesus's return for his bride. We must walk as children of light exposing the darkness, the evil systems of the world, "For everyone practicing evil hates the light and does not come to the light, lest his deeds should be exposed. But he who does the truth comes to the light, that his deeds may be clearly seen, that they have been done in God" (John 3:20–21 NKJV).

This is a great time not only to be alive but also to live—be the vibrant, loving, joyful, thriving, prosperous, healed, kingdom-compliant bondservants who unite as one body to bring the seven mountains of societies under the lordship of our Lord, Jesus Christ.

Our mental state should be focused on *here* and *now*! We are the "I am" on the earth. As we abide in the presence of the Lord and walk by faith that is settled in his word, we have victory through our Lord and Savior Jesus Christ, who always causes us to triumph in every place as we manifest the fragrance of his knowledge.

The world is witnessing the glory of the Lord like never before. The glory of God is upon the global church, and God is raising the church to be the light by which the world is drawn to his light. It's reformation time! It's awakening time! "But all things that are exposed are made manifest by the light, for whatever makes manifest is light. Therefore He says: 'Awake, you who sleep, Arise from the dead, and Christ will give you light.' See then that you walk circumspectly, not as fools but as wise, redeeming the time, because the days are evil. Therefore do not be unwise, but understand what the will of the Lord is" (Ephesians 5:13–17 NKJV).

ENTER INTO THE JOY OF THE LORD

What does the joy of the Lord look like? Unfortunately, few believers have asked this question. Christians sometimes make the mistake of displaying joy as an outward expression, a natural emotion. And by doing so, they confuse joy with being happy. But there is a distinct difference between the two, and that difference is pivotal to whether or not believers actually experience living in the joy of the Lord, and whether or not they are truly happy—blessed.

If we are to truly enter into the joy of the Lord, we must first understand that the Lord, Jesus, is the possessor of joy; then we will better understand what the joy of the Lord is, what it consists of, and what it looks like in physical demonstration.

The Greek word translated to *joy* as used in this context is *chara*, taken from *chairo*, which means cheerfulness—that is, calm delight;

gladness, be exceeding joyful, calmly happy or well-off; be well; farewell, be glad, Godspeed, rejoice.[85]

The English definition of *joy* is a feeling of extreme happiness or cheerfulness, especially related to the acquisition or expectation of something good; luck or success; a positive outcome; gaiety, merriment, festivity.

Happy means having a feeling arising from a consciousness of well-being or of enjoyment; enjoying good of any kind, such as comfort, peace, or tranquility; blissful, contented, joyous; experiencing the effect of favorable fortune; favored by fortune or luck; fortunate, lucky, propitious.

Makarios is the Greek word for *happy*, and it means to be supremely blessed; fortunate, well-off; blessed, happy.[86]

The joy of the Lord signifies, in principle, the circumstances attending cooperation in the authority of the Lord. God himself is the ground and object of the believers' joy.

So what is it that distinguishes joy from happy? From our physical application of joy and happy, there isn't much difference. Both are viewed as an emotion of the soul with little to no spiritual application and is derived from experiencing favor, fortune, luck, success, expectation of something good, and a positive outcome; a consciousness of well-being. So, from our physical experience, both joy and happy are expressions of one's feelings derived from emotions.

But the distinguishing factor between *joy* and *happy*, from a spiritual context, has less to do with the emotion of feeling and more to do with position—"Enter into the joy of the Lord."

Calmly happy, calm delight, well-off, and Godspeed relate to being supremely blessed, well-off, cheerful, and rendered holy through divine connectivity—sanctified and set apart to enjoy the Lord exclusively, in his presence, where saints are always in a place of rejoicing. So, from a spiritual application, both joy and happy denotes a blessed position or status in the Lord. When one enters into the joy of the Lord, he is happy—blest and blessed.

The joy of the Lord originates from the Holy Spirit's fruit of joy,

---

[85] *Strong's Exhaustive Concordance of the Bible, NT*, 5479, 5463.

[86] *Strong's Exhaustive Concordance of the Bible, NT*, 3107.

which is reflected in the lifestyle of spiritually mature believers and is not based on the circumstances of life. All believers should experience the joy of the Lord in their life as a wellspring that floods their spirit, soul, and body—their minds and heart filled with happiness because of their position in the Lord.

> If you abide in Me, and My words abide in you, you will ask what you desire, and it shall be done for you. By this My Father is glorified, that you bear much fruit; so you will be My disciples. As the Father loved Me, I also have loved you; abide in My love. If you keep My commandments, you will abide in My love, just as I have kept My Father's commandments and abide in His love. These things I have spoken to you, that My joy may remain in you, and that your joy may be full. (John 15:7–11 NKJV)

> Therefore you now have sorrow; but I will see you again and your heart will rejoice, and your joy no one will take from you. And in that day you will ask Me nothing. Most assuredly, I say to you, whatever you ask the Father in My name He will give you. Until now you have asked nothing in My name. Ask, and you will receive, that your joy may be full. (John 16:22–24 NKJV)

The Lord only comes in one measure—full! Obeying the Lord brings a constant flow of joy into the believer's life, filling him with the joy of the Lord. Obedience and love go together and are explicit in the manifestation of the blessed state or position of the believer and his ability via the Holy Spirit to bear much fruit. By this, the Father is glorified. The Lord wants our joy to be full or complete at all times. Therefore, as we abide in Jesus, and his words abide in us, we can ask what we desire, and it will be done for us. It's a knowing that erupts from our inner being. Mature believers know their position is one of joy as they remain in the presence of the Lord.

> *And we know that all things work together for good to those who love God, to those who are the called according to His purpose.*
>
> **—Romans 8:28 NKJV**

> *Now this is the confidence that we have in Him, that if we ask anything according to His will, He hears us. And if we know that He hears us, whatever we ask, we know that we have the petitions that we have asked of Him.*
>
> **—1 John 5:14–15 NKJV**

> *You will show me the path of life; in Your presence is fullness of joy; at Your right hand are pleasures forevermore.*
>
> **—Psalm 16:11 NKJV**

> *But as it is written: "Eye has not seen, nor ear heard, nor have entered into the heart of man the things which God has prepared for those who love Him."*
>
> **—1 Corinthians 2:9 NKJV**

Entering into the joy of the Lord is not some place we enter after we die and go to heaven. It is our current reality—our position in him—through our love, faith, and obedience to the Lord, "who gives us richly all things to enjoy" (1 Timothy 6:17 NKJV). He causes all things to work for our spiritual good and physical enjoyment as we abide in his presence, his word, in love.

As spiritually mature believers, our joy is also equated to our strength. Remember, joy in the Lord is the believer's position in his presence through abiding in his word in love, faith, and obedience. In this assimilation joy being identified with strength, strength, too, becomes our position in the Lord. If we've entered into his joy, we've also entered into his strength.

The Hebrew word translated *strength* is *maowz,* which means a fortified place; a defense: force, fortress, rock, a stronghold. It also means to be stout: harden, impudent, prevail, strengthen self, be strong.[87]

> And Nehemiah, who was the governor, Ezra the priest and scribe, and the Levites who taught the people said

[87] *Strong's Exhaustive Concordance of the Bible, OT,* 4581, 5810.

> to all the people, "This day is holy to the Lord your God; do not mourn nor weep." For all the people wept, when they heard the words of the Law. Then he said to them, "Go your way, eat the fat, drink the sweet, and send portions to those for whom nothing is prepared; for this day is holy to our Lord. Do not sorrow, for the joy of the Lord is your strength." So the Levites quieted all the people, saying, "Be still, for the day is holy; do not be grieved." And all the people went their way to eat and drink, to send portions and rejoice greatly, because they understood the words that were declared to them. (Nehemiah 8:9–12 NKJV)

Our understanding of the Word of the Lord in which we abide is a key to our entering into his joy and strength. Each day believers abide in the word, hearing and understanding the word via Holy Spirit revelation, is a day that is holy to the Lord our God. No need to sorrow or grieve anymore, but celebrate his pleasures—joyous occasions—afforded to us forevermore while remembering the less fortunate.

Understanding of the Word of the Lord is our invitation to a celebration to "eat and drink, to send portions and rejoice greatly." For the spiritually mature believer this becomes a lifestyle of giving and receiving exponentially multiplied—blessed to be a blessing!

> *Go, eat your bread with joy, and drink your wine with a merry heart; for God has already accepted your works.*
>
> **—Ecclesiastes 9:7 NKJV**

The meaning of life and true pleasure are experienced only in God. In him, acknowledging and reverencing him, we find fullness of joy and pleasures forevermore. Strength in him is our fortified place, and from that position in the Lord we prevail: "Not by might nor by power, but by My Spirit, says the Lord of hosts" (Zechariah 4:6 NKJV).

This is why believers must stay tuned-in to the frequency of heaven—God conscious, Christ centered, and Holy Spirit focused—abiding in and replicating the very nature of God, his word, and his holy character on earth. In this place, or spiritual state of mind, "Your will be done on earth as it is in heaven" (Matthew 6:10 NKJV), becomes a good work that flows continuously from the inside out.

All kingdom all the time is a current manifestation of the Lord's divine will to transition the church from "the religious church age" into the kingdom age. In other words, the mentality of the saints is being transformed from loving this present world to prioritizing first the kingdom of God and his righteousness.

We will consciously embrace our royal position as kings and priests unto God (Revelation 1:6 NKJV) as we mature spiritually and raise sons and daughters who will reflect their spiritual parents, and like them, leave their legacy of faith to succeeding generations.

The kingdom of God is a government of increase, peace, order, justice, and judgment established forever. God never intended for generations of believers to "reinvent the wheel" and start over at zero. His will is for his sons and daughters of the faith to daily embrace and enjoy the benefits of being citizens of the kingdom of heaven.

As we prioritize our citizenship in heaven above our earthly citizenship, we will think from an eternal perspective, our supernatural mindset, and fresh manna will await us each morning. We will learn from the revelation of preceding generations and increase in revelatory knowledge of present truth; each generation will expand the revelation of who Jesus is. The Father is pouring new wine into new wineskins and restoring the positions and authority of the apostles and prophets as the foundations of the New Testament Church of grace and truth.

The third great awakening of the church has begun, and this reformation will ensure that believers possess, as our heavenly Father does, the mentality of victory. God is the possessor of all victory, as he alone possesses every component of victory. God is love, and all his character traits flow from his pure nature and are passed on to his sons and daughters through our faith in Jesus Christ. We are victorious through him.

Spiritual battles were lost in the old order of the religious church age, as many Christians were corralled by fame and fortune, the attainment of celebrity status rather than credibility before God. But as the kingdom age unfolds, we will increasingly see the glory of the

Lord released upon his spiritually mature sons and daughters who have become commissioned kingdom-compliant servant-leaders, and who will fill the earth with his glory like waters cover the sea, (Habakkuk 2:14 NKJV), sparking the global wildfire revival that will usher in the billion-soul harvest.

The church will embrace the twenty-first-century apostolic model of the kingdom-compliant servant-leader. God will use apostles and prophets and other spiritually mature believers mightily. The apostles and prophets will be the spearheads—the commanders—who diligently heed their call and rally to their position as the foundation of the household of God, "Jesus Christ Himself being the chief cornerstone" (Ephesians 2:20 NKJV).

Kingdom-compliant sons and daughters will know how to fight their spiritual battles as warriors who possess the mentality of victory. And the church will press forward with a great faith that will not only destroy but also obliterate demonic activity with the name of Jesus!

Kingdom-compliant servant-leaders arise! Take the rightful place as the bride of Christ, who without spot or wrinkle, holy and blameless, comes to the wedding and stands beside the bridegroom with royal confidence, having possessed the kingdoms of the world for our Lord and his Christ (Revelation 11:15 NKJV).

Stay tuned-in to the frequency of heaven—the rate of occurrence in which we frequent the relationship and abide in the presence of our heavenly Father. The nature of our Holy Father's divine character operating in and through us is our authorization to plug in to where the real power may be found. Our divine assignment on earth is our frequency assignment, as we cannot complete it without the source of all bandwidth and power.

Our frequency channel is locked in through our abiding in his presence. The Holy Spirit is the satellite of heaven on the earth, and he resides in our spirit. Tune in to our specific band or channel—our divine calling—who Father says we are in and through Him.

As we learn more and grow to spiritual maturity, we will become a distributor of our frequency to spiritual sons and daughters who will have been nursed at our side and raised to become commissioned kingdom-compliant servant-leaders who will use our channel to tune in to the frequency of heaven by use of their own sound wave, modulating the sound to their personal frequency or intimate relationship with Abba Daddy.

Stay tuned-in to the frequency of each moment of his presence, and anyone can become God conscious, Christ centered, and Holy Spirit focused. At all times and under any circumstance, we must be conscious and alert that we walk with God—*all kingdom all the time.*

> *"For if these things are yours and abound, you will be neither barren nor unfruitful in the knowledge of our Lord Jesus Christ."*
>
> **—2 Peter 1:8 NKJV**

Printed in the United States
by Baker & Taylor Publisher Services